Brennon Williams

Microsoft® Expression Blend® 4

UNLEASHED

SAMS | 800 East 96th Street, Indianapolis, Indiana 46240 USA

Microsoft® Expression Blend® 4 Unleashed

Copyright © 2011 by Pearson Education

ISBN-13: 978-0-672-33107-7

ISBN-10: 0-672-33107-1

Library of Congress Cataloging-in-Publication Data is on file

Printed in the United States of America

First Printing, April 2011

Trademarks

All terms mentioned in this book that are known to be trademarks or service marks have been appropriately capitalized. Sams Publishing cannot attest to the accuracy of this information. Use of a term in this book should not be regarded as affecting the validity of any trademark or service mark.

Warning and Disclaimer

Every effort has been made to make this book as complete and as accurate as possible, but no warranty or fitness is implied. The information provided is on an "as is" basis. The author and the publisher shall have neither liability nor responsibility to any person or entity with respect to any loss or damages arising from the information contained in this book.

Bulk Sales

Sams Publishing offers excellent discounts on this book when ordered in quantity for bulk purchases or special sales. For more information, please contact

U.S. Corporate and Government Sales
1-800-382-3419
corpsales@pearsontechgroup.com

For sales outside of the U.S., please contact

International Sales
international@pearson.com

Editor-in-Chief
Greg Wiegand

Executive Editor
Neil Rowe

Development Editor
Mark Renfrow

Managing Editor
Kristy Hart

Project Editor
Andy Beaster

Copy Editor
Water Crest Publishing

Indexer
Lisa Stumpf

Proofreader
Jennifer Gallant

Technical Editor
Bruce Johnson

Publishing Coordinator
Cindy Teeters

Book Designer
Gary Adair

Composition
Nonie Ratcliff

Contents at a Glance

Table of Contents

About the Author

Brennon Williams is the Chief Technology Officer for the award-winning UK design and development agency, Splendid. Brennon is also a technical advisor to several companies around the world, specializing in the implementation of designer/developer collaboration and workflows.

For almost two decades, Brennon has worked in several countries as a consultant software developer and technical advisor.

Owner of the ExpressionBlend.com website which is due to be launched in 2011, Brennon's technology insights can also be followed at his personal blog, brennonwilliams.com

Brennon was awarded a BS in Computer Science from NYU and has received the Microsoft MVP award for Expression Blend 2008, 2009, 2010, 2011.

Dedications

To my family, friends, and loved ones.

You probably still don't know what it is that I do.

That's OK.

*Just know that I love you all and feel truly blessed
to have you in my life.*

Note to self...

Get some sleep, idiot.

4:18 AM. February 14, 2011.

Acknowledgments

I feel really happy about this book.

That's pretty important, and I hope that comes through as you read through the book.

Most of the time, authors will say writing a book is a killer, and although it's been a tough endeavor, I have to say that my editor at Pearson (Neil Rowe) is one of the reasons why I have managed to do it again.

Neil understands me; he understands that I am very time poor and that I wanted to get this book done as soon as possible, even though it sometimes isn't a schedule that I can stick to, because of the unknowns.

Neil and I agreed to write this book on nothing more than a handshake after a dinner in Las Vegas in 2010 (that reminds me... I need to sign the contract). He understood that I needed to rewrite this topic from scratch because it means more to me than just punching out some text. For me, this book needs to be "the book" on Expression Blend.

Thank you, Neil, for giving me this opportunity. Blackjack and steak in Vegas again this year?

To the Expression Blend team and Expression Management at Microsoft: Thanks for supporting me and listening to me—the good and the bad.

The speed at which you all reply to my questions is very much appreciated and certainly makes me feel like a valued part of your extended team. I hope this book honors the skill and creativity that you have all injected into Blend.

To Bruce Johnson: Thank you for your patience, waiting for chapters, and navigating the instructions that I have stitched together. Your exacting skill is what keeps me honest and what in the end gives the readers an accurate path to follow.

To all the Pearson staff who came together to make this book possible—the reviewers who make sense of my direction and the editors who guide me to creating a better product. Thank you for your endless help.

To my colleagues and associates, who I am privileged to work with at Splendid and around the world. Thank you for the encouragement, support, and belief, which gives me the confidence to write a book. Cheers to you all!

We Want to Hear from You!

As the reader of this book, *you* are our most important critic and commentator. We value your opinion and want to know what we're doing right, what we could do better, what areas you'd like to see us publish in, and any other words of wisdom you're willing to pass our way.

You can email or write me directly to let me know what you did or didn't like about this book—as well as what we can do to make our books stronger.

Please note that I cannot help you with technical problems related to the topic of this book, and that due to the high volume of mail I receive, I might not be able to reply to every message.

When you write, please be sure to include this book's title and author as well as your name and phone number or email address. I will carefully review your comments and share them with the author and editors who worked on the book.

E-mail: feedback@samspublishing.com

Mail: Neil Rowe
            Executive Editor
            Sams Publishing
            800 East 96th Street
            Indianapolis, IN 46240 USA

Reader Services

Visit our website and register this book at www.informit.com/title/9780672331077 for convenient access to any updates, downloads, or errata that might be available for this book.

Introduction

There are many ways that Expression Blend can be described—who it is aimed at and how it should be used.

My view will be different from the next guy or gal, and the one after that. All I know is that I have used this tool almost on a daily basis for several years now on every platform that it supports, and it just keeps getting better and better.

User experience and interactive design is an ever more important part of the solution creation life cycle and the richer the platforms become that Expression Blend supports, the greater the need for this tool, which can assist that process to be imparted into the production solution, working from initial sketches, wireframes, and prototypes, and then through to production implementation.

Expression Blend 4 represents a real step forward in providing designers and developers with the ability to collaborate, as well as to help developers who need a more robust design tool (other than Visual Studio) when working with user interfaces. Blend has matured to the point that very little, if any, code or XAML scripting knowledge is required for the majority of tasks that it allows you to perform, and this book aims to show you how to work in that manner in clear and as much as possible non-technical language.

What Will You Learn in Expression Blend 4 Unleashed?

As you would expect, you will learn how to work with the core features of Expression Blend 4, the creation of compositions, and the structure of solutions in a generic setting.

By far, the most important features of Expression Blend to learn are the combination of several intrinsically connected concepts, as follows:

▶ Styles and templates

▶ Parts

▶ States

▶ Behaviors

▶ Animations

▶ Resources

▶ Data

Understanding these features collectively will open up the world of user experience design and interactive development on the .Net platform to you. There are many other features to embrace with .Net and indeed with Expression Blend 4, but these concepts specifically are the key areas in terms of UI implementation.

If you are new to Expression Blend, you will find that you can read this book from start to finish and build your knowledge step by step, from beginner concepts through to complex interaction.

The Topics Covered in Expression Blend 4 Unleashed

Expression Blend 4 Unleashed contains detailed instruction and discussion around the core functionality of the tool.

The topics covered are:

- ▶ Exploring the Expression Blend interface
- ▶ How to work with common properties of user interface elements and controls
- ▶ How to work with dynamic layout support
- ▶ How to create, edit, and manage Styles, Templates, Parts, States, and Behaviors
- ▶ How to work with data in your user interface
- ▶ How to apply animations and visual effects
- ▶ How to work with advanced controls
- ▶ How to work with resources and assets
- ▶ How to use Blend to build solutions for Windows Phone 7

How This Book Is Structured

The book is written in a very explicit order, attempting to cater for as many readers as possible.

If you need a quick reference to refresh your understanding of a given topic, you should be able to find the chapter(s) that contains the correct content by logically reviewing the Chapter titles.

Even if you are a veteran WPF or Silverlight developer, if you jump straight into trying to work with Data in Blend, you will become frustrated at both the tool and this book, guaranteed.

Designers should not assume that just because Blend looks similar to other tools one may have previously used in the past, that Blend will work the same. Often, it is simply not the case.

Developers should be aware that Blend is not about XAML. Yes you can edit XAML script in Blend (and I concede that in some advanced cases you will need to do that), but in general, working with Blend to drag and drop, draw and define elements, is lightning fast by comparison of hand cranking the XAML.

There are few shortcuts to working with Expression Blend efficiently, so you should work through this book sequentially. After a few of the early chapters, you will start to gain familiarity with the discussion points and topics of the chapters and once you have traversed the initial learning curve of Expression Blend, you will find that it is quite an intuitive tool to use.

The best part is that you will be able to transfer your skills across platforms from WPF to Silverlight and beyond.

Sample Applications Covered in This Book

Most of the samples in this book are authored for the Silverlight web platform that, combined with the introduction of the Windows Phone 7 Silverlight platform, gives the greatest reach of your potential skill. You should find it easy to work from one to the other at any stage, as well as with WPF and Surface, should they be your platform of choice.

I have written the book by taking the view that you know your way around a Windows PC—you understand where File Explorer is located, and you are comfortable finding images and media files.

What I don't assume is that you have any prior knowledge of .Net, C#, Visual Studio, or any other specific platform package, such as Silverlight. Even if you have done little more then start Windows on a PC, you should be able to work through this book comfortably and with minimal stress.

Before You Begin with Expression Blend 4 Unleashed

It is essential that you have downloaded Expression Blend 4 or Expression Studio. It will also help if you have a version of Visual Studio installed. All those packages can be found by going to Microsoft's website and searching for the relevant download.

CHAPTER 1

Expression Blend 4 Overview

In this chapter, you will be quickly taken through some of the high-level concepts of Blend as a tool and be introduced to what is new in Expression Blend 4.

As you may have heard, there are currently several rumors surrounding the longevity of platforms such as Silverlight and WPF. Understanding a brief history of the platforms that Expression Blend supports will open you up to the future directions and changes that need to be made and why Expression Blend will play a pivotal role alongside the changing platforms in years to come.

Finally, I am going to show you what I think is coming and why it is so important to learn Expression Blend right now.

This chapter is completely non-technical and is the only one in the book that takes this format.

What Is Expression Blend and Who Is It For?

"As a WPF and Silverlight developer, Expression Blend makes my team and I much more productive; it allows us create user interfaces that are more visually engaging and compelling. We have been able to implement higher quality designs, faster, and more accurately using the full spectrum of WPF/Silverlight functionality. Areas of WPF/Silverlight that produce verbose and complicated XAML, such as animations, visual states, custom control templates and so forth, are easy and simple to do using Expression Blend."

—Sam Bourton, Developer

"As a developer, Blend allows me to concentrate on the final result and seeing it growing step by step without worrying excessively about technical aspects, it also makes the code and view integration very easy and smooth. Without Blend, I honestly do not know if I would still be able to create a user interface."

—Corrado Cavalli, Microsoft MVP Client App Dev

"Before Expression Blend I had a helpless feeling that no matter what I created in tools, such as Photoshop or Illustrator, I would be unhappy when the UI went through the development process. With Expression Blend I am empowered and know that my UI will look as expected in the final form. It makes a huge difference that I can control layers to create separate, named controls in Blend and that I feel like I have a part of the development process...even though I am not coding."

—Jennifer Smith, VP, Avlade

The quotes you have just read are from people who I have come to know and respect over the last few years. These people are the guardians of Expression Blend. They all do different things, all work in different disciplines, and all clearly have their own views on how and or what Expression Blend is.

Expression Blend means different things to different people, even inside Microsoft. How you use the tool differs, as a matter of course, depending on what you need to get out of it.

Read that paragraph again—it's important.

All too often, I hear feedback from users, frustrated (and, in some cases, infuriated) that Blend isn't working for them—in the manner in which they want it to work, that is. Mostly this is due to these people using the tool in a completely different context to the way in which a sample is projecting Blend use. Confusion reigns.

This is nobody's fault; it is just that most samples and discussions about Expression Blend are taken from one person who uses the tool in a specific way for a specific purpose.

In this book, completely different from the last, I show you how to use the tool in respect of the tool's functionality, rather than how to use it for a single persona or context. Also you will participate and discover just how much you can achieve without code; that is not to say that there won't be any code, however...there will be a very small amount.

This book is about using Expression Blend 4—not about learning how to use Visual Studio, learning how to write code, learning how to design experiences or user interfaces, or becoming a phone guru. It's not even about a specific platform, such as Silverlight or WPF.

> **NOTE**
>
> **Nobody Said Anything About Code?**
>
> Don't panic just yet.... The code should be relatively simplistic. If you need to understand in greater detail what code can offer you, I advise you to purchase one of the excellent books available based around the usage of your preferred .Net language, C# or VB.Net.

Learn to use Expression Blend 4 as a tool, and you will be able to work with all the supported platforms with only slight changes between them.

What's New in Expression Blend 4?

If you are an experienced user of past releases of Expression Blend, it might be the subtle changes to the interface that you first notice, but dig a little deeper and you see a bunch of new features that are available.

Expression Blend 4 adds several new and exciting features, yet also continues to build on previous functionality, improving the workflow for both designers (of differing ilk) and developers.

The following are some of the primary new features controls and improvements this book covers:

> **TIP**
>
> **What About the Old Features?**
>
> Don't worry if you have never used Expression Blend before—in the first few chapters, you get an understanding of how Blend works, how you can work with the most important panels of the UI, and how to use the basic controls that are used in 80%–90% of your applications.

- ▶ Silverlight 4.0:
  - ▶ Silverlight for Windows Phone 7
  - ▶ PathListBox
  - ▶ ListBoxItem layout states
  - ▶ Shapes
  - ▶ New behaviors:
    - ▶ Conditional behaviors
  - ▶ Design-time resource dictionaries
- ▶ WPF 4.0:
  - ▶ Visual state manager-aware controls
  - ▶ Easing functionality for animations
- ▶ Visual Studio 2010 interoperability
- ▶ SketchFlow:
  - ▶ Player improvements
  - ▶ Authoring improvements
- ▶ Support for M-V-VM templates
- ▶ Data store:
  - ▶ Design-time improvement
  - ▶ CLR type sample data

Some of the items in the preceding list might be completely alien to you—which is all part of learning a new tool. I also explain (in high-level detail, in some cases) parts of Expression Blend that are helping developers to work with Blend—business-type applications (also known as Line of Business (LOB) applications), for example.

A Brief History Leading to the Future...

You can move straight into the book from this point if you just can't wait any longer to start working with Blend!

I started working with WPF back in the pre-pre-Blend days, so I have seen Blend change very rapidly and adjust and modify to work better with what the vast majority of users want in a design-focused tool. Sure, there are some sticking points that are not quite right, such as the language used in tooltips and other small areas of significance, but on the whole, the tool has made leaps and bounds in its mission to assist a wide variety of designers and, dare I say, developers.

Interestingly, I am using the term "designer" here. In the earlier versions, especially in the Expression Interactive Designer days, the tool could have arguably been said to be focused on both designer and developer—then things cleaned up a whole lot!

> **NOTE**
>
> **My Personal Thoughts**
>
> This part of this first chapter is where I get on my soapbox, so to speak. It's where I like to voice a few predictions with a more generalized conversation feel, as compared to the rest of the book's tone (which drives one of my editors crazy); I promise this is the only section that takes this format.
>
> These are really my personal thoughts rather than some version of industry messaging, so hopefully it gives you a different perspective to how someone who uses the tool every day sees the tool and related technologies developing.

If you don't already know, Expression Blend also supports a wide range of platforms and devices. Most people are first introduced to Blend as a tool to help them author Silverlight applications, and although this is a considerable focus for the teams working on Expression Blend, it is not the only focus. Expression Blend also works with Windows Presentation Foundation and the Surface platform. It supports custom template types that work with Windows Phone 7 (as mentioned in the "What's New in Expression Blend 4?" section) and a prototyping extension tool called SketchFlow that I also cover in this book.

Why the Focus Shifted Away from WPF

Windows Presentation Foundation (WPF) was the forefather of the technology change we are all currently involved with. It brought about new ways for teams to work together and a shift in the "developer creates all" type of mentality that persisted with WinForms development.

Along with WPF came a related technology called X-Baps that allowed a browser-hosted WPF application to be authored using Expression Blend and Visual Studio. X-Baps are still used today, albeit very rarely, but obviously continue to offer a solution to some folks.

The mechanisms for delivery and installation are still routed deeply with a desktop application methodology and this just doesn't fly for a web-delivered solution to the masses. Also, WPF's core classes are tied heavily into the functional operations of the Windows OS, so that means working across platforms like Mac and Linux is always going to be impossible.

A new technology needed to be created that was based on the WPF platform, but could run on practically anything—from PCs to Macs to mobile devices and TVs.

Enter Silverlight

Silverlight was called WPF/E (with the "E" standing for "everywhere") in the beginning. At first, it was pretty underwhelming (and that's being nice, I think). You couldn't do very much with it except play media content and generally get really annoyed at the lack of functionality by comparison to WPF. Microsoft worked on making the platform perform more like WPF, work in and out of a web browser (user choice), and work with the existing tooling of Expression Blend and Visual Studio—and all this while maintaining a very small download footprint as a browser plugin to compete with other rich media plugins like Flash.

It's also important to note that at this point in time, Microsoft was starting to talk up their cloud-based solution called "Azure"—but more on this in a moment.

As the combined teams inside of Microsoft worked extremely fast (and collaboratively, to an extent) to make multiple versions of Silverlight possible within only a few years, a ground swell began to take place. More and more developers and designers started to understand the commercial ramifications for a mass-deployed platform that performs like a desktop platform.

Don't forget that Silverlight sits on top of the trusted corporate technology stack that Microsoft has in place globally with many of the world's leading businesses. All of a sudden, banks, financial houses, health providers, governments, and many others announced that they were building their next infrastructure works (large and small) with it—something they would never consider doing with Flash.

Silverlight... A New Version Coming Soon!

Silverlight as a platform is already very powerful and will become increasingly so in the next version with full hardware accelerated 3D engine support and many other features.

I was invited to a Silverlight 5 planning day in Las Vegas at the end of the MIX 2010 conference, where a wide range of future topics were covered. The tooling support in Expression Blend and Cider designer in Visual Studio were very interesting—things I can't discuss in detail at the present, but that makes me very excited (as a geek) for what is coming. To give you an understanding of how fast things move inside Microsoft, that Silverlight 5 planning day was held before the release of Silverlight 4. So, as far as platform development speed is concerned, multiple overlapping teams are working on the future—at hyper speed!

Silverlight authoring is not restricted to just web application-type scenarios, though, and people using Silverlight need different functionality and tooling support, depending on their target for deployment. You can understand just how hard it is to try to please all the people, all the time.

What Does This All Mean for the Big Picture?

I like to tell people that it's about connecting all the dots, and when you step back and look at the reach of the Silverlight platform (apparently 70% installed on all globally internet connected desktops), it holds a lot more opportunities and commercial viability than other competing technologies, but — and this is a very big "but", what it doesn't offer is flexibility and reach into the next generation of hardware and consumer based solutions. This is not a kill order on Silverlight but a directional change required on two fronts for Microsoft to strategically compete in the coming years. It may indeed by Microsoft's last chance to do so if they don't get it right.

Enter Project Jupiter

Project Jupiter is an extreme secret inside of Microsoft at the present time and the assumed reasons for this is because it represents the next evolution in XAML based UI frameworks that Microsoft *may* implement in Windows 8 (or whatever it eventually is named).

Silverlight and WPF have some specific engineering issues around high performance rendering and also some difficulties in efficient handling of Data Templating (and other areas) that make these two platforms useful for specific development solutions in the future — embedded device solutions which should remain as a *"Silverlight type"* platform (in terms of being cut down) and Line of Business (LOB) application development, both not really requiring or being able to harness desktop size power and chip design changes that mean more and more work being offloaded to from the CPU to the GPU(s).

It is my belief that Windows 8 will be the first operating system from Microsoft deliberately aimed at moving consumers away from the desktop computing of today and full speed towards mobile computing of tomorrow with Smartphone, Tablet, Console (inclusive of Set Top Boxes), TV and Slate level devices.

Microsoft has already announced the support of Windows 8 running on ARM chips which means that it is not unfeasible for a full and complete Windows OS to run on all of these devices with massive rendering capabilities and what I predict to be native support for Azure storage features.

Why Would Microsoft Throw Away All the Work Done with WPF and Silverlight?

Microsoft won't throw anything away and you will still be able to build Silverlight and WPF solutions for quite a time to come as most large corporates will still work with desktop computers.

What will come with Project Jupiter is a "Super UI Framework" re-engineered to fix the mistakes made previously and to put all the learning and efficiencies into a new platform.

1

Microsoft knows they have the right tooling solution in place now with applications like Expression Blend, Expression Web, and Visual Studio. Perhaps by accident, they inadvertently created a scripting language in XAML that can be compiled to .Net compliant code as well as a script that can be transformed on compilation to a new super script called HTML5 and a Style definition script called CSS.

What Does Expression Blend have to do with HTML5, CSS, and Expression Web?

It's wrong at this point to go into great details of why I think HTML5 is a game changer and why I think Microsoft will go after it hard in 2011 (most likely around MIX 2011 timeframe). Let's just say that there is a lot of similar functionality to XAML being defined by the HTML5 standard, and the optimum word here is "standard."

Adobe is all but killing off Flash after the Apple slap-downs and has declared its intention to concentrate on HTML5 tooling along with supporting Google.

There are a few pieces missing at the moment (data context, bindings, and so on), but by possibly combining Expression Web and Expression Blend, there is no reason why Microsoft doesn't already have most of the tooling they need to support the standard and allow their collective developer audience to output compliant content for all devices (iOS IPhone, IPad and Android Tablets and smart phones, most notably).

Learning Expression Blend now will ease your path towards this future should the reality of Project Jupiter and Windows 8 come to fruition; the same designer/developer workflows and conceptual implications of .Net fundamentally will not change—only the breadth of where you can deploy your solution to.

Summary

There is quite a lot of new functionality inside Expression Blend 4, and this book aims to assist you in discovering it. The focus of this book is around Blend's core functionality, but for the most part, that functionality is shown in the context of Silverlight usage in this book because of the points I make in the last section of this first chapter.

To really make Expression Blend sing, you need to understand how to work with the component parts that all come together in the UI's that you are assembling. It's OK to know how to animate something or how to lay out content, but if you don't understand how styling works correctly, or understand the visual state manager, you will never be efficient with Expression Blend. Take the time to understand the core parts of Blend, and you will be rewarded.

Keep in mind that you will use Blend differently than I do, and differently than the person sitting next to you.... But, after reading this book, you will be using Blend—how *you* do.

CHAPTER 2

Discovering the Expression Blend Interface

The Blend UI has changed dramatically from the first version, but there have been a lot of incremental changes that have evolved each step of the way. Expression Blend 4 has the fewest new editions to the UI directly of any release to date, but it still has some secrets that are waiting to be let out of the box.

In this chapter, you learn about the core parts of the Expression Blend UI, understanding the key changes to the user interface (which is dependent on project type) and focusing on those panels that provide the functionality that you will use most moving forward.

The Expression Blend Interface Theme

Amazingly, one of the first questions that many users new to Expression Blend ask is: "Can I change the UI theme?"

The short answer is yes—you have a choice of two themes, "Expression Dark," shown in Figure 2.1, and "Expression Light," shown in Figure 2.2.

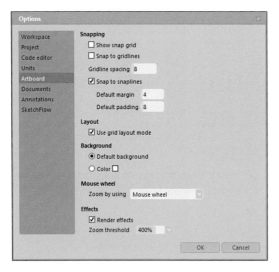

FIGURE 2.1   An example of the Expression Blend Light theme.

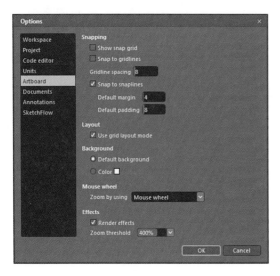

FIGURE 2.2   An example of the Expression Blend Dark theme.

There has been several requests over the years to enable the user to customize the theming of the Blend interface, but as of yet, it hasn't been a high-enough priority of the production teams to include this feature.

During this chapter, you see the Options panel, which enables you to modify a lot of settings to suit your needs and, of course, switch between the two themes and change the background color and fonts used.

As you can clearly see from Figure 2.3, the interface in its default state can look a little overwhelming and uninviting at first. Most designers probably would feel more at home compared to developers, but after a short time using the application, you will no doubt change it to provide a more natural flow for your eyes.

You Have Two Choices

I must admit that I am yet to see anyone (other than myself) use Expression Light in normal day-to-day usage, but it's a personal choice. I change it mainly to fool myself into thinking that I am doing something different every once and a while.

NOTE

Why Only Two Themes?

In earlier versions of Expression that were being trialed by insiders, there were several themes available, but testing of the users revealed that the dark theme was the most heavily used—thus the default setting of Expression Dark.

FIGURE 2.3   The general default Expression Blend 4 user interface.

Focus on the Artboard

The decision to create this dark theme and panel layout was born from the idea around directing the users' focus to the design surface (a.k.a. the artboard) and allowing it to stand out. This theory is not uncommon in a lot of high-end design applications, and after using the application for around 50 odd hours straight at times (CES 2010—Venetian Hotel, room 1210, Las Vegas), I find the usability still very comfortable, although by that stage I am usually hallucinating anyway.

How the Experience Changes

The user interface and indeed the user experience changes in the product depending on the project type that you select. There are several panels that become exposed or hidden depending on their relevance to the task at hand.

In the following sections, you are going to have a quick look at those changes so you are not surprised when you change project type later in the book and wonder where a certain panel has gone. First, however, it will be best for you to familiarize yourself with the most common panels that are almost always present. At the end of this chapter, you take a quick look at the Options panel and customize your experience even further.

Common Panel Framework

The Expression Blend common panel framework is very flexible in terms of how you can position and move panels and tabs to suit your working style.

In the following steps, you will create a new project and learn about the options available when performing this function.

1. Open Expression Blend, and on first use, you will be presented with a dialog similar to that shown in Figure 2.4.

2. Close this dialog. You look at this in detail in Chapter 3, "Using Expression Blend for the First Time." Don't be concerned if this dialog isn't showing at present, though.

   At the top of the Blend UI, you see the main menu system providing many options of which you are interested in the File option in the lefthand corner.

3. Select "File" and then select "New Project..." from the drop-down menu items.

FIGURE 2.4   The default start-up dialog for Expression Blend.

> **Menu Instructions**
>
> From here on out, when being instructed on a specific menu sequence you will be guided by arrow format describing the sequence of menu items to select as the following example shows:
>
> File->New Project...

You will now see the New Project dialog, as shown in Figure 2.5.

Collapse/Expand Toggle

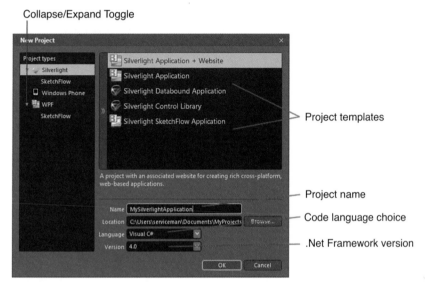

FIGURE 2.5   The New Project dialog.

Project Types

With the item highlighted at the top of this list, you see all installed project templates in the right side of the dialog. Subsequent selection of the items "Silverlight", "Windows Phone" or "WPF" show the specific template(s) included with each project type.

Hide/Close Project Types

Toggle to show or hide the respective template list.

Project Templates

You see varying project templates for you to select, which have specific implications for how your project solution will work and function.

Name

It goes without saying for most people that you should name your solution as descriptively as possible. Try to ensure that you don't use spaces or strange symbols in your solution name.

Location

You see a Browse button next to the input that opens a dialog enabling you to select the master location of your solution files. Make sure you remember where this is for future use, although there exists some helpers in Blend to return you to this location in Windows Explorer.

You also see in the screenshot of Figure 2.5 that I have created a location specific for the examples I create in this book.

Language Dropdown

You see that you have two language options to choose from in this drop-down; C# and VB.net are both .Net-compliant languages that Expression Blend supports. As mentioned previously, C# is the language that you will be using in this book.

Version

Expression Blend supports Versions 3.0 and 4.0 of Silverlight and Version 3.5 and 4.0 of the full WPF-based .Net framework; therefore, the choice is simple in those respects. Each version of the .Net framework offers differing functions and features with the later versions offering more choice and hopefully better performance than the predecessor.

> **NOTE**
>
> **Why Use C# Over VB.net?**
>
> This is a question that really opens Pandora's Box in many development circles, as people claim one language is better than the other for various reasons. I won't weigh into this argument if I can help it, because fundamentally both languages compile to the same codebase that .Net uses, although there exists several differences, both positive and negative.
>
> The choice is yours, and neither is a wrong or right choice. I began as a VB developer a very long time ago, so I do have a soft spot for it; commercially, however, it is clear that C# is the language of choice for vastly more job opportunities, so why limit yourself?

Expression Blend 1 and 2 do support early versions of the .Net framework before version 4.0, but it must be noted that the project types created by Expression Blend 1 and 2 only associate with Visual Studio 2008.

Expression Blend 4 creates and support Visual Studio 2010 project types.

This book will focus on targeting the .Net framework version 4.0 for both WPF and Silverlight, as well as Silverlight 3.0 + WP7 enhancements for Windows Phone 7.

> **NOTE**
>
> **Why Don't You Have the Same Project Types Showing?**
>
> Depending on what you have installed, Expression Blend shows different project template options, and this should not concern you at present. In the following sections, you see where to get copies of various Expression Blend add-ins, which give you similar project template options as shown.

4. In the project template list, select the Silverlight Application + website option.

5. Leave the default name and, if suitable, location as is provided.

6. Ensure that you have C# selected as your language type.

7. Ensure that you have version 4.0 selected.

8. Click OK.

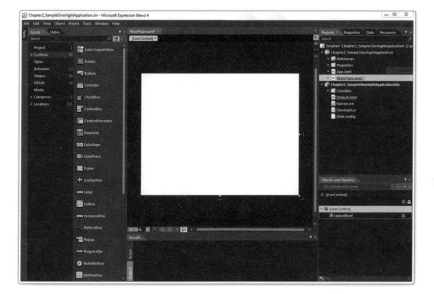

FIGURE 2.6   The Expression Blend user interface for Silverlight applications.

As shown in Figure 2.6, there is a lot going on in the user interface, as the default Silverlight Application + Website template specifies which panels should be visible.

Moving Panels Around

Figure 2.7 shows an example of the panel and tab collections in Expression Blend, which offer a robust mechanism for customizing your layout and preferred workspace requirements. The movement of the tabs and docking is very similar to that of Visual Studio if you have previously experienced that product.

> **Specifying Which Panels are Shown by Default**
>
> Once you make a change to the panels that are shown, Expression Blend will remember those settings and from there on out, the same panels and layout in the Blend UI should remain in place for all project types.

Tab Collection

Tabs are held in collections in the Blend interface, and you have the options to change the order of the tabs by simply dragging them left and right to re-order them.

Auto Hide

This option enables you to hide/unhide the selected tab collection. You can choose to "float" any tab by click and holding your chosen tab and moving the tab away from the collection. When you move the tab back toward the collection, you will be given a hint of its new placement by a floating blue border, as shown in Figure 2.8.

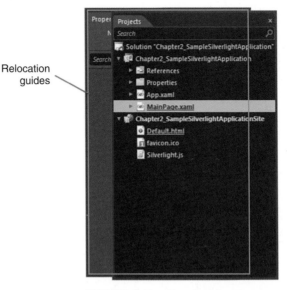

Relocation guides

FIGURE 2.7   The Project/
Properties/Resources/Data tab
collection.

FIGURE 2.8   How to relocate a
Tab panel.

Figure 2.9 shows that the Properties tab has been floated and the rest of the tab collection is now in Auto Hide mode, which you can mouse over any of the hidden tabs to view that specific tab. Click on the pin again on any of the tabs, which will return the entire collection back to its original position.

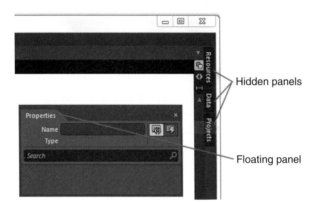

Hidden panels

Floating panel

FIGURE 2.9   The collapsed panel collection and the floating Properties tab.

Docking

You can drag a tab item to roughly the location on the screen where you would like it to free float, including an edge of the UI to dock the panel. You should be again presented with the blue border guide that gives an indication of a new docking position, as shown in Figure 2.10.

Panel docking indicator

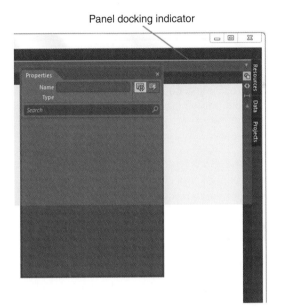

FIGURE 2.10   The indicated position of a docked tab is shown in the interface.

Project Panel

The Project panel represents all the pieces of your solution, including files, resources, settings, and any references to external assemblies and application parts that you may be using. Figure 2.11 shows a breakdown of the Project panel in a typical Silverlight Application + Website project.

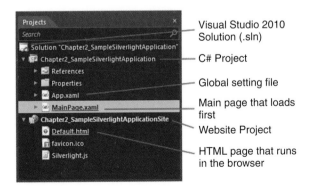

Visual Studio 2010 Solution (.sln)

C# Project

Global setting file

Main page that loads first

Website Project

HTML page that runs in the browser

FIGURE 2.11   An example of a Silverlight Application + Website project.

You become more familiar with what layouts of varying projects are best as you gain more experience with Expression Blend, and it is important that if this is your first use of the product, you don't allow yourself to be overwhelmed with any perceived complexity.

Solution development is a complex subject that has many variants to understand; therefore, covering such a topic is beyond the scope of this book. You will, however, gain further understanding of some of the more typical usage and creation scenarios of solutions while reading the rest of this book. Specifically, you learn how to create and reference entirely separate projects when using resources, as detailed in Chapter 13, "Skins, Themes, and Resource Dictionaries."

> **TIP**
>
> **Can I Customize the Project Types?**
>
> There exists several project types that you get out of the box with Blend, but it is also possible to load additional types and to create your own. The methods of doing that is beyond the scope of this book, but a particularly good article on how you might go about performing such a task is located here: http://goo.gl/7HGzc

Expression Blend Options Dialog

The Options dialog in Expression Blend enables you to specify a host of features, as well as some default settings that might help you work more efficiently. You can access this dialog by selecting the Tools menu and then the Options menu item at the bottom.

> **NOTE**
>
> **Navigating Menus**
>
> From here on out, you will be directed to access menus with the following format: Tools->Options.

Workspace

As Figure 2.12 shows, the Workspace options are extremely limited, allowing you simply to select either the Dark or Light Theme.

Project

Consisting of five options shown in Figure 2.13, you have a choice of some self-explanatory settings and a few that are probably a little cryptic to the new user of Expression Blend.

The first option simply enables you to enforce a name on the creation of a new element on your artboard. By default this is off, so when you add a new Button element, for example, you see that it doesn't have a name and appears in the Properties panel as <No Name>. With the option selected, your Button being added would be named "Button," the next will be named "Button1," and so on. It is my advice to leave this option unchecked and to only name elements that you strongly feel need a descriptive title.

There are many technical reasons as to why you shouldn't name elements but such discussions are outside of the scope of this book.

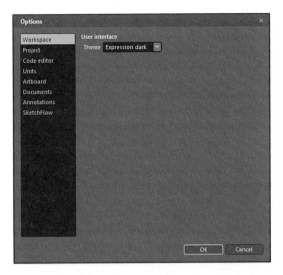

FIGURE 2.12   Expression Blend Workspace options.

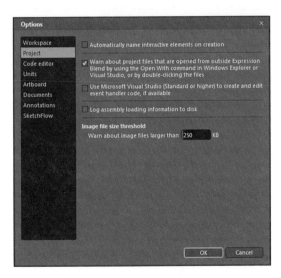

FIGURE 2.13   The Project options.

What you should know is that if you intend to do a little bit of coding to interact with elements, you need to have a name for any elements that you want to work with in code. Also, elements that are used in storyboards, for example, are named by Blend if not already done so by you, because the code or markup needs a key reference in order to manipulate the right elements.

The next option is on by default. This is quite handy as a warning system to let you know that a file inside your project has been opened by an external application. This can save versioning issues that can arise from file modification in multiple locations.

The next option is quite explicit about Visual Studio. It states that if you have Visual Studio (Standard or Higher) installed on your machine, you have the option to open and edit code files from within Visual Studio rather than Expression Blend.

As you see shortly, the code editor in Expression Blend is rather limited. It serves a purpose in some respects, but again my advice is that if you have Visual Studio installed, you will get a far better code editing experience in that tool compared to the limited code editor in Blend.

Log assembly loading to disk refers to a Debug assist mechanism that is used when reporting issues to the Expression Blend team. It generates a file that can assist in identifying issues with the Blend application.

Image file size threshold by default is set to 250kb. Allowing Blend to add large files to the output structure of your application can sometimes make it easier to manage your solution package. Typically, you would do this is you know this same file will be used continuously in your solution.

Code Editor

As shown in Figure 2.14, the Code Editor options are quite small. It is interesting to note is that the first option allows you to specify changes for either the code editor or the XAML editor.

These settings are all personal choice, and it's handy to note that if you make a real mess of setting your options such as font and size, you can hit the Reset to Default button to get it all back again.

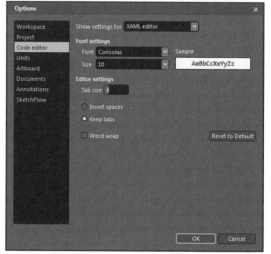

FIGURE 2.14   The Blend Code Editor options.

Units

Specifically referring to Type units of measure, my personal preference is to show pixels here as most of my design software such as Illustrator also uses pixels as a unit of measure for font types. As Figure 2.15 demonstrates, you have the choice of pixels or points.

Artboard

Under the title "Snapping," you see six settings, as shown in Figure 2.16. The first two will be detailed later in this chapter when investigating the Artboard, as these settings can also be turned on and off directly from settings available locally. It is also much easier to explain what the differences are between Snapping to grid and gridlines, as well as the fourth setting of Snap to snaplines.

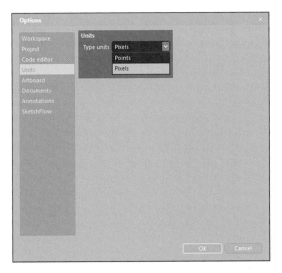

FIGURE 2.15   The available unit of measure options.

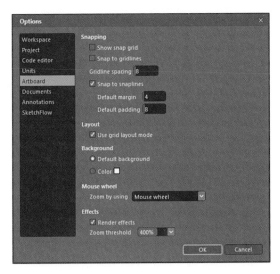

FIGURE 2.16   The Artboard options.

The setting for Gridline spacing should be pretty self-explanatory, but what is important to note here is that the default value shown of 8 is the same value of the Default padding setting and the Default margin value is half of that at 4. You should try to maintain these ratios if you change the settings to see consistency in your snap layout scenarios.

Default margin is shown in Figure 2.17, as the pink area between the two buttons and Default padding is shown as the pink area between the border of the Parent Grid element and the buttons that are sitting inside of it.

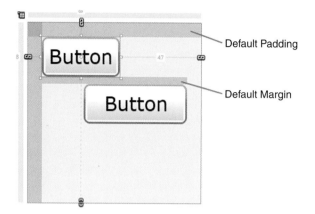

Default Padding

Default Margin

FIGURE 2.17   Default margin and padding settings are applied and shown on the artboard.

Under the heading of "Layout" resides a single setting, enabling you to set Use grid layout mode. You are advised to ensure this is turned on. More details around the reasons for that will be explained in Chapter 5, "The Art of Layout."

The Background settings enable you to specify a background color for behind the collections of controls you are working on, or you can just stick with the default.

The Mouse wheel settings are again self-explanatory.

The Effects settings might be a little cryptic until you understand what they are referencing and why you can set a threshold value in percentage terms. Effect rendering is discussed in the Artboard part a little later in this chapter. For now, you can leave it at its default of 400%.

Documents

Figure 2.18 details the choice you have for setting the default view when opening a document in the artboard. Split view, as you would imagine, splits the view into one-half design surface and one-half XAML view.

> **NOTE**
>
> **Snap to Snaplines**
>
> For the Default margin and Default padding indicators, you must have Snap to snaplines enabled either in the Artboard options, or toggled on the design surface.

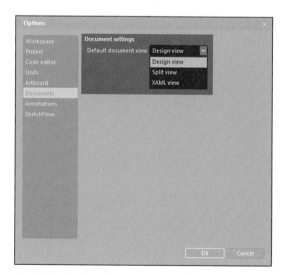

FIGURE 2.18   The settings options available for the Document section.

Annotations

Annotations (with their options shown in Figure 2.19) are available to post all over your applications and can be extremely helpful in guiding teammates to areas of concern or specific notes for items as well as indicating to multiple audiences your point of view. More detail will be provided later in this chapter under the design surface, explaining how to create and view annotations.

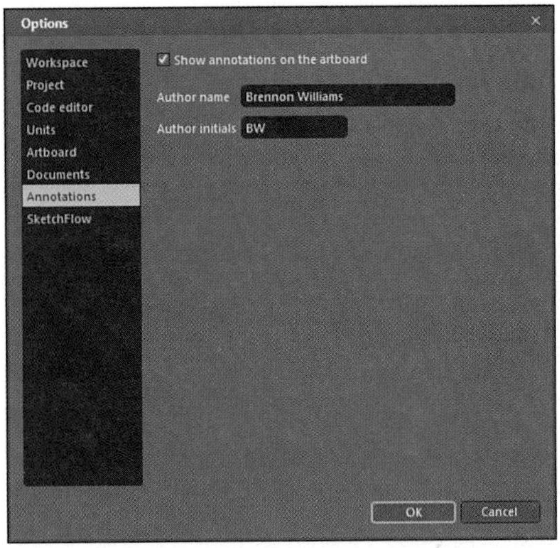

SketchFlow

The SketchFlow Options panel shown in Figure 2.20 is really very much out of context in this part of the book but is shown here for completion. For this reason, the specifics of the settings will be detailed in Chapter 9, "Working with SketchFlow." Most of the settings should be recognizable to you, as they mirror other settings in this section.

The Artboard

The Artboard is contained within a primary viewing area of the Blend UI that consists of three main display types: the Design Surface, the XAML viewer, and the Code viewer.

The design surface is similar to other WYSYWIG (what you see is what you get) type editors you might have seen before. It is a rich interactive surface enabling you to drag and drop elements onto it from multiple panels, as well as to manipulate the visible elements with ease and simplicity.

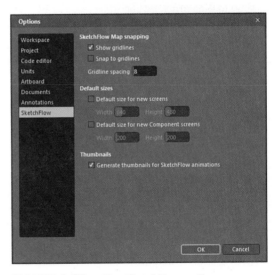

FIGURE 2.19   The Annotations options.

FIGURE 2.20   The SketchFlow options.

Figure 2.21 shows how most elements have what are called "adorners" that allow you to directly modify the elements with your mouse. You can also directly manipulate other properties, such as layout of elements and grouping, and in the case of path elements, you can also use tools to create artwork at will.

The design surface can also be directly interacted with the use of shortcut keys and shortcut keys, plus the mouse as a combination, which Table 2.1 has a breakdown of some of that functionality.

Button
Adorner controls

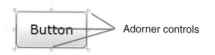

FIGURE 2.21 A sample of control adorner on the artboard.

TABLE 2.1 Handy Keyboard Shortcuts

Function	Keys
Cycle workspaces	F6
Show/Hide all panels	F4
Pan around the workspace	Spacebar and move the mouse
	Hold the Shift key to pan left and right while scrolling
	Select an element in the Objects and Timeline panel and double-click the Pan tool in the toolbar to pan to the selected element
Switch to element selection while keeping the same toolbox element selected	Hold Ctrl key down
Zoom	Mouse wheel
Zoom—fit selection	Ctrl + 0

Figure 2.22 shows some of the functionality attached to the artboard itself. The following gives some detail as to what each function is and how to use them.

Zoom

As you have read in Table 2.1, scrolling your mouse will zoom in and out on the artboard. You can also use some preset values in the Zoom dropdown, shown at the bottom of the artboard space. The last item, "Fit selection," shown in Figure 2.23 can be especially handy and is also documented in Table 2.1. You also note that the toolbar has a Zoom tool that performs similar functions all with just a little more control.

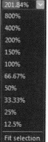

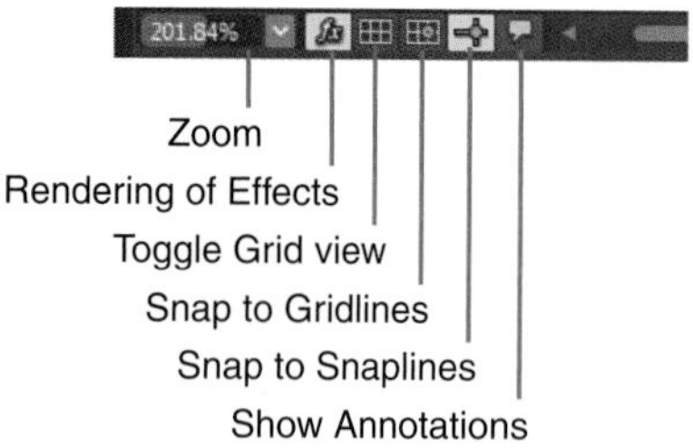
201.84%
Zoom
Rendering of Effects
Toggle Grid view
Snap to Gridlines
Snap to Snaplines
Show Annotations

FIGURE 2.22 The attached artboard function controls.

201.84%
800%
400%
200%
150%
100%
66.67%
50%
33.33%
25%
12.5%
Fit selection

FIGURE 2.23 The Zoom option dropdown.

The View menu item also details several Zoom options, including Actual Size.

Rendering of Effects

As the name suggests, rendering of effects controls if effects (such as Blur and DropShadow) are seen in design time on the artboard. Why would you care about this? The rendering of effects inside the design time preview can be quite expensive in computation cycles, which can reduce performance of Blend considerable, especially when you are zoomed in heavily on items.

For this reason, you also note that previously in the Artboard Options section of this chapter, you could specify a Zoom Threshold. This setting constrains Blend so as it will not render effects regardless of whether you have this option selected or not.

Toggle Grid View

Figure 2.24 shows the Grid effect that is overlaid on your artboard, helping you to guide elements. You might also adjust the spacing of the grid (default is 8 pixels) inside the Options panel. Grid usage is a personal thing, and I find myself turning it on and off depending on how I feel at the time.

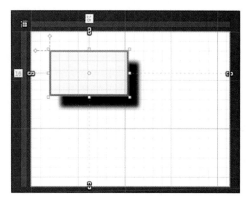

FIGURE 2.24   The default Grid effect applied to the artboard.

Snap to Gridlines

As you would most likely surmise, snapping to Grid enables you to move elements around the screen and have those element positions snap to your grid guides. Interesting to note is that you don't have to have the Grid shown to make elements continue to snap to grid.

Snap to Snaplines

Similar to smart guides in other applications, snaplines are approximations for boundaries that element share and other points of reference within your UI element collection. These snaplines can make it much more efficient to quickly place elements on the screen and get the alignment pretty close. Figure 2.25 shows two button elements that show the snaplines when one button is being moved close to it.

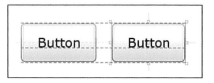

FIGURE 2.25   The snaplines alignment feature.

Show Annotations

Annotations are a feature used within Expression SketchFlow applications, enabling you to mark screens and components up with points of discussion visible to other users.

Figure 2.26 shows the creation of an annotation in against a SketchFlow button, whereas Figure 2.27 shows the same annotation collapsed, but remaining next to the element as the focus is shifted onto another element on the artboard.

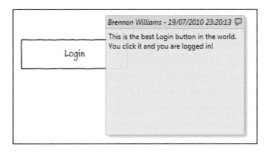

FIGURE 2.26   A new annotation is displayed.

The XAML Editor

FIGURE 2.27   A collapsed annotation.

Figure 2.28 is showing a split view of both the artboard and the XAML window. In this case, it is the XAML markup that corresponds to the two buttons also shown on the artboard.

You can view just the XAML markup by itself if that is your preference, and you can also cycle between the design/markup/split view windows by clicking on F11. As shown in Figures 2.29 and 2.30, under the View menu, you have many choices within the submenus of the first two options.

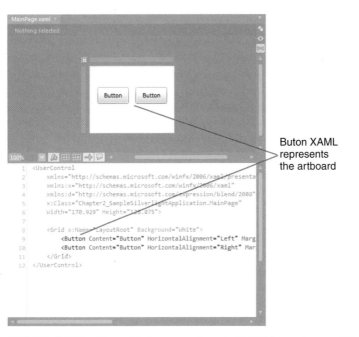

Buton XAML represents the artboard

FIGURE 2.28   The split view comprises both XAML markup and the artboard.

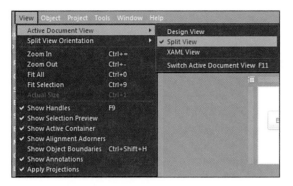

FIGURE 2.29   The Active Documents View options.

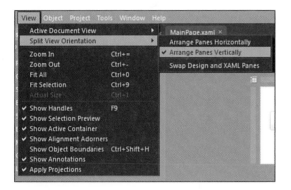

FIGURE 2.30   Split View Orientation options.

The first menu option, "Active Document View," enables you to switch between the three split and solid view windows.

Split View Orientation options allow you to define exactly how you prefer to see the split in your windows. Horizontal or vertical, the choice is completely yours.

You should note that these options are not saved in custom workspaces, though.

The Code Editor

The code editor in Expression Blend has been added, removed, and then added again, much to a mixed reception. Some folks really want it to be in there, in case Visual Studio isn't installed, or in some cases for simple editing of code where Visual Studio just isn't required.

The art of writing code is very much out of the scope of this book, and there are many other texts that take you through the very beginning into the deepest of details around how code works and how you can write it, even with limited historical skills.

For coders, it does matter, though. The functionality of a coding editor and its ability to improve productivity are very much sticking points, and so it is no surprise that many people use Expression Blend 4 and Visual Studio 2010 together as an integrated toolset.

Intellisense Comparison

Figures 2.31 and 2.32 show how similar functionality in Intellisense is provided for in Blend versus Visual Studio, but as Figures 2.33 and 2.34 show, when you need to add library references fast and you can't remember the name of them, Visual Studio really shines through as the tool of choice.

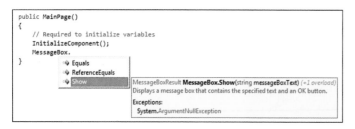

FIGURE 2.31   The Expression Blend 4 Code Editor Intellisense.

FIGURE 2.32   The Visual Studio 2010 Code Editor Intellisense.

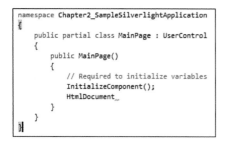

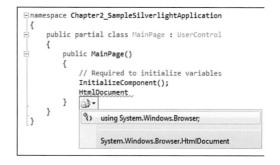

FIGURE 2.33   Expression Blend shows nothing but a little red squiggle after the word "HtmlDocument," offering no help to find and use the correct code library.

FIGURE 2.34   Visual Studio gives single-click fast insert for the correct library.

You might think that is just a little bit of more help, but with literally thousands of libraries that are available in the .Net Framework, trying to remember them all is next to impossible. Without the inclusion of those libraries (as indicated by the using statements in the code), you can quickly see how Visual Studio offers a much more robust coding experience.

Expression Blend and Visual Studio Integration

To enable Blend to work with Visual Studio seamlessly, you need to check a setting in the Tools->Options->Project dialog, as shown in Figure 2.35.

To try this out, the following steps show you how an event is handled between the two tools.

1. Create a new Silverlight Application + Website project.

2. Locate your Tool panel and the very last item ICON should be a Button element. Double click it to add a Button element to your screen.

3. Locate the Properties panel.

4. Name the Button element, as shown in Figure 2.36. Take note of the Event Viewer Mode button, detailed also in Figure 2.36, and click it after you have named your button.

5. Figure 2.37 shows you the large array of events that are available for a button. At this point, you should save your work by using the key combination: Ctrl + Shift + S at the same time or by selecting File->Save All.

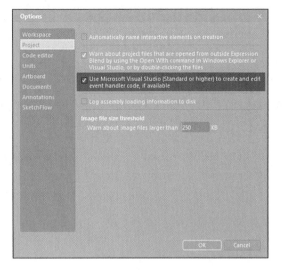

FIGURE 2.35   The setting to enable Visual Studio integration.

> **NOTE**
>
> **Don't Worry If You Don't Understand the Code!**
>
> This is a simple exercise that is designed to show the integration between the Expression Blend and Visual Studio tools. Not understanding the code or the concept of event handlers is perfectly fine at this stage of the book.

> **NOTE**
>
> **Properties Panel Overview**
>
> Shortly, you will be given a detailed tour of the Properties panel and how it works. For this example, you will have minimal interaction with it.

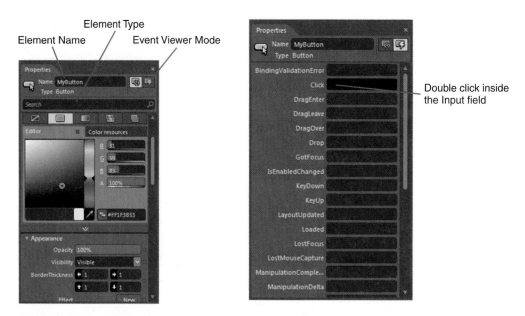

FIGURE 2.36   The Properties panel contains an area where you can give your elements a name as well as change the view of the panel to show all available Events.

FIGURE 2.37   The Events view of the Properties panel.

6. Figure 2.37 also indicates where you should double-click in the event input field.

7. When you double-click in the "click" event input field, you might briefly get a message, as shown in Figure 2.38. This is always shown when Visual Studio is busy loading up.

FIGURE 2.38   The alert that Expression Blend is trying to set up the communication between the two tools.

8. Visual Studio should have appeared after a quick load. If it hasn't, you might need to save all your work and open Visual Studio separately to ensure that it's working correctly. Also note that the Expression Blend 4 -> Visual Studio 2010 integration is only available for versions of Visual Studio that are standard or higher.

9. Figure 2.39 shows you the event handler code added by Visual Studio -> Blend inter-actions, as well as the code that you should write specifically into the generated handler inside Visual Studio.

```
private void MyButton_Click(object sender, RoutedEventArgs e)
{
    MessageBox.Show("Hello World!");|
}
```

FIGURE 2.39   The newly generated event handler and the code to add inside the handler method.

10. Run the application from within Visual Studio by pressing the F5 button, which is the same as in Blend.

Figure 2.41 shows another dialog asking for the specific location of the debug file that must be generated and added to your project. You can simply opt OK at this stage, where a Web.Config file will be added to your project solutions.

Your application should now start up and run inside your default browser, and if you have installed Silverlight correctly, you should see your button showing on the screen where you can now click on the button, and a MessageBox should be presented with "Hello World" contained, as shown in Figure 2.42.

Setting Debug Mode
What you should get the first time you run the application from within Visual Studio is the dialog shown in Figure 2.40. This dialog is asking about adding some debug settings to the solution, which you should add now if you know that you will need to debug your appli-cation either now or at a later stage.

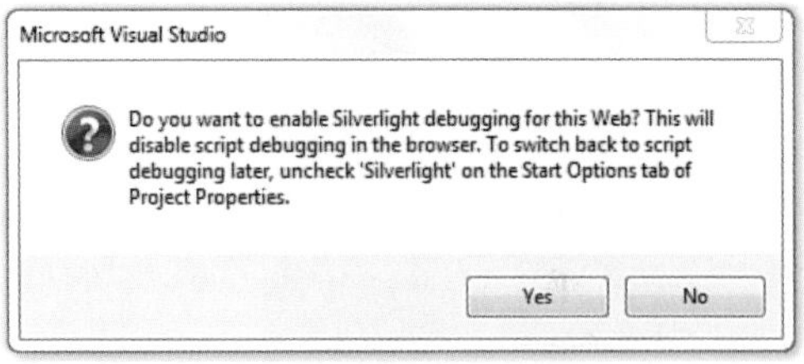

FIGURE 2.40   The dialog asking about Debug mode from within Visual Studio.

FIGURE 2.41   How Visual Studio asks you where it should generate the Debug file.

You can do it over and over, but that
will get tiring very soon.

11. Close the web browser for now
    and then return to Visual Studio.
    Save your work by pressing the
    Ctrl + Shift + S combination and
    then return to Expression Blend.

12. Locate the Project tab and, as
    shown in Figure 2.43, locate the
    ".cs" file that represents the code-
    behind file of your
    MainPage.xaml. By double-clicking
    on this file, you will again see the
    code editor in Blend, and it should
    now show the updated code that
    you added to the event handler in
    Visual Studio.

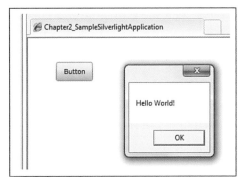

FIGURE 2.42   The result of the button click
calling the event you added in code and raising
the MessageBox.

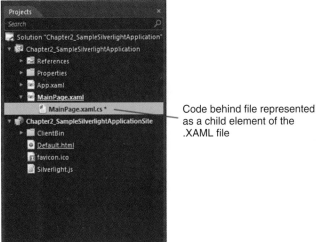

Code behind file represented
as a child element of the
.XAML file

FIGURE 2.43   The location of the code-behind file in the Project tab.

Simple Edits Inside of Blend

You can now inside the Blend code editor, change the "Hello World" string to anything
else you want, and run the application with F5 directly from Blend. This simple example
demonstrates that it's easy to modify and work with code inside of Expression Blend, but
anyone thinking they would be easily be able to code up a fully-fledged application in it
would be met with frustration very quickly.

Objects and Timeline Panel

The Objects and Timeline panel represents hierarchical views of all the elements that are currently in the scene you are working in. You can translate that simply to mean that it shows parent-child relationships.

The Objects and Timeline panel also provides a visual representation for attached objects, such as Behaviors (see Chapter 3 for more details), that don't necessarily have a visual representation on the screen but are indeed attached to a specific element.

As the name of the panel also suggests, it contains the primary Timeline manager for the Blend application, which you cover in depth in Chapter 11, "Animations and Transitions."

Figure 2.44 details the most important parts of the Objects and Timeline panel, and it is very important that you become familiar with it as quickly as possible because this will be one of the main panels you interact with when using Expression Blend.

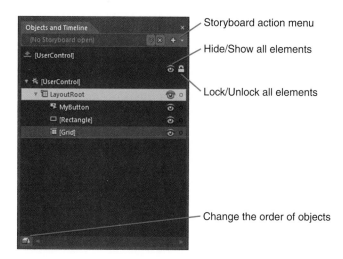

FIGURE 2.44   The Object and Timeline panel details specifically for objects.

Locking Elements

Figure 2.44 also points out that you can control the locking state of individual objects or elements and their children simply by clicking on the Lock icon. When locking is engaged, you are restricted from selecting the item on both the artboard and in the Objects and Timeline panel.

Dragging Elements

The collection on display is simple to move around in terms of Z-Order. Z-Order refers to how elements sit on top of one another on the screen. You can simply drag elements up and down the list shown to change their parent relationship or how they are presented

on the screen. You can actively drag items from the Assets panel and toolbar onto the
Objects and Timeline panel, as well as various Behaviors and effects, as shown in
Figure 2.45.

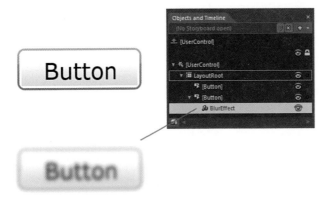

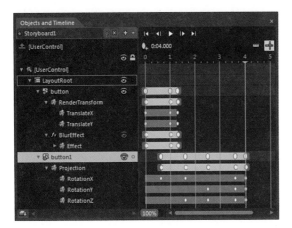

FIGURE 2.45   A Blur effect applied to a Button element.

Even in the scenario shown in Figure 2.45, you can simply drag the Effect element from
one Button element to another.

The Objects and Timeline panel contains a multitude of functionality that is exposed
even further when working with storyboard animations. Figure 2.46 shows how the panel
expands and contains a fully-fledged Timeline editor. See Chapter 11 for further details.

FIGURE 2.46   The Object and Timeline panel in full flight with storyboard editing.

Tools Panel

The Blend Tools panel hasn't seen much evolution since version 1, with the exception of being dockable and the modification to some of the Gradient tools that are available from it.

As Figure 2.47 demonstrates, the Tools panel changes slightly depending on the application type: WPF or Silverlight.

The Tools panel is made up of several collections of controls, including primary artboard tools such as Pan, collections including layout controls, shapes, text controls, and common controls.

Selection Tools

The Selection tools contain two conceptually similar tools that are used within different context of editing.

Selection Tool

The Selection tool enables you to grab elements and move them around the artboard.

Direct Selection Tool

The Direct Selection tool, as shown in Figure 2.48, is used for selecting path segments.

View Tools

The View tools collection contains three tools used to control your view of the design surface.

Pan Tool

The Pan tool enables you to literally grab the entire artboard and move it around your screen. The shortcut key to allow you to do this at any time is to hold down the spacebar and move your mouse to the location of your choice.

WPF
Silverlight

FIGURE 2.47   Displayed is the slight variation in WPF and Silverlight Tools panel.

— Selection

— Direct Selection

FIGURE 2.48   The two Selection tools available.

Zoom Tool

The Zoom tool enables you to accurately click on an point of the artboard and zoom in or out. To enable zoom out, you simply hold down the Alt key and continue clicking your mouse until you reach the desired zoom level.

Camera Orbit Tool

This tool is only available when you are authoring a WPF application and is quite cool to play around with.

The following steps take you through creating a fast and simple 3D element to help you experience the Camera Orbit Tool.

1. Create a new WPF application.

2. In the Project tab, right-click on the project name element and select Add Existing Item, as shown in Figure 2.49.

3. You should be provided with an "Add Existing Item" dialog box where you can navigate your files. I have chosen an image of tulips, which is part of the Windows 7 Sample Pictures file, but you can choose whatever image you want to use.

4. If you have chosen a moderately large image, you see the dialog showing in Figure 2.50. This is an alert from Blend that tries to make you conform to the good practice of packaging your large image files with your EXE files. I also recommend you accept this advice and select Yes to continue.

5. If all has gone as expected, you should now be able to see your image inside the Project panel and being an image, if you role your mouse over it, you should see a small Thumbnail image, as shown

Selection

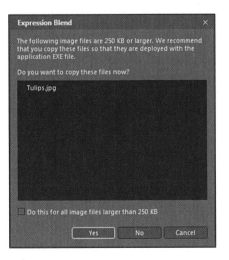

FIGURE 2.49   Add an existing item to your project.

FIGURE 2.50   Showing the large file alert provided by Blend.

in Figure 2.51. All you need to do now is drag that image file directly from the Project panel to the artboard, or you could right-click on the image and select "Insert" from the context menu that appears.

6. Most likely, the image will be massive and might indeed be larger than your artboard. Use the Selection tool to resize the image so you can work with it in the center of the artboard.

7. Take a quick look at the Objects and Timeline panel, as shown in Figure 2.52, and note that currently you should simply have an Image element as the child control of the LayoutRoot element.

FIGURE 2.52   The Image element is shown as a child element of the LayoutRoot element.

FIGURE 2.51   Image resources are presented in the helpful thumbnail provided by Blend in the Project panel.

8. With the Image element selected, click on the Tools menu and then select the "Make Image 3D" menu item.

9. Nothing will look like it has changed, but if you now take another look at the Objects and Timeline panel, you see that the Image tag has gone, and in its place is a Viewport3D element, as shown in Figure 2.53.

10. There is a lot you can do from here, but at the moment, you are looking at the Camera Orbit tool in the Tools panel. Select the Camera Orbit tool, click on the image with your mouse, and keep your mouse button down, dragging across the image.

FIGURE 2.53   The Objects and Timeline panel change.

11. You should see your image appearance change, which is indeed the 3D Camera position changing.

To view some more accurate details around this Camera Orbit, you can drill down through the Viewport3D element in the Objects and Timeline panel, finding and then selecting the PerspectiveCamera element, as shown in Figure 2.55.

12. Open the Properties panel, which you should now see has some very specific properties for the camera, as shown in Figure 2.56. Move the Camera Orbit tool back over the image on your artboard and keep an eye on the Position, Direction, and Up Vector properties specifically, and you should see them changing to actions you are performing on the artboard.

Experiment with those tools and property values inside the Camera properties, changing camera and dragging on the interactive property setters, as also referred to in Figure 2.56.

FIGURE 2.54   Showing the result of Camera Orbit tool used against the 3D element.

FIGURE 2.55   The PerspectiveCamera element in the Objects and Timeline panel.

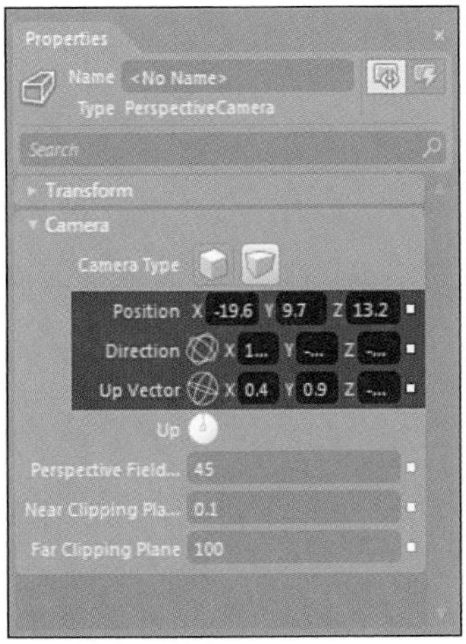

FIGURE 2.56   The camera-specific properties affected by the Camera Orbit tool.

Brush Tools

The first tool I believe is incorrectly named or incorrectly propositioned as an eyedropper control. You would naturally associate an eyedropper with a color selection tool, which it is in the case of Blend; what this particular eyedropper tool does, however, is duplicate some matching properties of one element to a matching property collection of another element, not just color.

It sounds confusing, so follow through with this example to understand the usage of the tool:

1. Create a new Silverlight Application + Website project.

2. Add two Button elements, a rectangle and a Border control, so your layout is the same as shown in Figure 2.57. Take note of the content of the buttons, identifying them as Button 1 and Button 2.

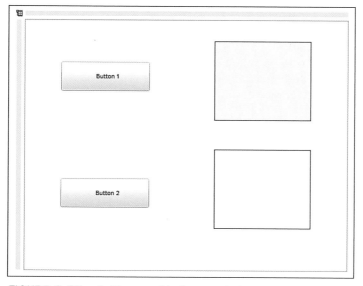

FIGURE 2.57   Setting up with the sample layout.

3. Select Button 1, and note specifically in the Properties panel that the Button element has a background, BorderBrush, and a foreground color property.

4. With Button 1 still selected, change the Background property to a solid color bright green, the foreground to a bright pink/purple and the BorderBrush property to a solid color bright red. You end up with something like the image shown in Figure 2.58. Note that I have increased the BorderThickness property of both the buttons to 4 pixels all

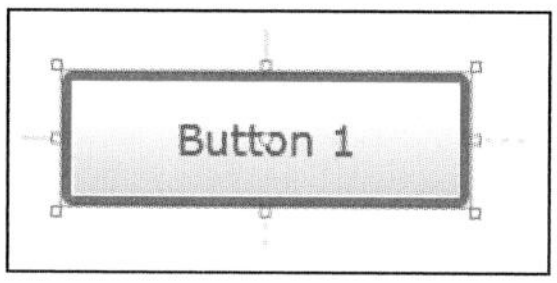

FIGURE 2.58   The setup properties.

around and increased the font size to 18 pixels to accentuate the effect.

5. Select Button 2.

6. Select the Eyedropper tool from the Tools panel and click once on Button 1. You should notice that Button 2 instantly takes across the entire set of matching color properties, as well as the font size from Button 1 to Button 2.

> **NOTE**
>
> **Why Is the Button Background Not a Solid Color?**
>
> This is entirely expected and is because of the default template applied to the Button element. For now, don't worry too much about this. Chapter 6, "Element Styles and Templates," walks you through this entire process.

7. If you now select the Rectangle element (which is the top right) and again select the eyedropper, click again on a button with the Eyedropper tool. You see that nothing happens at all. This is because the properties don't match for a rectangle and a Button element. The rectangle has a Fill property instead of a Background property.

8. Select the Border element and again select the eyedropper and select a button. Did you get what you expected? The background of the border is the solid color of the Buttons Background property, and the BorderBrush property is duplicated as well, but as you can see, the BorderThickness is not copied, as shown in Figure 2.59.

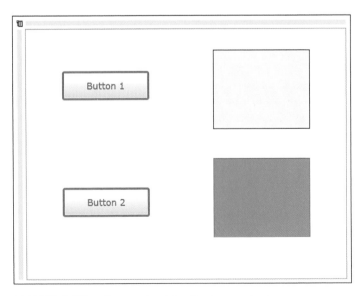

FIGURE 2.59   The result of the Eyedropper tool.

It's confusing, and I have made these points to the Expression Blend team. You might find some use for it—I can't.

The Paint Bucket tool is the same sort of confusion, but in reverse. To try this out, the following sample quickly shows the effect:

1. Change the layout of your app slightly and add another Border element, as shown in Figure 2.60. I gave the new Border element a thicker border (4 pixels), and you can apply similar colors.

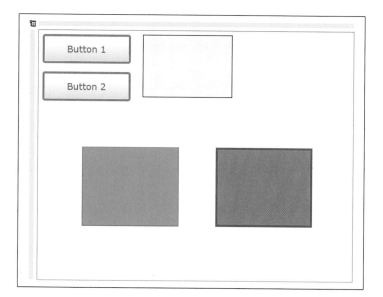

FIGURE 2.60   The new layout of the sample application.

2. With the new Blue Border element selected, select the Paint Bucket tool and then click on the existing green Border element.

I am sure you noticed that the BorderThickness property was not translated.

The next two tools are true Brush modifiers, the Gradient tool and the Brush Transform tool, and are shown in the collection detailed in Figure 2.61.

FIGURE 2.61   The Brush modifier tools collection.

You now use these two tools to understand each one in isolation; later in Chapter 4, "Common Properties and Functionality," you see how these two tools can work even further to adjust and help you work with patterns and image brushes.

The following steps walk you through creating and modifying a GradientBrush created with the Gradient tool.

1. Modify the layout of your solution so the Rectangle element takes the most space, as shown in Figure 2.62.

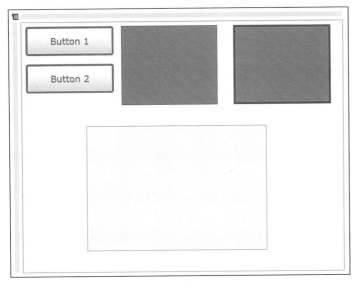

FIGURE 2.62   The new sample layout.

2. Select the rectangle and then the Gradient tool (the one with the Arrow icon).

3. Place the mouse cursor slightly inside the top-left corner of the Rectangle element. With the left mouse button held down, drag your mouse to the bottom right of the rectangle.

4. You should end up with a weird-looking gradient, black and white, stretching across the rectangle. Notice in Figure 2.63 the Gradient Stop modifiers. You can now select either one of those little rings and move them up and down the gradient guide line to change the weight of either color.

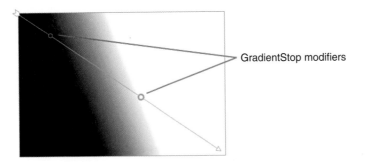

GradientStop modifiers

FIGURE 2.63   The Gradient Tool guide.

5. You can move the guide directly with the mouse, or you can move the mouse to either end of the guide (the arrow tip or end), and you see that you can shorten or lengthen the guide. You can also rotate the guide by moving the mouse slightly past the end of the guide.

6. Hold down the Shift key while rotating the guide, and you see that the guide turns in locked 15-degree increments.

7. Select the Brush Transform tool.

8. You see that the guide system changes considerably to present you with a rectangle type shape, as shown in Figure 2.64. This guide is easy to move around and independently change the depth and width of the guide, which gives you more accuracy when working with specific gradients.

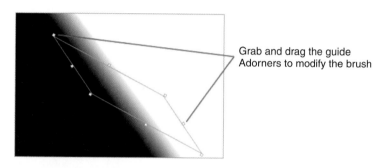

Grab and drag the guide
Adorners to modify the brush

FIGURE 2.64   The Brush Transform tool guide system.

Object Tools

The Object tools are multiple collections that contain a mixture of common controls, Layout panels, and Path and Shape tools. Most of these tools are covered in depth throughout the rest of the book, so to save on confusion at this point, I will detail the collection in the following and point you to the chapters that contain more details.

Path Creation Tools

The Pen tool, as shown in Figure 2.65, is used to create fixed-line path elements, connected from point to point. The tool has multiple key modifiers to help you create very accurate arcs and tangents.

FIGURE 2.65   The Path creation tools.

The pencil represents a freehand drawing tool, enabling you to plot path line elements everywhere that you hold the mouse down on the artboard.

See Chapter 12, "Shapes, Paths, and Effects," for details on using the Path creation tools.

Shape Tools

As you would expect, the Shape tools enable you to create and modify simple shapes, such as the rectangle, ellipse, and line, as shown in Figure 2.66.

See Chapter 12 for more detail on using the Path creation tools.

Layout Panel Collection

As shown in Figure 2.67, the Layout panel collection contains several panels that specifically control the layout of controls that you use in your user interface. The primary Layout panel is the grid, and it is very important that you understand how to use this control property in order to master your use of Expression Blend.

FIGURE 2.66   The Shape tools.

Also note that in Figure 2.67, WPF type projects have more tools available, which is because of the larger control set that WPF contains.

See Chapter 5, "The Art of Layout," for greater detail on how to correctly use layout.

Text and Input Controls Collection

Some Text input controls have specifically defined functionality such as the PasswordBox, which enables you to help conceal sensitive information. The TextBox is an input control, whereas the TextBlock and Label controls have specific usage around the display of text back to your user.

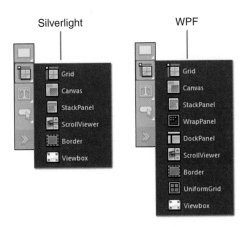

FIGURE 2.67   The Layout panel collection for both Silverlight and WPF.

As shown in Figure 2.68, both Silverlight and WPF share some common controls such as the TextBox, PasswordBox, and RichTextBox, for example.

See Chapter 4, "Common Properties and Functionality," for more details around using Text input controls.

Common Controls

The most commonly used controls such as the Button and ListBox are always in

> **NOTE**
>
> **Why Does WPF Have More Controls Than Silverlight?**
>
> Silverlight is a subset of Windows Presentation Foundation (WPF), and in order to reduce the install size of the Silverlight solution, many classes and controls were removed from the .Net Framework version that supports Silverlight. Most of the removed controls are available from the Silverlight SDK or additional libraries.

easy reach for both Silverlight and WPF by being part of the common controls collection, as shown in Figure 6.69.

See Chapter 4 for more details around using Text input controls.

Asset Tools

The Asset library tool button gives access to the Assets panel, which will be detailed in the next section.

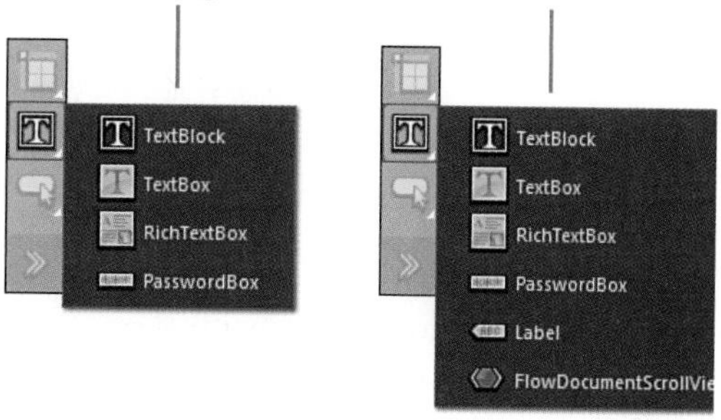

Assets Panel

The Assets panel represents collections of all available controls, media, effects, Behaviors, and much more, as shown in Figure 2.70.

What Figure 2.70 doesn't indicate is that a WPF projects contains the same layout and functionality of the Assets panel, but different controls that are not available in Silverlight (this is the same in reverse) and WPF projects typically contain many more reference locations.

Usage is pretty self-explanatory, in that you find a control or behavior, for example, that you want to use, and you either double-click the item or drag directly to the artboard or the Objects and Timeline panel.

Searching

As you become more familiar with various controls and elements, you will naturally start to remember the names of the controls and elements, so the Search mechanism of this panel is very helpful. You only need to begin typing the name of what you are after and the collection will begin to modify to show you what is available, as shown in Figure 2.71.

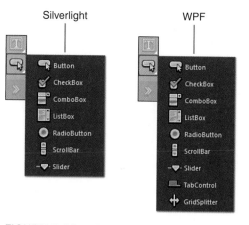

FIGURE 2.68   Some of the common controls shared by Silverlight and WPF.

FIGURE 2.69   The Common Controls collection for both Silverlight and WPF.

As I typed in the letters "he," you can see in Figure 2.71 how the collection has now reduced considerably, and you see that the collection count indicators also show relevance to the available result.

Properties Panel

The Properties panel contains a substantial amount of functionality and represents (along with the Objects and Timeline panel) one of the primary areas that you will spend most of your time in when working in Expression Blend, so learning how to navigate it is very important.

Search input

Collection count

Child groups

Drag elements
onto the
artboard

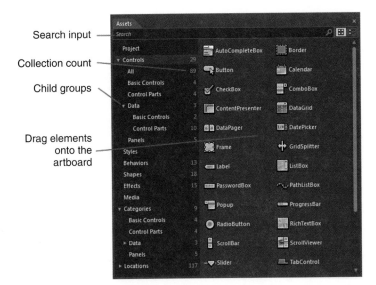

FIGURE 2.70   The Assets panel.

Result count

Resource online

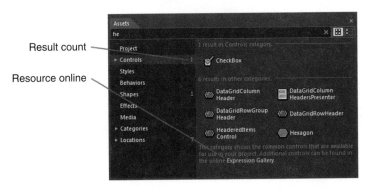

FIGURE 2.71   The Asset panel context change in the collection after searching.

The following section details the most-used features of the Properties panel, although it should be noted that the panel and the collections shown inside the Properties panel are context driven, and will change dramatically depending on what you are doing with Blend at the time.

Figure 2.72 indicates that the Properties panel also has an Event Viewer mode that will be detailed last in this section.

> **NOTE**
>
> **Changing Controls Changes the Category Collection**
>
> In this section, the Properties panel is detailed while a Button element is selected on the artboard, as this will show the most common functions and features of the panel.

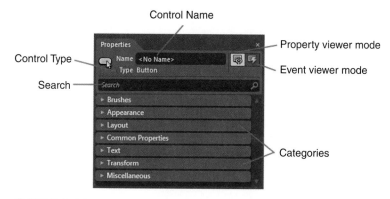

FIGURE 2.72   Overview of the Properties panel.

You see that several Property categories are very similar in their layout and contain simple input boxes that you can type values into directly, or use your mouse to drag values up and down in the case of numbers.

Name and Type

The name of any element is by default <No Name>, which means that the control or element has no Name value assigned to it. Depending on the architecture of your application, you might choose to use names and if so, it is advised you take on a constant naming convention for use in your applications. By default as mentioned, Blend does not assign a name to your controls, but this rule is broken when you apply behaviors or specific functionality to a control, such as animate a property of a button, in which case Expression Blend assigns a default name to your element. This is done so your application can represent the correct instance of your control elements. Think about it for a minute, if you had 10 buttons on your artboard and only wanted to animate one of those buttons, the application needs to be able to reference that specific control.

The *Type* of control is very specific and is well worth noting when you add or work with new controls. You can clearly see in Figure 2.72 that Button element is currently being reviewed and the Property collection also shown in Figure 2.72 is the property collection representation of the Button type control.

> **NOTE**
>
> **Property Changes Occur Implicitly**
>
> What does this really mean? Expression Blend will change the property value of your elements automatically when you work with them on the artboard, so for instance, if you select a Button element on the artboard and resize it, you see that the appropriate Width properties will also change. See Chapter 5 for more details on how properties are also affected by Parent elements.

Search

Search is a powerful feature of the Properties panel and can help significantly reduce confusion and aid in productivity. Figure 2.73 shows how the Category collection has been reduced, and only properties that contain a pattern match of "cont" are shown.

My advice is to use property searching as often as possible.

Categories and Advanced Properties

As you have seen in varying figures, there are plenty of categories that properties are divided into. What you also see in the Properties panel is that some categories contain an Advanced Property

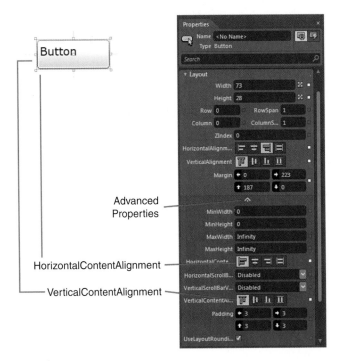

FIGURE 2.73   The result of searching the Property collection.

section that extends the property collection, sometimes with only a single property and sometimes much more, as shown in Figure 2.74.

FIGURE 2.74   The Layout category and Advanced Properties for layout.

Figure 2.74 also shows you the effect that the Advanced Properties of HorizontalContentAlignment and VerticalContentAlignment have on the Button element also shown.

Property Binding References

Ignore the fact that the control type in Figure 2.75 is a ContentPresenter; I wanted to show you here that Blend indicates if properties are not their default values, as well as indicating that the value supplied to the property is coming from somewhere else.

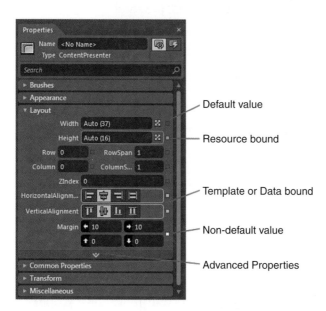

FIGURE 2.75   Different property binding notifications.

In the case of the green border and box, this is indicating that the value supplied is coming from a resource within the application. A resource is a value that is usually fixed—it could be a template, or it could be a number, as in this case. See Chapter 13, "Skins, Themes, and Resource Dictionaries," for more details on resources.

If the border and box are orange, this indicates that the property value is "bound" to a property somewhere else in the application. This is a complex concept that is out of scope for this section of this chapter, but reviewing Chapter 6, "Element Styles and Templates," gives you the detailed understanding of what this all means.

A white box means that the value applied is not the default value of that particular property and, conversely, an empty or clear box means that a default value is applied.

Advanced Options

The Advanced Options dialog, as shown in Figure 2.76, is a combination of extended functionality and shortcuts. The options as they are shown become enabled/disabled when working in specific context.

An example of this is that Figure 2.76 is shown as the result of clicking on the green box for the property that is currently bound to a resource; you will see that the options to "Edit Resource..." and "Convert to Local Value" are enabled.

For the most part, these options are explained in context throughout the rest of the book and will not be detailed here. The last advanced option, "Record Current Value," is only available when working within a storyboard for instance, so its usage will be shown in Chapter 11, "Animations and Transitions."

FIGURE 2.76   The Advanced Options context menu.

Brushes

The Brushes category, as shown in Figure 2.77, carries significant functionality that takes a little practice to really come to terms with. Understanding where everything resides is half the battle, but you should quickly become comfortable with working in the color pallets for SolidColorBrush and GradientBrush types. Case in point is locating where you can switch from RGB to CMYK color values, which is hidden away completely. Figure 2.78 shows that you can click on any one of the letters of RGB, and you will be presented with a little context menu offering your choice for saturation, hue, and other modifiers.

Resources play a large part in how you will interact with brushes and the properties that they are applied to and, as such, will be detailed in Chapter 13, "Skins, Themes, and Resource Dictionaries" As a matter of practice, you will use the Brushes category heavily throughout the rest of the book.

Active Icons

Some specific categories such as brushes have their own unique property editing experience, but it's interesting to note as well that some categories have what appear to be just icons but are, in fact, interactive property assistants.

One of the most common property categories is called Transform. You will learn more about Transform in Chapter 11, but for now, it serves as a great example of active icon assistants in Blend.

If you create a Silverlight Application + Website project and add a simple button to the artboard, you should see that the Transform category is available in the Properties panel.

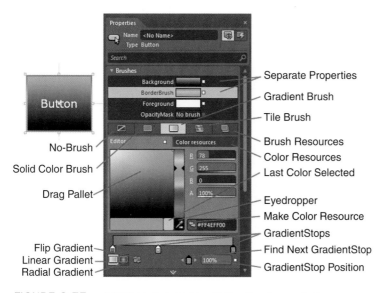

Separate Properties
Gradient Brush
Tile Brush
Brush Resources
Color Resources
Last Color Selected
Eyedropper
Make Color Resource
GradientStops
Find Next GradientStop
GradientStop Position

No-Brush
Solid Color Brush
Drag Pallet
Flip Gradient
Linear Gradient
Radial Gradient

FIGURE 2.77   A high-level overview of the Brushes category.

Figure 2.79 is showing the effects of a Plane Projection Transform applied to the button element, which in this case is rotating the element in all three axis. What I am pointing out here, though, is that I didn't need to enter the values into the X, Y, and Z input boxes. You can simply drag your mouse of the active icon on the left.

Most Transform properties have an active icon, so have play around with the effects that they create.

Events

Events occur when a user or dynamic parts of your application cause something to happen to an object. The easiest way to understand this is to consider a Button element. When you physically click on a button, you are causing an event to occur—the Click

FIGURE 2.78   The very well-hidden options to switch color modifiers.

event, to be specific. Events enable you to react to the Click and perform whatever task suits your requirements. For instance, a click could mean that someone has entered a value on a form, and the button is a Submit button, and so on.

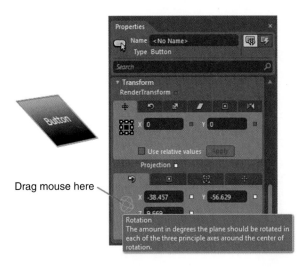

Drag mouse here

FIGURE 2.79   Demonstrating an active icon in the Transform category.

Expression Blend provides an Event viewer mode so you can hook up controls that you are creating in Blend to code-behind file that let you go off and dynamically work out what to do next.

The key word here is "dynamic."

The user interface layer you are creating in Blend is not dynamic at all. It might appear to be that way when you start animations and add effects, but the truth is that Expression Blend is simply creating a static mark-up language for you (called XAML), which defines what objects are where and how you might want to use those objects.

The code layer is very different to that as you can work with conditional logic, add and remove elements, and do all sorts of magical things.

Think of the user interface layer in Blend being a static design time layer that is more akin to drawing on a board, and think of the code layer as being all that power when your application is running—so-called runtime.

Figure 2.80 shows the Event viewer mode for a Button type and as you can see, a value has been given for the Click event. This Click event is linked up in the code behind file waiting for the user to click the button.

FIGURE 2.80   The Button event collection with specifically the Click event being subscribed to.

Don't be overwhelmed by this concept, as it will be explained a little further in Chapter 3, "Using Expression Blend for the First Time" where you connect all the pieces together, including some simple events.

Resources Panel

The Resources panel contains a map to all the control element and property value mappings that are collectively referred to in Expression Blend as resources. Figure 2.81 provides an overview of the panel showing two resources in differing scenarios.

FIGURE 2.81   The Resources panel.

A concept that is key to using resources is that of the Resource Dictionary (RD), which is basically an XAML file that contains a collection of resource elements. You can push pretty much any type of resource into an RD, and when you edit any property value in the Properties panel, you can select the Advanced Options button; if applicable, you will be able to select "Convert to New Resource...."

When using an RD, the collections contained within it become accessible across your entire solution, so for example, you can create a default button style that you want to use everywhere and just by drag and dropping an element straight out of the Resources panel, your new button instance will appear. Any changes made to that style will be updated instantly across every button that references the style you have used.

As you can clearly see in Figure 2.81, there are two button styles added to this project. ButtonStyle1 is located as a child element of the [UserControl] element, whereas ButtonStyle2 is a child of ResourceDictionary1.xaml. This means that if you open the Assets panel and look at the Style collection, you see that only ButtonStyle2 is available as a global style, as shown in Figure 2.82.

Figure 2.83 shows that I am now filtering my resource collection by the current control that I am working on, so the Resources panel shows me the ButtonStyle1 style that I don't have in the RD.

Chapter 13 will help you understand in greater detail how to work with the Resources panel and Resource Dictionaries.

FIGURE 2.82   The ButtonStyle2 style available globally.

FIGURE 2.83   The ButtonStyle1 element available locally.

Data Panel

The Data panel contains a large amount of functionality specifically designed to get you working with structured and strongly typed data. This means that you can be sure of the data that you are working with, regardless of it being in designtime or runtime. Expression Blend enables you to create sample live data, which lets you style and present data in a meaningful way, all without having to write any code or get anyone else involved with providing data to your solution.

Figure 2.84 shows a sample data collection that has been created just for design time. You can see that the data collection is in use because of the orange binding border notification. The bottom half of the Data panel is also showing that the same data collection (in this instance, named SampleDataSource) is also providing the DataContext to the current scene. In essence, this means that any control I add to the artboard could get its display value and other settings directly from the DataContext.

FIGURE 2.84   The Data panel in use.

Granted that if you haven't worked with data collections before, the preceding information probably sounds very confusing and very complex, but Chapter 10, "Expression Blend Data Support," shows you just how simple it is to work with.

Summary

This is one of the largest chapter of the book, and you have covered quite a lot of ground to this point—some very high-level views of certain areas of working with Expression Blend and some interesting discoveries to help you position the tool in your mind. You now have seen the vast majority of the panels and understand that you can set up Blend to work how you want and need it to.

Chapters further on from this one are about digging into the detail of all of these concepts, teaching you as easily as possible about how Expression Blend works.

Chapter 3

Using Expression Blend for the First Time

It doesn't matter what type of application you are attempting to build—Windows Phone 7, WPF, Surface, SketchFlow, or Silverlight. Being able to work with the basics is applicable for all of them.

In this chapter, you begin to work around the Blend UI, understanding the core components by applying property changes and some simple animation to basic application components or UIElements (used interchangeably with element and control) to use their correct name.

Keeping Things Simple to Start With

> **Walk Before You Try to Run**
>
> I can't emphasize enough just how important it is to understand the core functionality and features of Expression Blend before jumping off the very deep end and trying to create something that is going to be extremely complex and ultimately very frustrating for you.

You can learn a considerable amount about Expression Blend by experimenting with a few simple elements. The humble button is, of course, the most ubiquitous control, but in XAML-based applications such as Silverlight and WPF, the layout panels (such as Grid and Canvas) are also leveraged highly. You review their respective functionality and cause and effect in Chapter 5, "The Art of Layout."

It's interesting to note that in the first release of Silverlight, the control set was pretty much limited to a MediaElement and anything else that could be cobbled together with a few shapes. The control collection has blossomed, especially in Silverlight 3, and now with Silverlight 4, an exceptional collection of functionality is available. The good thing with this is that for the most part, you won't have to reinvent the wheel and roll-your-own. Of course, sometimes that is the fun part!

It All Starts with a Button!

I love buttons. They are almost always a simple, yet effective, interaction. You mouse over and get some feedback (developers take note), and you should also be able to tell from a glance what the state of a button is: enabled or disabled. If you click on a button, something should happen. By comparison to other controls, it doesn't get much easier than that, does it?

That is the theory, but in practice, previously there was a bit more heavy-lifting to actually get the "something" to happen.

One of the continuing goals of the Expression team is to empower you to create as much of the functional user interface without the need for code or code understanding, so along came the concept of behaviors.

Behaviors attach to elements and, as the name suggests, enable you to specify how a nugget of interactivity should be applied and how the control should behave—without you ever needing to see code, much less understand it.

Expression Blend 4 is the full embodiment of the "Behavior" direction that the Silverlight (and WPF) platforms needed to take. The inclusion of behaviors from Expression Blend 3 onward meant that you as a designer or developer can hook up interactions with nothing more than a drag-and-drop action, which becomes extremely productive and reduces runtime errors and state complexity.

Work through this chapter and take in the simplicity of the button and the Blend user interface. By the end of the chapter, you will be working with a control in both a static and animated context and also be using a behavior to get some functionality added.

You should start the following task by creating a new Silverlight Application + Website project type.

> **NOTE**
>
> **Project Creation**
>
> From subsequent chapters, you will be directed to create your projects autonomously, and you can safely assume that you should use default settings unless otherwise directed.

Creating a New Silverlight Application

The following steps show you how to create your first Silverlight application.

1. Open Expression Blend, and use either the default Welcome dialog to create a new project, as shown in Figure 3.1, or select the File menu item and then the New Project menu option.

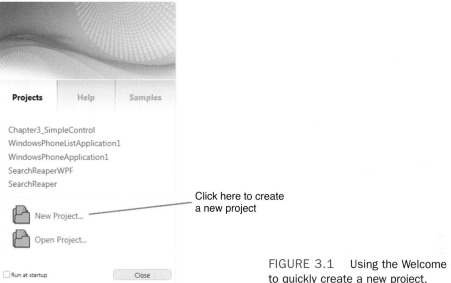

Click here to create
a new project

FIGURE 3.1   Using the Welcome screen
to quickly create a new project.

2. Select the Silverlight project types
   option and ensure that "Silverlight
   Application + Website" is selected,
   as shown in Figure 3.2.

3. You can name this project whatever you want, but for this
   example, I have called it
   "Chapter3_SimpleControl." The
   location of the application is in a
   specific folder created for this
   book's projects.

TIP

**What Happened to the Welcome
Dialog?**

You can always bring the Welcome dialog
back up at any stage by going to the Help
menu and selecting the Welcome Screen
option.

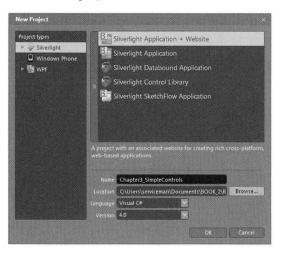

FIGURE 3.2   The New Project dialog
and the project settings to use in this
sample.

You now have the basic parts of a Silverlight application and a small website also created in the solution to handle the pages you will create. You can open the Project tab (by default, located with the collection of tabs on the right side of the Blend UI), and you see the structure that Blend has created for you in order to fulfill the basic requirements. This is shown in Figure 3.3, and it is worthwhile to take a moment to understand the breakdown of the solution.

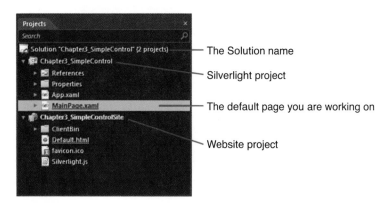

FIGURE 3.3   Exploring the Silverlight Application + Website project Blend has created, using the Project tab.

> **NOTE**
>
> **A High-Level Solution Breakdown**
>
> You can clearly see in Figure 3.3 that the solution is broken into two main parts. One of those parts represents the Silverlight project that you are currently working on and the other is the website that was also created for you. In general, you don't work on any of the website project files inside Expression Blend. Expression Web is a much better tool for this particular piece of work.
>
> What you continue to do as your projects get more complex is add more and more controls and resources to your projects, which also show up in the Project tab. You can also access the code behind files for any of your XAML files from this view, not to mention being able to right-click on the Solution label and open up the entire solution in Visual Studio.

Without adding any controls or changing any settings, you can now run the application by selecting the Project menu item at the top of Blend and then selecting the Run Project option (Project->Run Project), which (as you have most likely guessed) will run the application as a blank white screen inside your default web browser.

Interestingly, when you run your application, you should note that Expression Blend creates and starts a Development Server for you (shown in Figure 3.4), which enables you to emulate a web server on your desktop. This is important to note because later on, you will need some of these details in order to test certain functionality in Silverlight.

Note the icon that is added to the Windows Notification area. You can right-click on this icon, and you should be able to select the Show Details menu item, which displays a dialog similar to that shown in Figure 3.5.

It's important to note that in these details, you get to understand the port that your application is using to communicate with other applications and services, as well as the physical location of your application as you selected.

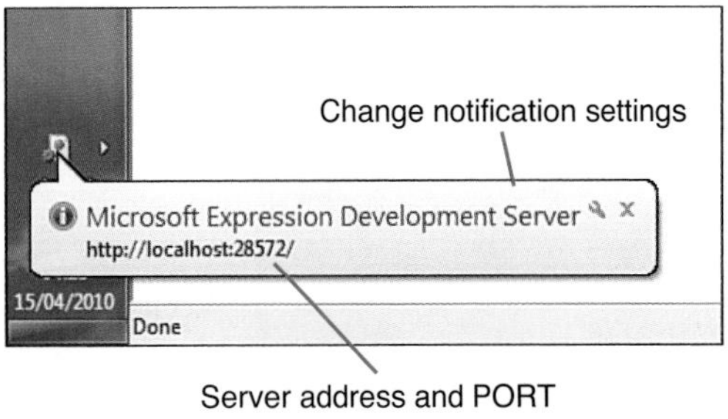

FIGURE 3.4   The Development Server successfully being created for you.

Close the dialog shown in Figure 3.5 by using the "X"; don't click on the Stop button. You should now also close the web page that is showing your completely blank application.

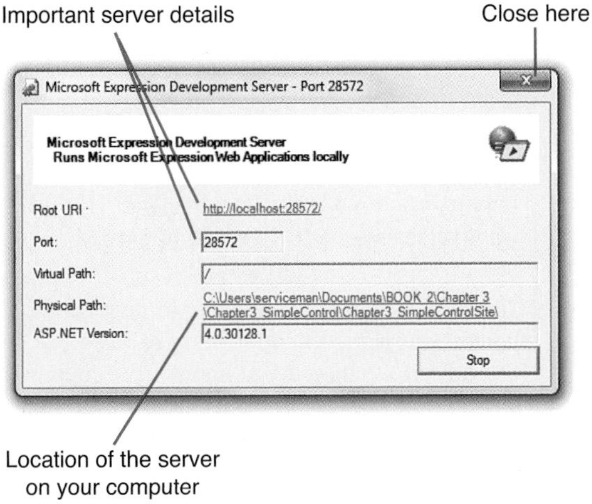

FIGURE 3.5   Exploring the details of the Development Server.

Your application is not very exciting at this point. You now add some basic controls and change some properties to liven things up!

Objects and Timeline Panel Basics

On the left side of the Blend UI, you should see a tab that is titled "Objects and Timeline," and under this is the start of what looks like a tree and some "eyes" and a "padlock" type icon(s), as shown in Figure 3.6.

You will note that there are two elements visible in the tree (as shown in Figure 3.6), with the first item showing as [UserControl] and another item underneath it called LayoutRoot.

Nested control (parent/child relationship)

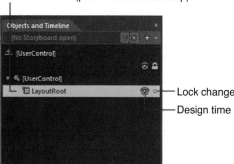

Lock changes to the control
Design time visibility toggle

FIGURE 3.6   The default Objects and Timeline panel.

This tree might in some cases become filled with lots of items, and they represent the visual hierarchy of not only the elements you place on the design surface, but also various behaviors and effects that you apply to each element. This can sometimes appear to get quite complex, but you learn how to navigate this panel in further detail throughout the rest of the book as needed.

You should ensure that you have the Properties tab open because you are about to make some simple changes.

Forgetting the top element in the Objects and Timeline tab for a little while (you will come back to it later),

> **NOTE**
>
> **Have You Lost the Properties Tab?**
>
> If you lose the Properties tab (or any of the other tabs), there is a simple way of getting them to appear on the screen.
>
> Open the Window menu item at the top of Blend, and you see a list of panels that should be shown. If the tab or panel that you want to see has a tick next to it, simply select it to remove the tick.
>
> The menu will close, but you can now go back through the Window menu to re-select the tab or panel, and you should see your choice now appear on the screen.

you should ensure that you have the LayoutRoot selected; it should become highlighted with a blue border to visually indicate this.

Reviewing the Properties tab, you should now see that the name of the element is indeed LayoutRoot; note that it says Grid next to the "Type" option. This is important much later on, but for now, you should get into the habit of always checking the *type* of element you are working on and become familiar with the relevant properties of that element.

For those of you who have used various design applications previously (and indeed developers), as you would expect, the property collections shown changes depending on the *types* of element you are working on.

1. Ensure that the Brushes category is fully expanded and open, as shown in Figure 3.7.

2. Select the Background property.

3. Select the GradientBrush option tab.

4. Select the right Gradient stop

5. Change the color gradient bar by dragging your mouse over it or clicking when the indicator is close to the middle of the blue area. Then, select a nice vibrant blue from the color palette, as shown in Figure 3.8.

FIGURE 3.7   The default color properties of the LayoutRoot element.

Run your application again (you might want to just press the F5 button this time), and you should see that indeed your application shows the new color gradient applied.

Why isn't the entire web browser showing the gradient, you might ask? This is because the default `UserControl` element in your project has its `Width` and `Height` properties set to a fixed value by default, which you are going to change in the following steps.

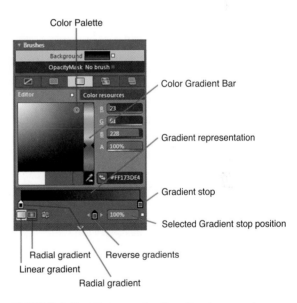

FIGURE 3.8   The new Gradient Brush property settings applied to the Background property of the LayoutRoot.

1. Return to the Objects and Timeline tab, and this time, select the [UserControl] named element (referred to as simply UserControl from now on).

2. Note the Properties panel change to reflect this (remember to check the element*Type*).

3. Locate the Layout category of the Properties tab and expand it, as shown in Figure 3.9.

4. As also shown in Figure 3.9, you can select the Auto button options for both the `Width` and `Height` properties. This changes the values in the property input box to show "Auto (0)" as the value.

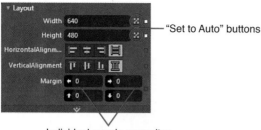

"Set to Auto" buttons

Individual margin properites

FIGURE 3.9   The Layout category of the Properties tab and specifically the Set to Auto buttons.

You might experience a weird change in your screen at this point, where your design surface elements appear to have disappeared.

This has occurred because of the change to the property value, which shows the "(0)"; in this particular case, the 0 represents the design time size applied to the property. Simply select the UserControl element in the Objects and Timeline tab and press your "Control" and "0" buttons at the same time (Ctrl + 0) to center your design surface. You should see some adorners on the screen, as highlighted in Figure 3.10. Grab and stretch the resize adorner by dragging down to the right, and you see your gradient colored LayoutRoot element again. Just make sure that you drag it all back out to a sufficient size again, so the property values now read something like "Auto (1024)" for Width and "Auto (768)" for the Height. Don't worry if you don't get it exact; you just need it large enough to keep working on.

Click and drag down to resize the control and keep Auto size settings

FIGURE 3.10   The resize adorners of the UserControl element when it is set to Auto (0) sizing.

Running your application (F5) should now render a full screen result, as you might have been expecting previously.

Using the Button

In the following steps, you are going to use a button and apply some basic behavior values to it. This realistically

> ### TIP
>
> **Auto Size and Keep Values**
>
> Although it's difficult to discover, you can select an element in the Objects and Timeline or the artboard and right-click to show a context menu containing an "Auto Size" menu item. One of the sub-menu items from there is "Both," which when clicked will maintain the original design size of the element while applying the Auto Size property value.

gives you quite a bit, considering you are just dragging a few elements onto your screen and making some clicks with your mouse. Simple, isn't it?

1. Select the LayoutRoot element in the Objects and Timeline panel.

2. In the toolbar at the fixed-left position of the Blend UI, you can locate the Button element in the common controls collection, as shown in Figure 3.11.

3. With the Button element selected, draw a large button on your artboard so you end up with something similar to Figure 3.12.

4. The Objects and Timeline tab should also now reflect that the Button element you added is indeed a child element of the LayoutRoot element, and by default naming convention shows

Click and hold to show additional items in the ToolBar collection

FIGURE 3.11   The location of the Button element in the common controls collection of the toolbar.

that you have a [Button] element, as shown in Figure 3.13. You can again check that with the element *Type* property on your Properties tab.

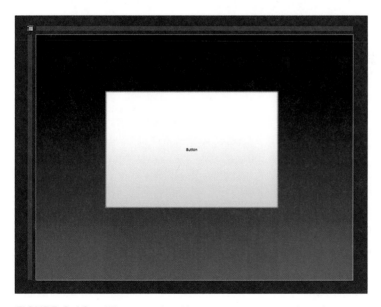

FIGURE 3.12   What you should now see on your artboard.

Collapse/Expand collection

[Button] is the new child element of the LayoutRoot element

FIGURE 3.13   The new child element of the LayoutRoot.

Properties Are the Highest Level of Importance

When it comes down to it, almost everything you do in Expression Blend is directly affecting the property values of the elements you are working on. In other words, you are effectively modifying property values for every action you apply to an element, whether that be by animation, behavior, or action, for example; this underscores the importance of understanding the Properties tab and what it can do for you.

Obviously, there are many more advanced discussions to take place around how to work with those advanced options, which come later in the book, but for now you should be noting the "cause and effect" of the actions you perform.

To demonstrate this, ensuring that you have your Button element selected, you should take note of the Margin properties. The Margin values live inside the Layout category of the Property tab and, as shown in Figure 3.14, the values applied to my sample are 227 for the Left margin, 243 for the right, 178 for the top, and 227 for the bottom.

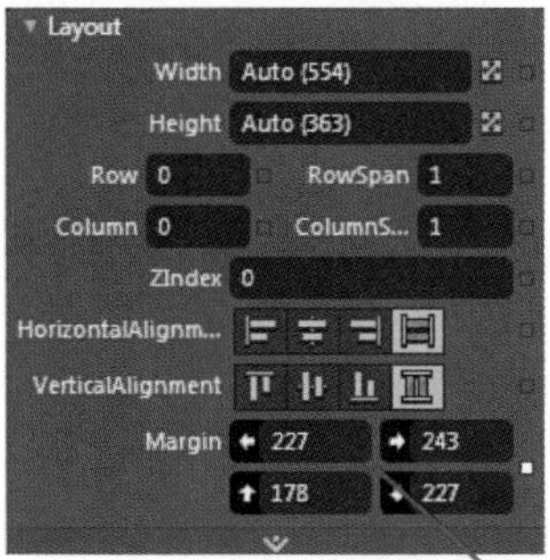

What are these Margin values saying?

The numerical values are saying how far away the edge of the Button element **must** always remain from the outer edge of its parent element (which, in this case, is the LayoutRoot). This means that if I resize my browser (or application in WPF), the Button element changes size to honor those property values.

Margin properties fix a distance that the element must always remain from the parent element boundary.

FIGURE 3.14   The Margin property values for the Button element added.

Chapter 5, "The Art of Layout," gives you greater detail around how to work with different panels and the layout effects that can be achieved.

The following steps show you how to rotate the Button element.

TIP

How Does the Button Know to Change Size?

The button's resize logic is effectively moot because it doesn't change its own size. The parent element is what determines the child size, as it performs several steps of measuring when it becomes resized, and so on and so forth up the tree of elements. Each child is resized by its parent.

1. Selecting the Button element in the Objects and Timeline tab, move your mouse position to just above one of the corners of the button; you should see your mouse change to show a double-headed curved arrow, which indicates that you can rotate the element.

2. Left-click and hold and drag your mouse around to change the rotation value of the button. What should remain is something similar to Figure 3.15. Notice that the original position of the button is also shown by the adorner on the artboard.

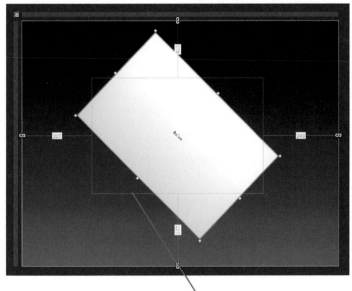

Physical location of the button
in its original presentation

FIGURE 3.15　The rotated Button element.

3. Open the Properties tab, and in the Property Search box, type in the letters "tra," which narrows the property categories shown. Specifically, you want to be looking at the Transform property group; within that group, the second tab that represents

the Rotation Transform has been applied to the selected element, as shown in Figure 3.16.

Manually change the value in this input box
Drag on this disk to change the rotation value

FIGURE 3.16   The Rotate tab of the Transform category.

4. You can manually change the value of rotation directly either with your mouse by dragging on the little disk type image or by modifying the values in the input box.

5. Reset the value to 0 when you have finished having fun.

Transformations

While you are working inside the Transformation category in the Properties tab, you should get an understanding of the difference between transforms and fixed property value modification before you start to animate the button; animations are mostly applied as a transformation rather than direct element changes, such as Margin values. You get a much deeper understanding of transformations in Chapter 11, "Animations and Transitions" when you work with much more complex animation samples.

The following steps demonstrate simple Translations

1. Ensure that you have the Button selected and the Transform category open in the Properties tab.

2. Select the first Tab inside the Transform category, which is called Translate and is shown in Figure 3.17.

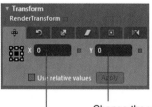

Change the vertical position of the selected element
Change the horizontal position of the selected element

FIGURE 3.17   The Translate tab of the Transform category.

3. Modify the value in the X property value, and you should see that your button has moved position, again noting the adorner showing the original position of the Button element.

Perhaps you are asking the question at the moment: "What is the difference between moving the element with the Transform versus just changing the Margin property?" At a high level, you can achieve the same thing using either property, but when you start working with more than one element, things start to get a bit trickier.

As I mentioned previously and demonstrate next, Transforms are generally applied to an element when it is being animated. Transforms on an element also affect the element's presented location rather than its position in a physical sense (thus the importance of the bounding box)—in other words, if you modify the Translate X and Y values of a control, its physical location position (of X, Y) doesn't change, but its presented position does.

Take this example: You have two buttons side by side, and they are nested inside a layout type control called a StackPanel. The job of the StackPanel, as its name suggests, is to "stack" the controls on top of each other or side by side, as shown in Figure 3.18.

StackPanel element forces the two buttons to "Stack" side by side. This can also be set to make child elements to stack on top of each other

FIGURE 3.18   A basic scenario of two buttons stacked side by side inside of a StackPanel.

When you change the left Margin value of Button 1, note in Figure 3.19 how both buttons are still stacked; in this case, the StackPanel shown in gray simply grows to facilitate the Margin requirements of its child buttons.

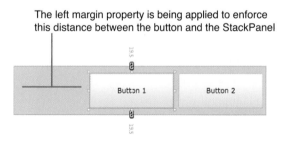

The left margin property is being applied to enforce this distance between the button and the StackPanel

FIGURE 3.19   The Margin effect inside the StackPanel.

What if you want only Button 1 to move and Button 2 to stay in the same location? This is where the Translate property is applied to the element's presented location, but the physical location of it doesn't change, so the layout logic of the StackPanel and Button 2 remain correct, as shown in Figure 3.20.

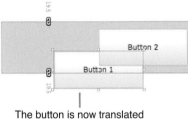

The button is now translated
in both the X and Y axis

FIGURE 3.20   Button 1 with an individual Translation applied.

Simple Animation

Now that you understand the high-level concept of the transformation, it would be nice for you to be able to apply a simple animation to move the button around the screen when the button is clicked.

The following steps show you how to achieve this, although it must be said that this is an extremely simple sample. I am sure you will have lots of questions about animation and storyboarding, which will be answered in Chapter 11.

1. With the Button element selected and highlighted inside the Objects and Timeline tab, you can click on the New animation button, which is shown in Figure 3.21.

2. Figure 3.22 shows the default dialog that enables you to name your storyboard, but for now, just leave it as Storyboard1.

3. You should now see the Storyboard composition view of the Objects and Timeline tab, similar to that of Figure 3.23, which might be a familiar sight for some of you with previous animation experience.

Create Storyboard being edited   Create new Storyboard button

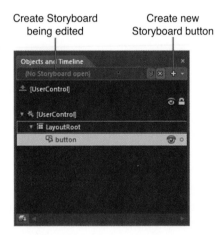

FIGURE 3.21   The current element tree indicates where the New Storyboard button is.

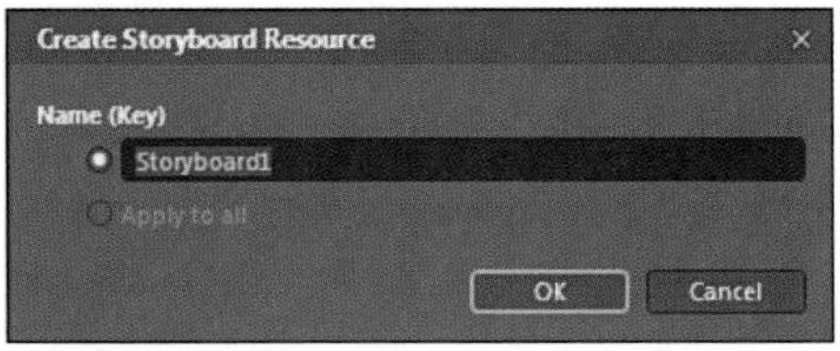

FIGURE 3.22   The default Create Storyboard Resource dialog.

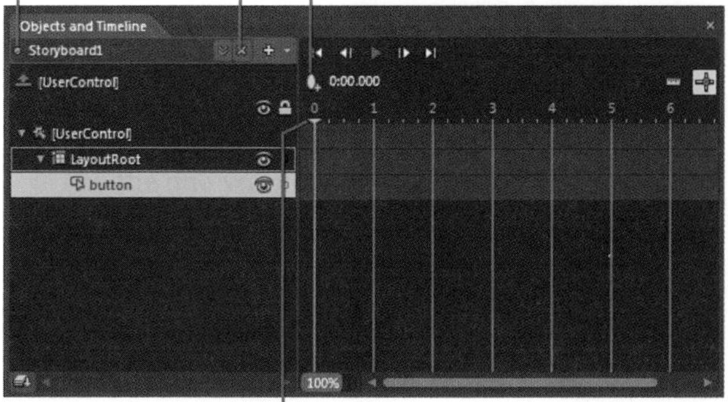

Storyboard in Record mode

Close Storyboard ¬   ┌ Record Keyframe button

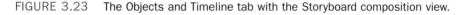

Playhead position

FIGURE 3.23   The Objects and Timeline tab with the Storyboard composition view.

4. Figure 3.23 also shows you where the Record Keyframe button is; ensuring that you have the Button element selected and the Playhead indicator (the yellow line you can drag from the top) at position 0, you should now click on the Record Keyframe button.

5. Move the Playhead indicator to position 1.

6. Move the Button element to the bottom-right side of the screen; using the adorners on the artboard around the button, reduce the size of the button by dragging the adorner in the top-left corner, as shown in Figure 3.24.

Did you notice that a keyframe was created for you after you changed the properties of the button's size, and now a RenderTransform item has been added under the button in the Objects and Timeline panel? You can expand that item to see the properties that have been animated, as shown in Figure 3.25. Take a look at the Translate properties inside the Transform category in the properties tab as well.

Notice the dots on the screen showing the original center position of the Button as well, also shown in Figure 3.24.

There is a lot going on here for such a simple little animation, so you can see why you are doing simple things first.

Figure 3.25 also shows you how to close down the animation view and return to the default Objects and Timeline view.

- ▶ Slider
- ▶ ComboBox
- ▶ ListBox
- ▶ TabControl

With the release of Expression Blend 4, tooling support is now provided for even more controls (and some new controls) that help provide even greater levels of simplicity and ease of use. You will find that this chapter looks at the standard controls that are available across most of the platforms that Blend supports, but don't despair—Chapter 14, "Advanced Controls," gives you a closer look at some specific platform controls for Silverlight and WPF, as well as some of the more obscure controls.

In Chapter 6, "Element Styles and Templates," you also look at the concepts of how to create your own styles and templates for common controls. For now, however, you will be concentrating on the Property sets available and some ideas around user experience with them.

To get started with this chapter, create a new Silverlight Application + Website project type.

Border

For those who have already had a look around Expression Blend or will be upgrading to this new version, sometimes it is unclear what a Border offers that the Rectangle shape doesn't. As you can see in Figure 4.1, both can take the same visual appearance (almost).

The Border control differs in property set from the Rectangle by enabling you to do four specific things that the Rectangle can't, as follows:

- ▶ The Border enables you to host child controls where the Rectangle doesn't.
- ▶ The Border enables you to specify each corner with a different radial curve, whereas the Rectangle provides for a RadiusX and RadiusY property that constrains the pairs of corner curve.

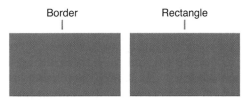

Border   Rectangle

FIGURE 4.1   A Border element and Rectangle element looking the same.

TIP

Looks Like a Rose, Smells Like a Rose; Surely It Must Be a Rose? Not Quite.

The answer is indeed in the latter part of the last sentence in the first paragraph stating that although the Border element is a control, the rectangle is a shape. It sounds like just a terminology difference, but in reality, the differences are vast. You look at shapes in Chapter 12, "Shapes and Effects," in greater detail, as Expression Blend 4 now contains a nice collection worth reviewing.

▸ The Border enables you to set different side thickness values for each side, whereas the Rectangle maintains a singular value for all sides.

▸ Create a Style for the Border that is transferable to other Border elements.

To be technically accurate, the Border is a `ContentControl` *type*. This means that although *Panel*-based controls such as a `Grid` enable you to add as many child elements as you like, the Border enables you to host only a single child element.

The following steps help demonstrate this concept.

FIGURE 4.2   The border located in the Layout panel collection of the Tool panel.

1. Figure 4.2 shows you where to get a Border control from the toolbar to which you should add to your artboard. Make it a large arbitrary size and give it a background color by modifying the Background property in the Properties tab.

2. With your border selected in the Objects and Timeline panel, locate and double-click on the `Button` control in the toolbar to add it as a child of the `Border`. Your Objects and Timeline panel should resemble Figure 4.3.

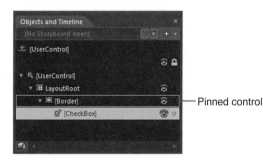

FIGURE 4.3   The nested child Button inside the Border control.

3. With the Border control selected again, right-click on it and select the Pin Active Container menu item. This fixes the Border control as the parent container control and puts a yellow border around the element in the Objects and Timeline panel, as shown in Figure 4.4.

4. Go to the collection of common controls in the toolbar, find a CheckBox control, and double-click it.

FIGURE 4.4   The button has been removed from the Objects and Timeline tab.

What should have happened is that the Button control has been removed from the Border, and now the Objects and Timeline tab looks like Figure 4.4.

What is the point of a single child element?

At first, a single child element appears like a design fault and in practice, without understanding the reasons, only having a single child is frustrating.

There is nothing stopping you from adding a Grid element (or any other type of layout container) instead and then adding as many child elements to the Grid, all presented nicely inside the bounds of your Border.

Aside from the Border hosting elements that, as I wrote previously, the Rectangle can't do, you can perform several other features with the Border that you will look at now through property modification in the following steps.

> ### Why Pin an Element?
>
> Pinning an element allows you to manipulate the elements on the artboard in a much more efficient manner, especially if you have a lot of child elements. It's a workflow habit that is more about personal preference than a requirement.

> ### TIP
>
> ### What Other ContentControls Are There?
>
> The Button is also a ContentControl, along with the CheckBox and ComboBox, plus a few others. I wanted you to understand this functionality so you don't get frustrated moving forward, wondering why controls keep disappearing. It is also important later on when you need to decide how to architect a custom control and the choices you have.

1. With your Border element selected, right-click and again check on the Pin Active Container menu item.

2. You should have also noted that there exists a BorderBrush property that you can modify to suit. In the Appearance category of the Properties tab, you will see two border-specific properties of interest. The first is the BorderThickness property, which enables you to set individual side thickness values. Modify each one to various sizes, as shown in Figure 4.5.

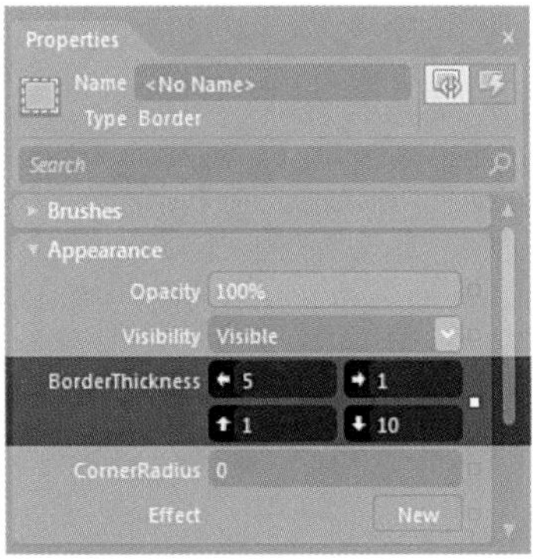

   Set all the BorderThickness values to 5.

   In the Appearance category of the Properties tab, you will find another property called

FIGURE 4.5   Mismatched side BorderThickness values applied in the Properties panel.

CornerRadius. At first, this looks like it only takes a single value, and if you change the default 0 value to a 15, you see that all corners now have a 15-pixel corner radius. You can enter comma-separated values to modify each corner individually, though, and you should now enter 5,10,25,40, as shown in Figure 4.6.

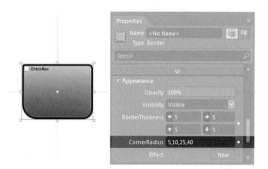

FIGURE 4.6   The individual CornerRadius ability of the Border element.

The comma-separated values represent a clockwise transformation of the corners, starting at the top left and moving to top right, bottom right, and finally bottom-left corner radius.

The Checkbox

The CheckBox is one of those controls that feel like it has been around since the beginning of time. Let's face it—the CheckBox's functionality is pretty well known, and it might appear at first that there is not much to look at from a design perspective.

You should review some of the properties for this control so you are a little more aware of the choices for usability and styling that you will be looking at in Chapter 6 in detail.

You should now add a CheckBox control to your artboard. You should be able to find that inside the Common Controls collection in the toolbar; just double-click on the CheckBox item, and one should be added to the default top-left corner of your artboard.

With the CheckBox selected, have a quick look through the property list. You see that there are plenty of properties to modify, but in the default Silverlight Style of the control, some of these properties would appear not to work. Don't be alarmed, as the properties are simply not wired up in this CheckBox *Style*.

One such property of the CheckBox is the BorderThickness. You can go ahead and change the default values of 1 to anything you like, and you won't see any change at all.

The BorderBrush property, on the other hand, is wired up in this default Silverlight Style, so you can change that value by selecting a new color; you will see the border of the "Check" part change, as shown in Figure 4.7. You should note that the change in this Border property is applied to two parts of the control. Also shown in Figure 4.7 is the very faint change that the Background property applied to.

The most important properties for you to take notice of at present are located inside the Common Properties category.

> **NOTE**
>
> **Confused About Properties Being Present But Not Working?**
>
> As will be detailed in Chapter 6, a Style is effectively a template that can be applied to control types, which can change the functionality in a user experience (UX) sense, but most often changes the visual appearance of a control. Within the *Style*, the author has the ability to "Bind" properties to the Style so that you as a user can change—for example, a Background property value and that value will be applied to the foreground property.
>
> Sounds confusing, doesn't it? All will become clear when you deep dive into Styles, but for now you need to understand that nothing is broken. Just be aware of when you might need to modify a Style to get some of the properties to work the way you want them to or the way you believe your end user will want them to work.

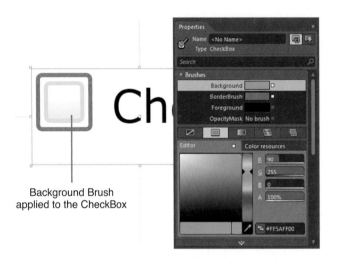

FIGURE 4.7   The BorderBrush and Background brush change applied to a CheckBox.

The ClickMode Property

The ClickMode property is by default set to Release, which translates to the user being able to click the CheckBox and then drag the mouse away from the control without releasing the mouse and the property won't change. Only when the mouse button is clicked and released on the control surface will the check show. You have two other choices—Press and Hover, which you should set now from the dropdown, as shown in Figure 4.8, and run your application to see the differences.

The IsChecked Property

The IsChecked property is self-explanatory in that when the property is set to True, you should see the little tick inside the CheckBox. This property represents a Boolean value that changes when your user checks or unchecks the CheckBox. Take note of this property as you will most likely use it heavily in triggering a storyboard or change notification in later applications.

The IsThreeState Property

You should translate this property value option as Yes, No, Maybe. Click on this property to set it to `True` and run your application; you see that you need to cycle through your clicks to enter different property *states*. Figure 4.9 shows the CheckBox control in the three states.

You should also note that the `CheckBox` control is a `ContentControl`, the same as the `Border` control, as mentioned previously. The difference between the `Border` and most other `ContentControls` like the `Button` and the `CheckBox` is that the `Content` property enables you to either add a child control (like another `Button` or a `Grid`), but it also enables you to supply a *string* value that, in this case, shows up as the word CheckBox.

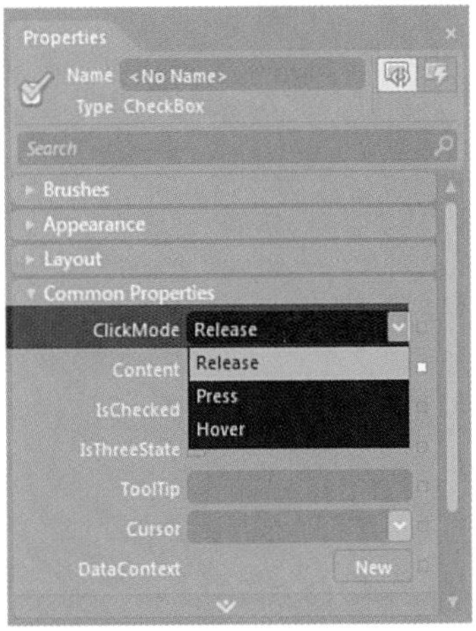

The RadioButton

The `RadioButton` control appears to be at first identical to the `CheckBox` control, and it shares almost exactly the same property set with one specific difference—the `GroupName` property value. The following steps demonstrate the use of the Group functionality.

FIGURE 4.8   The ClickMode property drop-down choices.

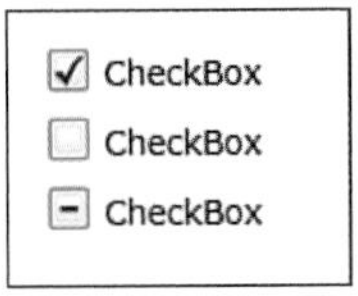

FIGURE 4.9   The difference in states applied to a CheckBox with IsThreeState set to true.

1. Remove the previous controls or start a new Silverlight Application + Website project.

2. Select the `LayoutRoot` element in the Objects and Timeline tab.

3. Locate the `RadioButton` control inside the Common Controls collection of the toolbar and double-click to add one to the artboard.

4. Add two more `RadioButton` controls and drag the entire group of controls close to the center of the artboard.

5. As shown in Figure 4.10, with all three of the `RadioButton` controls selected, right-click on the controls and navigate to the "Group into" menu item. In this particular case, select the `StackPanel` from the submenu.

6. In the Objects and Timeline tab, select the `StackPanel` and locate the `Orientation` property inside the Properties tab, which you will find located inside the Layout category. Change the drop-down property option to `Horizontal`.

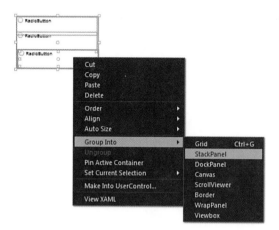

FIGURE 4.10   The Group into menu options.

TIP

Where Have My Controls Gone?

If, after you have grouped your controls, it looks like one of the RadioButtons has disappeared, this is because Blend fixes the `Width` property of the `StackPanel` to that of the first RadioButton. The solution is to navigate to the `Width` property of the `StackPanel` and set the `Width` property to `Auto` by clicking on the Set to Auto button, as shown in Figure 4.11; you also reset any margin values back to 0 and set the `HorizontalAlignment` and `VerticalAlignment` properties to `Center`.

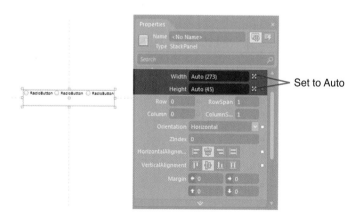

FIGURE 4.11   Where to click to set the StackPanel Width property to Auto, which will reveal both RadioButtons seated side by side.

7. Change the `Background` property of the `StackPanel` to a gray color.

8. Now add a fourth RadioButton control to the artboard so you can clearly see the three grouped and one ungrouped control.

You now have three RadioButtons that are grouped into a separate layout container (you will learn more about layout containers in Chapter 5, "The Art of Layout") and a fourth control that is not a child or nested element, as shown in Figure 4.12 with the Objects and Timeline tab.

FIGURE 4.12   Four RadioButton controls on the artboard and the nesting relationship in the Objects and Timeline panel.

The GroupName Property

In the following steps, you will use the GroupName feature.

1. Select all the RadioButton controls inside the `StackPanel` and use the property search box to find the `GroupName` property by typing in the word "Group."

2. Add a property value that suits; in this scenario, displayed is the GroupName "Check," as shown in Figure 4.13.

FIGURE 4.13   The GroupName edit.

Run your application and click on any of the three RadioButtons inside the gray StackPanel.

You will see the behavior is fixed between these controls, and clicking on any of them will set the other controls "Check" mark on or off and vice versa — only one can be checked at any one time.

The fourth RadioButton, which is not bound to the GroupName, has no effect on the Group collection of controls and can be checked on or off independently.

You should note that you have placed the `RadioButton` controls inside a `StackPanel` in this example purely for relevance of separation, but it is not required to make the Grouping functionality work. You can place RadioButtons anywhere, and as long as their `GroupName` property is set to the same, they will work as a group with only a single `RadioButton` control containing a check (dot) at any given time.

TextBlock Versus Label

The TextBlock control is heavily used inside your applications to show a non-editable field value or, in the case of Silverlight, mostly it is used as a common Label control. A lot of new users don't realize that WPF and Silverlight both have specific Label controls, with the difference being in the property sets available to each control, and mainly to do with the layout of the contained text and the font scenarios applied.

Table 4.1 shows a high-level overview of the differences between the two controls in context of the Silverlight 4 platform.

TABLE 4.1   The Silverlight Label and TextBlock Controls

Property Category Set	Label	TextBlock
Brushes	▶ The Label control contains Background and BorderBrush properties.	▶ The TextBlock has only a Foreground property. ▶ **Advanced Properties.** The TextBlock control contains a global Opacity property.
Appearance	▶ Label has a BorderThickness property.	
Layout	▶ **Advanced Properties.** Label has a VerticalContentAlignment and HorizontalContentAlignment property collection.	
Common Properties	▶ Label has PropertyPath and Target properties for easier MVVM DataContext support. ▶ **Advanced Properties.** Supports TabNavigation, IsEnabled, and IsTabStop properties.	
Text		▶ Supports LineHeight and TextAlignment properties. ▶ **Advanced Properties.** Supports LineStackingStrategy, TextHintingMode, TextTrimming, and TextWrapping properties.
Miscellaneous	▶ Supports DataTemplating with ContentTemplate properties.	▶ Supports the FontSource property, as well as Inlines collection for rich content embedding.

As you can see from Table 4.1, the differences are quite varied, and realistically, it completely depends on your task at hand to what control is better suited. With both controls (as will all controls that contain text in the Content property value), you can click on F2 to automatically begin editing the text value in context on the artboard.

> **NOTE**
>
> **The Importance of Looking in the Advanced Properties Section**
>
> There are many properties to be found in the Advanced Properties sections of all controls. This should be a marker for you to understand that you need to investigate controls deeply to understand their full functionality.

The TextBox

The TextBox control is another heavily used control, and aside from being the point of input for your user's text, there are several properties that are interesting to note that give you quite a lot of control of the experience that the control provides. There are also quite a few differences with the control being used in either Silverlight or WPF, with some of those pointed out in the following section.

With a TextBox control added to your artboard in a Silverlight project, select it and have a look at the property collection in the Properties panel. The Brushes category specifically shows that you have a fantastic amount of control as to how the selection of text and appearance of the caret look, as shown in Figure 4.14.

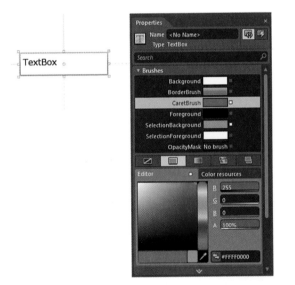

FIGURE 4.14   The Brushes category of the Property panel for the TextBox control.

The Caret

The blinking line at the end of the text within the TextBox is called the caret. If you change the CaretBrush property, users will see that change when they enter text in the textbox at runtime, as shown in Figure 4.15. This property is also available in WPF.

As you may expect, a change to the `SelectionBackground` and `SelectionForeground` properties gives some very specific feedback to your user on selection of text in the control, as shown in Figure 4.16. In WPF, you see that there exists only a `SelectionBrush`, but you have additional control with a `SelectionOpacity` property that is not available in Silverlight.

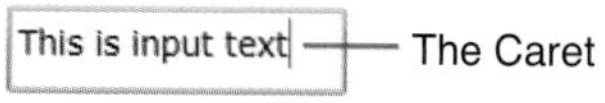

FIGURE 4.15   The CaretBrush change in the TextBox.

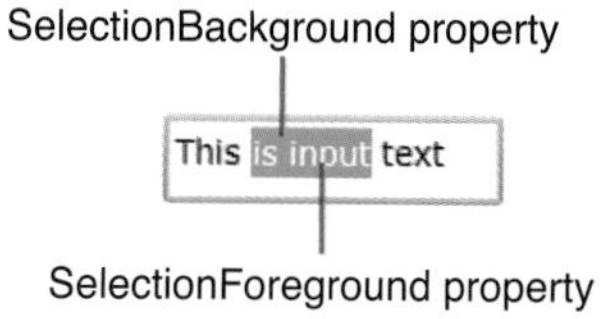

When creating with Silverlight, the Common Properties category contains two TextBox-specific properties called `AcceptsReturn` and `IsReadOnly`.

SelectionBackground property

This is input text

SelectionForeground property

FIGURE 4.16   The results of the Brush property changes for the selection of text in the TextBox control.

AcceptsReturn

When enabled, this means that you used can hit the Return or Enter button on the keyboard in order to add line returns to their input text. `AcceptsReturn` is available in WPF under the Advanced Properties section of the Text category, along with another self-explanatory property called `AcceptsTab`.

IsReadOnly

The `IsReadOnly` property is sometimes confused with the `IsEnabled` property. Specifically `IsReadOnly` when activated means that the TextBox control is still very much enabled and is selectable by the end user, only the text that is contained inside the TextBox control is not editable.

The WPF Common Properties category contains substantially more properties for the TextBox, as displayed in Figure 4.17. This shows the differences between Silverlight and WPF.

Silverlight   WPF

FIGURE 4.17   The Common Properties category for both Silverlight and WPF TextBox control.

WPF Spell Checking

It is interesting to note that the WPF
TextBox comes with a property called
SpellCheck.IsEnabled, which is also
seen in Figure 4.17. When this property
is checked, your users will see the familiar red squiggle underneath any incorrect text, and an automatically
generated context menu provides the
correct spelling, as shown in Figure 4.18.

The TextBox control also contains quite
a lot of functionality to control the way
in which the contained text is displayed,
so as you would expect, the Text cate-

FIGURE 4.18   The simple spell checker with
WPF TextBox.

gory (especially the Advanced Properties section) contains quite a few property settings to
let you really control the user input. The difference between Silverlight and WPF is also
shown in Figure 4.19.

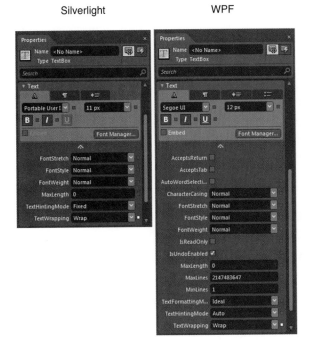

FIGURE 4.19   The Advanced Properties of the Text category for the TextBox control both in
Silverlight and WPF.

Specifically, the MaxLength property enables you to control the maximum amount of
characters that the user can enter. 0 is the default, which means that it is unlimited. You

will see that WPF contains a lot more control, which also allows you to specify Undo functionality as well as controlling the amount of lines the user can have.

The ProgressBar

The ProgressBar is a heavily used control to indicate, as the name would suggest, progress of a certain task that is being performed. It can also be used to indicate a busy state where the time remaining is unknown; though I am sure many designers among you will no doubt prefer other visual mechanisms to indicate this.

> **What Is a Control Transform?**
>
> Transformations allow you to control specific positioning of an element such as Rotation or Skew. You will learn more about transformation in Chapter 11, "Animations and Transitions."

The ProgressBar controls used in both Silverlight and WPF are almost identical in features, aside from an Orientation property available in WPF, as shown in Figure 4.20. You can simply use a Rotation transform on the control in Silverlight to achieve essentially the same thing.

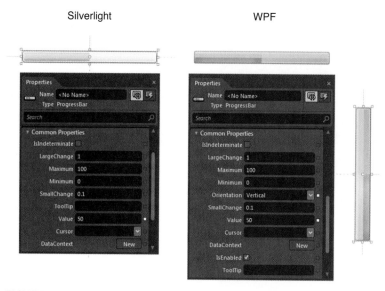

FIGURE 4.20   The ProgressBar controls for both Silverlight and WPF.

The only other obvious difference is that the ProgressBar by default shows a lovely bright green color, whereas Silverlight has a more relaxed pale blue.

The Value of the Value

The property settings for the ProgressBar are very simple, as shown in the following example.

1. In a new project, find and add a ProgressBar.

2. Inside the Common Properties category of the Properties panel, set the value of the Maximum property to 10.

3. Find and set the Minimum property to 0, if it is not already.

4. With your mouse, drag up and down or side to side on the property input for the Value property.

You see that the number inside the Value property increments or decrements by whole values of 1. This is not to say that the property only accepts integer values, and you could manually change the value to any valid fractional number such as 8.5 or 7.2, as shown in Figure 4.21.

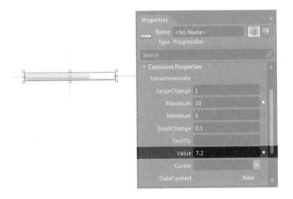

FIGURE 4.21   You can apply fractional values to the ProgressBar control.

The IsIndeterminate Property

The IsIndeterminate property is by default unchecked. When you enable this property, the value bar continuously moves along the length of the ProgressBar to indicate that something is happening, but an expected end is not known. It doesn't matter if you have fixed values specified for the Maximum, Minimum, and Value properties; IsIndeterminate takes over the control.

The Slider

The Slider control in both WPF and Silverlight reflect the property set available for the ProgressBar in both platforms amazingly closely. You can see the comparison of the WPF and Silverlight Slider control in Figure 4.22. Yes there are several new property values that are Slider-specific, such as TickFrequency and TickPlacement (for WPF only), but for the most part, the Slider control is also about Maximum, Minimum, and Value properties.

Silverlight   WPF

FIGURE 4.22   The Slider Common Properties for both WPF and Silverlight.

The following example explores the WPF version of the Slider control:

1. Add a new Slider control to a WPF project.

2. Set the Maximum property value to 50.

3. Set the Minimum property value to 0.

4. Set the value to 15.

Working with Ticks

Ticks can be shown either above, below, or both above and below the Slider control. The Foreground property value found in the Brushes category is what changes the color of the ticks as shown in the following steps.

1. Set the TickPlacement property to Both.

2. Change the Foreground property value to something like a green color.

Figure 4.23 shows the ticks lined up across the top and the bottom of the Slider control, looking similar to little spikes. The higher the Maximum value, the more those little spikes will blend into looking like a line, so you can always set the TickFrequency property to a value such as 10; this will again spread out the ticks.

The IsDirectionReversed Property

The Slider-specific property IsDirectionReversed simply makes the Minimum value applied the control Thumb to the far right (instead of far left as by default), and conversely the Maximum is then applied to the far left of the control.

FIGURE 4.23   The tick's top and bottom of the Slider control.

The following steps show how to Bind the Value of the Slider control to a Label so you can see the IsDirectionReversed property in action.

1. Add a Label control above your Slider control. Either click on the Pointer tool in the Tools panel or hit Esc so you are not editing the text in the Label.

2. With the Label still selected, find the Content property and click on the Advanced options box to the right of the control, selecting the "Element Property Binding...," option as shown in Figure 4.24.

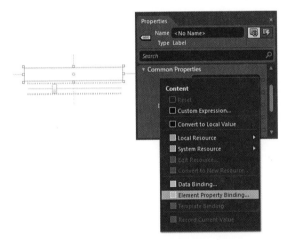

FIGURE 4.24   The Advanced options for the Content property of the Label control.

3. Your mouse cursor will now change and contain a target icon attached to it, indicating that you need to select a Target element. Move your mouse over the Slider control and click on it, which will present you with the Create Data Binding dialog, as shown in Figure 4.25.

    Figure 4.25 also shows that you need to scroll down the ComboBox next to the Property of slider label and find the entry "Value."

4. Click OK to continue. You should now see an orange border around the Content property, as shown in Figure 4.26.

FIGURE 4.25   The Value property selection in the Create Data Binding dialog.

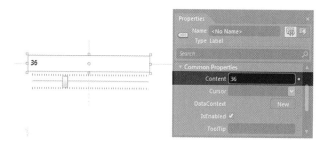

FIGURE 4.26   The binding indicator on the Content property.

> **NOTE**
>
> **What Is Binding?**
>
> Binding in Blend terms has several levels of complexity, which extends from the type of binding you are performing here called element binding all the way down to complex CLR-type binding. You don't have to worry about the mechanics of it at this stage; just know that what you are doing here is supplying the value of one control (in this case, the Slider) to the property of another control (the Content property of the Label. See Chapter 10, "Expression Blend Data Support" for more detailed information about binding.

5. Select the Slider control again, either from the artboard or the Objects and Timeline panel.

6. Change the `Value` property by moving the mouse up and down or side to side in the input box.

You should now see that the value in the Label corresponds to the value in the Slider `Value` property, as shown in Figure 4.27. You should play around with changing certain properties, such as `IsDirectionReversed` and the `Orientation` property, to really see what you can do with the Slider control.

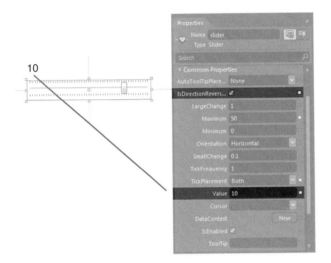

FIGURE 4.27   The data bound Label indicating the current value of the Slider control when IsDirectionReversed is checked.

The ComboBox

The ComboBox control is used frequently in the case where screen real estate is limited and requires multiple options to be presented to the user with only a single selection being possible. Although it's true that the WPF ComboBox control has more functionality in terms of decoration scenarios and grouping of children, the Silverlight control is largely comprised of the same common properties.

Figure 4.28 shows that after you have added a ComboBox element to your artboard, you can simply right-click on the control and add child items directly to the control (ComboBoxItem).

Child Items Collection

You see that the ComboBox control also contains an `Items` `(Collection)` property in the Common Properties category, which enables you to add other *types* of controls, such as Buttons and Checkboxes, directly to the ComboBox collection, as shown in Figure 4.29. Note that each child also has a functional property collection available to edit directly in the Collection Editor.

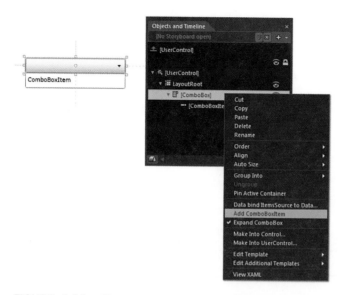

FIGURE 4.28   How to manually add ComboBoxItem child elements to the control.

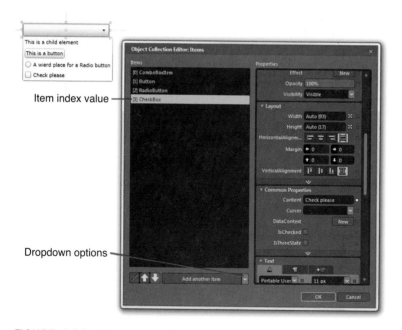

FIGURE 4.29   The Items (Collection) property editing experience.

The SelectedIndex Property

Items held in a collection in .Net are grouped in what is known as a zero-based array. This simply means that the first item in a collection is located at position 0, the second at position 1, and so on. The SelectedIndex property enables you to either change the default selected item, or when the user chooses another item at runtime, the SelectedIndex value will also change.

The following steps required that you add a ComboBox control to the artboard in a Silverlight project where you can then modify and experience the SelectedIndex property.

1. Right-click on the ComboBox and select the Add ComboBoxItem menu option.

2. With the ComboBoxItem element selected in the Objects and Timeline panel, you will find a Content property that you should change the value from ComboBoxItem to "Item 1."

3. Perform these steps twice more so you have a total of three ComboBoxItem child controls inside the ComboBox, as shown in Figure 4.30.

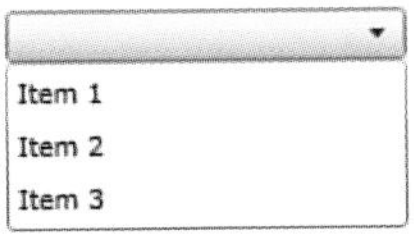

FIGURE 4.30   Three child ComboBoxItem elements are added to the ComboBox.

With the ComboBox control selected, you will find a property called SelectedIndex, which by default shows a value of -1. This effectively is stating that none of the child elements are currently selected. You can change the SelectedIndex value between 0 and 2, and as a result, you see the corresponding child element highlighted, as shown in Figure 4.31.

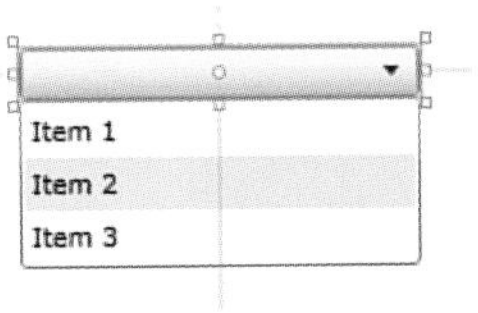

FIGURE 4.31   The element at index position 1 highlighted.

If you enter a value into the SelectedIndex property that is higher than the number of children in the collection, you see the error shown in Figure 4.32. If you do this programmatically at runtime, and error will be raised that you must handle or the application will crash.

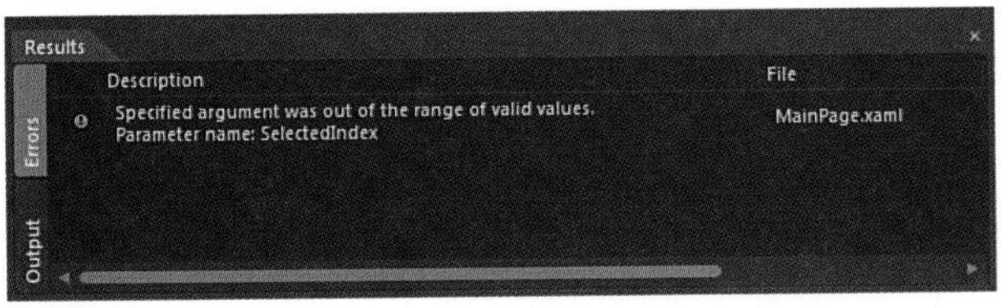

FIGURE 4.32   The error returned when changing the SelectedIndex value past the item count.

The ListBox

The ListBox control is almost identical to the ComboBox control in terms of properties and child item functionality. In point of fact, the only property difference in the Common Properties category between the two is the ability to set the ComboBox drop-down to visible, which of course is not applicable in the ListBox.

Figure 4.33 shows just how similar the controls are between platforms as well, although it should be noted that the WPF version has vastly more properties available in the Miscellaneous category. This enables you to specify alternate row styles and many other decorative functions.

Silverlight   WPF

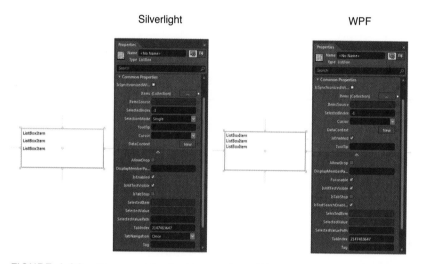

FIGURE 4.33   The near identical properties of WPF and Silverlight ListBox control.

The SelectionMode property is visible in the Silverlight Common Properties category, whereas the same property is in the Miscellaneous category for the WPF control. The SelectionMode property determines the functional difference between the user being able to select only a single item or multiple items by holding down the Shift or Ctrl keys when selecting items.

The SelectionChanged Event

Although it is easy enough to fill the ListBox with items (the same way as you did with the ComboBox), most often a developer will need to ascertain which child has been selected by the end user in order to work with the correct data context when working with the control at runtime.

The functionality to determine this is exposed though an event that is fired when the user makes the child selection; consequently, the event is called the SelectionChanged event.

The following steps help demonstrate the SelectionChanged event.

1. Add three child elements to a ListBox control in either WPF or Silverlight.

2. Give each child a different Content value of Child 1, Child 2, or Child 3.

3. With the ListBox selected in the artboard or Objects and Timeline panel, switch the Property viewer to Event viewer mode, which is shown in Figure 4.34.

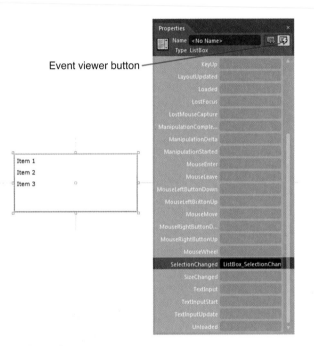

FIGURE 4.34   The Event viewer mode of the Properties panel.

4. Also shown in Figure 4.34 is the SelectionChanged event. Double-click in the input box, which should either open Visual Studio or a code-behind page.

5. Add the code shown exactly in Figure 4.35 to your code behind.

WARNING

What Does All the Code Mean?

Understanding code to any great level is beyond the scope of this book—not because it is too hard or you don't need to learn it, but because there are a lot of choices that you need to make when learning code, and you can do without the confusion at this point, considering you are trying to just learn the Expression Blend tool. The code shown in the snippet is by no means production quality and indeed has a host of bad practices associated with it. The concept here is to understand that an event fires, and you can by code ascertain what item has been selected.

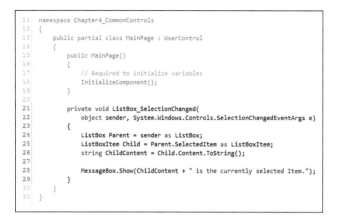

```
11   namespace Chapter4_CommonControls
12   {
13       public partial class MainPage : UserControl
14       {
15           public MainPage()
16           {
17               // Required to initialize variables
18               InitializeComponent();
19           }
20
21           private void ListBox_SelectionChanged(
22               object sender, System.Windows.Controls.SelectionChangedEventArgs e)
23           {
24               ListBox Parent = sender as ListBox;
25               ListBoxItem Child = Parent.SelectedItem as ListBoxItem;
26               string ChildContent = Child.Content.ToString();
27
28               MessageBox.Show(ChildContent + " is the currently selected Item.");
29           }
30       }
31   }
```

FIGURE 4.35   The code snippet to add to your application.

You should now be able to run your application, and every time you choose another item from the ListBox, a message will show detailing which item you have selected.

Summary

There are a lot of properties that have not been covered here, and for various reasons—chief among them is that you just don't need to understand them at this point. As you go deeper and deeper with controls, you will want to, and will most certainly need to, understand more and more properties in order to achieve various effects and of course to allow you to augment functionality to your requirement.

Simple control usage is a big step and a solid first start to working with different types of functionality, regardless of the platform choices that you need to make. WPF hands down offers a lot more functionality within its control collection as opposed to Silverlight, but you should expect that based on the nature of Silverlight being a much smaller runtime.

Play with the controls. Try to break the controls. Get used to where they are and what you will probably need them for. The rest will come as you become more experienced and more confident in what Expression Blend enables you to do.

The Art of Layout

Layout in Expression Blend can be a slightly confusing proposition to those who are unfamiliar with existing layout models that have been used over the last few years—starting with WPF and now predominantly with Silverlight.

In this chapter, you will experiment with the main layout container types, which gives you a basic understanding required to work in most platforms that are supported by Expression Blend.

Layout Panels

WPF was the first platform to be supported and used by Expression Blend and its introduction had an immediate and positive impact on the development community. The level of control was so refreshing compared to WinForms, and none more so than in the area of control layout.

WPF contains several more panels out of the box compared with Silverlight—such as WrapPanel, DockPanel, and Uniform Grid, to name a few—but most of these panel are available for Silverlight through extensions to the framework by way of toolkits or SDK.

Figure 5.1 shows the collection that is baked into the toolbar for Silverlight projects, and this collection is a fairly robust one that you will now go through one panel at a time, examining the most common features and properties. The Border container was reviewed in detail in Chapter 4, "Common Properties and Functionality," and will not be covered again in this chapter.

By understanding the layout panel principles, you will be able to work in more defined ways that are constrained by functionality and property options.

You start by working with the most common layout panel: the Grid control.

The Grid Control

The Grid can be confusing to new users because it appears to just move controls around at will; Expression Blend also appears to modify control property values by itself, which can be rather painful at times.

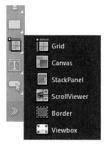

FIGURE 5.1   The Layout Panel collection for Silverlight projects.

There are several areas of the Grid that you should strive to understand really well, as this is the most commonly used layout container, and just changing one property can have a profound effect on how your child elements will respond to draw requests from the application when something like resizing occurs.

The first thing you should check when working with a Grid is what mode the Grid element is in. There are two modes that are discussed in the following examples. Grid in Grid mode and Grid in Canvas mode are the two behaviors that can be specified. Figure 5.2 shows the icon present at the corner of a selected grid. This is a toggle button of sorts, allowing you to simply click on it to change the current mode.

Click here to change Laout Mode

FIGURE 5.2   The clickable mode icon for grid elements.

The following steps walk you through experimenting with the modes of the Grid element.

1. Create a new Silverlight Application + Website project type.

2. Right-click on the [UserControl] top-level element in your Objects and Timeline panel, navigate to the Auto Size menu item, and select Both in the submenu if it does not already show a tick next to it. This allows your application to run fully stretched to the boundaries of your browser.

WARNING

Setting Expression Blends Global Mode of the Grid

You need to be aware that you can't set the Grid mode for just one Grid element. When you click the icon to change the layout mode, this mode change is applied to Expression Blend as a setting and therefore to all Grid elements you use in any project or application. You will also find this setting in the Tools->Options->Artboard (Layout-> User grid layout mode).

3. Click on the LayoutRoot element in the Objects and Timeline tab and then look at the type in the Properties panel. Notice that by default, the LayoutRoot element is indeed a Grid element. You are not going to work on this LayoutRoot element at this stage, so locate and add a new grid to your artboard as a child of the LayoutRoot. From herein out in these steps, Grid refers to this new Grid element you have added.

4. Change the Background color so you can easily see the Grid.

5. Ensure that you are working in Grid mode, as discussed previously and shown in Figure 5.2.

6. Name your new Grid element in the Properties tab to something similar to "MyGrid."

7. Set the Width and Height of your Grid element to Auto and set both the HorizontalAlignment and VerticalAlignment properties to Stretch and all four Margins to 150 pixels, as shown in Figure 5.3.

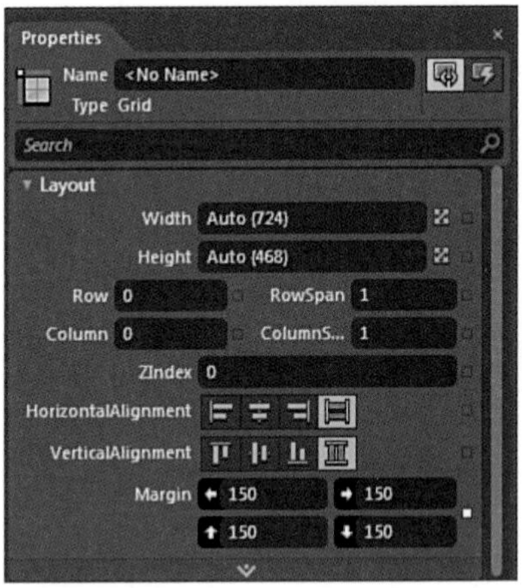

FIGURE 5.3   The layout category properties to set for the MyGrid element.

8. With the MyGrid element selected, add a Button element as a child control.

9. Resize the Button element to roughly 200 pixels wide and high.

10. Drag the Button on the artboard so that it is roughly in the center of the artboard.

11. Run your application by hitting F5.

   Spend some time resizing your browser to see the layout effects that are applied to the Button element inside the MyGrid element. You will be able to make the Button disappear with not too much effort. When you have done so, close the browser.

   Back inside Expression Blend, you should be able to select the Button element.

12. Inside the Properties tab, locate the Advanced Properties of the Layout category hide/show button, as shown in Figure 5.4.

13. You should now give your Button element a MinWidth and MinHeight property value of 50 each and set both the MaxWidth and MaxHeight properties to 100. Figure 5.5 shows the effect of the layout constraints on the Button element by revealing the original positions and the physical button with its layout constraint applied.

FIGURE 5.4   The Advanced Properties property collection.

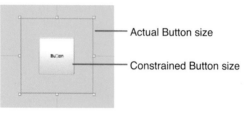

Actual Button size

Constrained Button size

FIGURE 5.5   The button not able to fill its designed space because of its layout constraints.

The entire point here is to get you used to the concept that the parent control (in this case, the Grid) is responsible for the layout of the child element (the Button), and child control boundary settings are maintained by the collection of properties found in the Layout category of the Properties panel.

Advanced properties such as `MaxHeight` and `MinHeight` give you the ability to control the tolerances of the effects of the margins and layout applied to your control.

Column and Row Sizing

By now, you have possibly noted that with your Button element selected, you have a property collection called `Rows`, `RowSpan`, `Column`, and `ColumnSpan`, as highlighted in Figure 5.6. These properties are known as AttachedProperties and are provided to the button from the parent grid.

> **NOTE**
>
> **What Are AttachedProperties?**
>
> AttachedProperties, as the name suggests, are properties that have been "attached" to your currently selected element from another element—in this case, the Grid. They work the same as any other property in the property editor that you are modifying.
>
> You could conceivable think of AttachedProperties as being generic and applicable to more than the just the element you are working with. For example, A Button, a RadioButton or any other control will contain the Grid.Rows AttachedProperty when either of those elements are the child of a Grid.

FIGURE 5.6   The AttachedProperty collection inside the Layout category.

In order for those properties to have any form of function, your parent Grid element needs to have either Rows or Columns specified:

1. Select the MyGrid element. Notice how it also contains the AttachedProperties—this is because its parent container is the LayoutRoot, which is also a *type* of Grid.

2. You can very easily manually add Rows and Columns to your Grid element by moving your mouse over the grid horizontal and vertical adorner bars, which present you with an indicative guide, as shown in Figure 5.7. For now, however, don't add these manually.

Mouse over the Grid Adorners to see the Row or Column guides

FIGURE 5.7   The Row guide shown when mousing over the grid adorner.

3. In the Property search box, type the word "def." This constricts the property collection to show two properties, ColumnDefinitions and RowDefinitions, as shown in Figure 5.8.

4. Click on the Ellipses next to the ColumnDefinitions property, which reveals the Collection Editor dialog.

5. Using the "Add another item" button, add three column objects as shown in Figure 5.9 and then select the first one. Note that the properties for the Column appear on the right side, and because you are working with columns, you see a Width property with a ComboBox next to it.

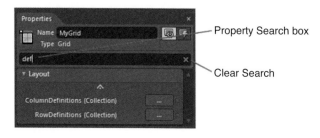

FIGURE 5.8   The constricted property set.

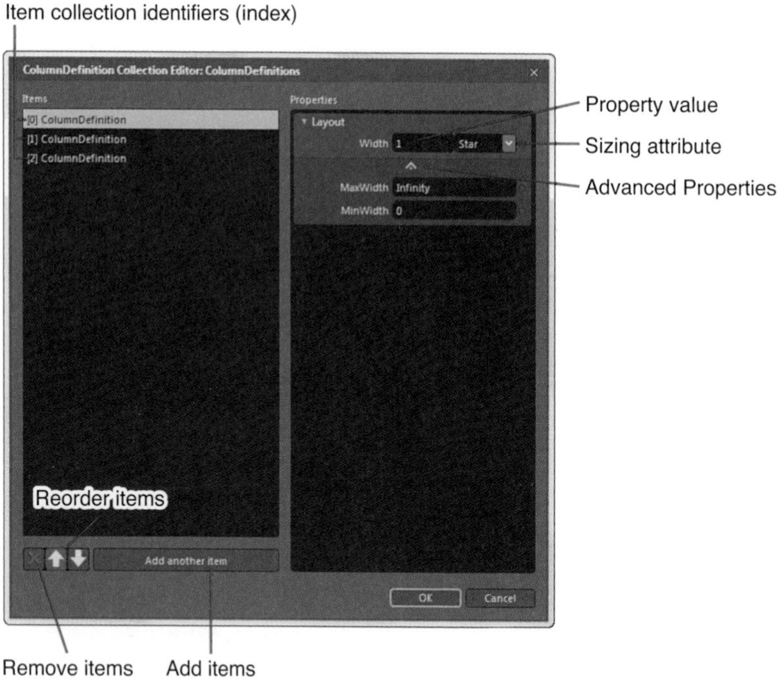

Item collection identifiers (index)

Property value

Sizing attribute

Advanced Properties

Reorder items

Remove items   Add items

FIGURE 5.9   The Collection Editor dialog box.

6. For the moment, take note of the three values in the ComboBox of the Width property, as highlighted in Figure 5.10.

7. Close the Collection Editor dialog by clicking on the OK button; you should now have your three columns present in your Grid, but either you can't see your Button element or it is now moved over to the left. This is because the Button element property values are being applied to the boundaries of the "cell" that the button now sits in—inside the Grid. Don't worry about it at the moment; you will move it shortly with property values.

It's important to note that the Columns created in your Grid now have an icon representing their current sizing state. The icon visual will change to one of three states if you click on it, and these states map directly back to the ComboBox property values (Star, Pixel, and Auto), as shown in Figure 5.10. Table 5.1 shows those three icons and describes the purposes.

FIGURE 5.10   The three ComboBox property values.

TABLE 5.1   The Sizing States of Columns and Rows within a Grid Element

Icon	Size State Name	Description
🔓	Star	Any column or row with a Star size applied will be given a dimensional value proportionate of 100% of the available Width/Height divided by the number of Columns or Rows. Don't confuse this with meaning 0.5 = 50%.
		An example is two columns that are exactly the same width; each would be given a Star Width value of 0.5.
		Three columns with a Star Width value of 0.5 each will also be exactly the same width.
		The column or row will maintain its width (grow or shrink) in ratio to the entire size of the grid, regardless of how big or small the grid becomes due to resizing of the browser or parent container.
🔒	Pixel	Pixel sizing represents a fixed pixel width or height size applied to the column or row. An example is a column given a 150-pixel Width value will always maintain a 150-pixel width regardless of the browser or parent container.
▨	Auto	With Auto Sizing, the column or row will automatically maintain the width or height of the element collection contained within it. An example is a row set to Auto Sizing that has a Button element inside of the row with a height of 47 pixels. The row will always be 47 pixels high. If the button is removed or collapsed, the row will shrink to 0 pixels.

Pixel Sizing

You will now continue with the existing example in the following steps, which will demonstrate the use of those three sizing modes. The first demonstrates pixel sizing, which constrains the width or height or a column or row, respectively.

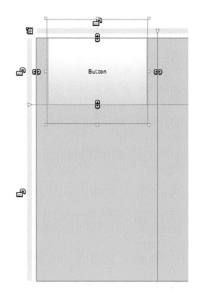

1. Manually using your mouse on the Grid element adorners, add a row about one-third down the Grid to give two rows, one small and one large, as shown in Figure 5.11. Again, don't be concerned about the Button element.

2. If you place your mouse cursor just above or below the open padlock icon, you see your cursor change to show a small grid next to the arrow. Click when you see that change, and you see the appropriate row or column become highlighted and the property editor changes to show you similar properties you viewed inside the Collection Editor dialog, as shown in Figure 5.12.

FIGURE 5.11   The new row added to the grid.

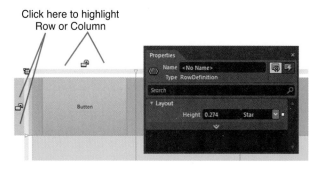

FIGURE 5.12   The highlighted row and the corresponding property collection.

3. Again, you could have clicked directly on the icon to change the Sizing state, but you can also change it directly in the ComboBox shown in Figure 5.12.

> **NOTE**
>
> **When 100% Is Not Quite 100%**
>
> Notice that the Height property value showing in Figure 5.12 is 0.274? My estimate of one-third of the grid size was pretty close. Even if you are not close to that value, you should change the Height value to 0.5 and keep the Sizing value as Star. You see now that something isn't right because both rows are not taking 50% each of the possible height, as shown in Figure 5.13.
>
> This is because the bottom row still has a Star Sizing value and a Height value that, when combined with the first RowHeight property, is now higher than 100%. What happens as a result is that the two Height property values are adjusted in ratio to the percentage of the combination and applied to the available height of the grid. You can fix that by selecting the bottom row definition and giving it a value of 0.5.

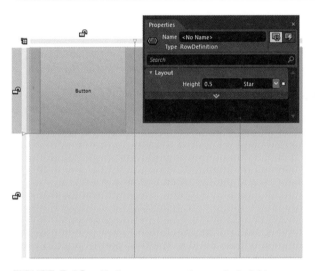

FIGURE 5.13   Both rows are not even in height.

4. Set the first row (which is technically called Row 0) to have a fixed pixel size and a Height property value of 150 pixels.

> **WARNING**
>
> **Why Is the First Row or Column Number 0?**
>
> In the .Net framework, collections and arrays of objects are known as zero based. There is a very long history to the reasons why this is which is beyond the scope of this book.
>
> It is extremely important to remember that **any and every collection** in Silverlight, WPF, or any other .Net-based language has its first element at position '0', the next is position '1', and so on. If you go back to Figure 5.9, you see that the Collection position of (0) is also detailed.

5. Set Column 0 as being fixed pixel size and also having a Width property value of 150 pixels.

6. Find and select your Button element from the Objects and Timeline panel.

7. Set the Width and Height properties of your Button element to Auto.

8. Set the HorizontalAlignment and VerticalAlignment properties both to Stretch.

9. Set the Margin values as each having 15. Figure 5.14 shows the result that your button should now have.

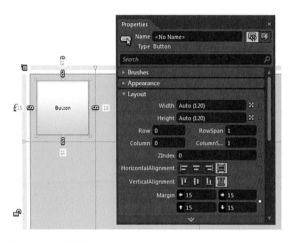

FIGURE 5.14   The Button element in the Grid and the Layout properties applied to it.

If you now run your application by hitting F5, you can resize your browser window, and you see that your button stays the same size and in the same position. You would expect this because the Button element is contained within a cell of the Grid defined by the row and column that are both fixed pixel sizes of 150 pixels.

Star Sizing
Star Sizing is akin to the type of layout experience in web development where percentages can be applied to Width and Height values to allow dynamic sizing of elements. This can be a tricky concept to get used to, but once you understand how to apply Star Sizing, you will become more comfortable with its use. The following steps walk you through working with Star Sizing.

1. Add a new button, drawing it directly into the middle cell of the first row of the Grid. Ensure that the Layout property values of this second button element are the same as the first in terms of Width, Height, VerticalAlignment, HorizontalAlignment, and Margin values. Note that this Button now shows a Column value of 1. This is because it is located in Column 1 of the Grid element.

   Only your first Column (Column 0) should be Fixed pixel sizing and the other two columns should both be Star sizing. You can check that at a glance by noting the icons above each column. If they are correct, run the application, and again resize the browser window.

You see that the second Button will grow and shrink in width because the column cell is set to Star sizing, but the height of the Button remains constant because Row 0 has a Fixed pixel size.

2. Add a third row to your grid, cutting the bottom row in two approximate halves.

3. With the Button in Column 1 selected, enter the Property panel Layout category, set the ColumnSpan value to 2, and set the RowSpan value also to 2. Your button should now take up four cells, as shown in Figure 5.15.

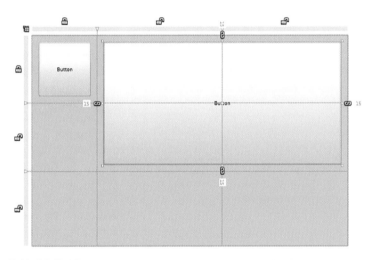

FIGURE 5.15   The addition of the third row and the Button element spanning four cells.

Run the application now and note the Button changing both height and width as you change the browser window size.

The button changes size because its VerticalAlignment and HorizontalAlignment properties are both set to Stretch, so it will always take as much space as it can as defined by the boundaries of the cells that it is assigned to. The Margin values ensure that the Button element maintains its distance from those cell boundaries.

Auto Sizing

As previously stated, Auto Sizing makes the column or row restrict in width or height to the boundary size of the element(s) contained within. The easiest way to demonstrate this is with an object changing size, which you will now add in the following steps.

1. Add a Border element to your grid and change its Background color to offset it against the parent grid.

2. Set the Row property value to 2.

3. Set the `Column` property value to `0`.

4. Set the `ColumnSpan` property value to 3.

5. Set the `Height` property value to `50`.

6. Set the `Width` property value to `Auto`.

7. Set the `HorizontalAlignment` property to `Stretch`.

8. Set the VerticalAlignment property to Top.

You should now have something that looks similar to Figure 5.16.

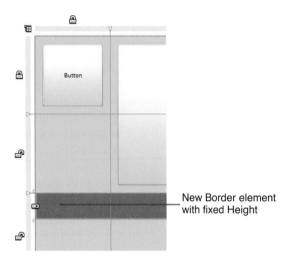

FIGURE 5.16   The new Border element.

9. Click on the unlocked padlock icon of the **third row** until it shows the Auto icon.

Oddly enough, the row doesn't change height. I say "oddly" because the rules are that the Auto Sizing attribute should resize the row height to the boundary of the contained element, which in this case is a Border with a height of 50 pixels.

You need to go a few steps further to get Auto Sizing working as you would expect. One little hidden property value is what almost always causes all the problems for new users understanding how to make this work—the `MinHeight` or `MinWidth` property (depending on if you are working with a row or column). The following steps help you to correct this issue.

1. Move your mouse cursor just above or below the Auto icon so you can highlight the row.

2. You now need to view the Properties panel and ensure that you expand the Advanced Properties to find the pesky `MinHeight` value that Blend sets for you. Set the `MinHeight` value to `0` and voila—your row will now constrain to the height of the Border element, as shown in Figure 5.17.

Auto constrained height
to the child element Height

FIGURE 5.17   The correctly collapsed Auto row, constrained to the height of the Border element.

When you run your application now and resize the browser window, you see that the Border grows and shrinks in width but always maintains the fixed height of the Border element:

1. To prove the constraint even further, you can now select the Border element in the Objects and Timeline panel and open the Appearance category.

2. In the ComboBox options for the `Visibility` property, select `Collapsed`.

You now see that Row 2 (the third row, remember) is now set to `0` pixels.

Grid in Canvas Mode

Canvas mode of the Grid affects the way in which child elements have their margins applied. In Grid Layout mode, the margins of the child elements are maintained as you resize the row and column cells of the grid.

In the previous example, you manually added a row by moving your mouse of the Grid adorner. If you move your mouse over the little arrow defining the row or column (as detailed in Figure 5.18), you can left-click down and readjust the size of the row or column.

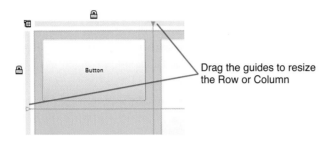

FIGURE 5.18   The Row and Column guides to move.

The following steps demonstrate the Grid in Canvas Mode:

1. Select one of your Button elements in the grid and make sure you can also see its Margin properties in the Properties panel.

2. Resize either a row or column boundary that is next to the Button. You see that the margins stay correct and the layout of the Button element updates to maintain its specified constraints.

3. Change the mode of the grid to Canvas Layout mode by clicking on the icon at the top-left of the grid.

> **NOTE**
>
> ### What Happened to the Row and Column Icons?
>
> My belief is that this is nothing more than a simple defect and one that I have raised with the Expression Blend team. You can still edit the column and row definitions by using the Property editor to launch the Collection Editor dialog.

4. Again, with a Button element selected and the Margin values visible to you, resize either a row or column adjacent to the element. Notice that the margins change the Button element, and it will stay fixed to its top-left position with the Grid, as shown in Figure 5.19.

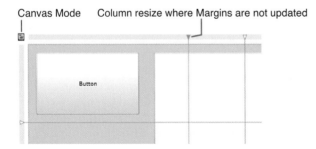

FIGURE 5.19   The column definition change and the button remaining in place.

Run the application again in Canvas Layout mode, and you see that the rest of the constraints placed against the button continue to work—for example, the second large button continues to grow and shrink as you resize your browser window.

Working with the grid is confusing at first to some, and it isn't made any easier with confusion around the differences between Grid Layout mode and Canvas Layout mode. My preference is to always work in Grid Layout mode, but as I said, this is just my preference.

Canvas

The Canvas layout works very similar to the previous layout that was provided in the older WinForms (pre-.Net 3.0 Framework) in that it provides for Absolute Fixed Positioning of its child elements.

To put it simply, you can add a child element to a canvas and specify that child elements X and Y (or Left and Top) positions as a pixel value, and the element is guaranteed to always stay at that location as demonstrated in the following steps.

1. Either create a new Silverlight Application + Website project or simply hide the grid you were working with previously in this chapter.

2. With the LayoutRoot element selected, add a Canvas element to your artboard. Change its Background color so you can see it.

3. Add a Button element as the child of your canvas and make it an arbitrary size, probably larger than you normally would.

4. With the Button element selected, open the Properties panel and specifically look at the AttachedProperties that are now present in the Layout category, as shown in Figure 5.20.

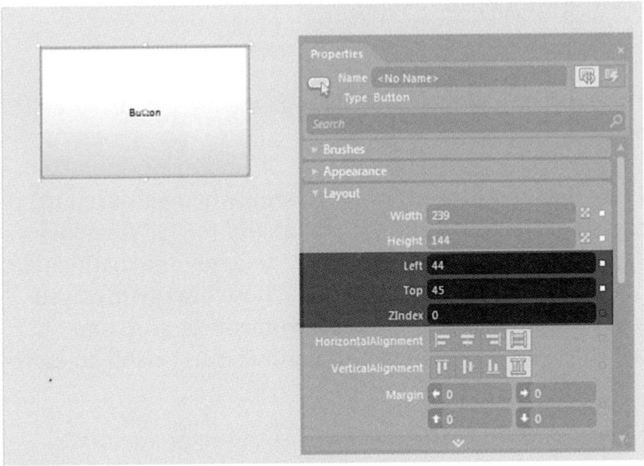

FIGURE 5.20   The Button element added to the canvas and the associated AttachedProperties now available.

Gone are the Row, Column, RowSpan, and ColumnSpan attached properties of the Grid, which have been replaced by three canvas ones: Left, Top, and ZIndex.

The Left property, as you might expect, sets the Button element (44 pixels, in this case) away from the left of the canvas. The Top property does the same in terms of pixel distance away from the top of the canvas.

What you see is that the Margin values shown in Figure 5.20 are all set to 0, but this is not to say that margins no longer apply—they most certainly do. You can test that by setting the Left and Top property values to 0 and then play around with the margins.

To demonstrate ZIndex, add another Button element to your artboard or simply select the first button, hold down the Alt key, and drag a new one.

What is confusing here is that both the buttons show a ZIndex property value of 0. You can go ahead and give them a unique value where the element with the highest value will always be the one on top, as shown in Figure 5.21.

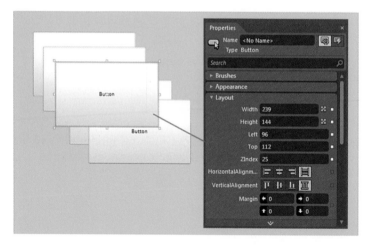

FIGURE 5.21   A Button element in the middle of the collection, with the highest ZIndex as being the element on top of all others.

The Canvas functionality of absolute fixed positioning is very useful when you need to dynamically change the location of items in code. Without the ability to give elements a fixed X and Y (Left and Top) value, it would be almost impossible to apply the mathematic algorithms that are often needed to correctly position elements. Those heavily involved with development and who have ever needed to create custom controls or grids and charts where plotting is concerned will understand how important it is to be able to ascertain an element's fixed position.

Another important role for the canvas is when you are working with vector artwork. Vectors use fixed positioning to define the lines and shapes (collectively called Paths) that make up a composition. If you created an icon inside a grid, for instance, each time the Grid is resized, the location of the paths would change either left and right or top and bottom positions; thus, your icon would never look right if your Grid changed size.

With a Canvas, however, it doesn't matter if the Canvas changes size, because all the elements stay in the same position, which means that the original Paths of the Vector elements stay in the right positions.

The Viewbox

The Viewbox element is very important but constantly overlooked because its functionality is not immediately apparent. The sole job of the Viewbox is to scale its child element collection to fit to the constraints placed upon the Viewbox.

The follow example demonstrates this using a new Illustrator Import feature of Expression Blend 4. You will be importing a simple icon Vector graphic into a Canvas (because you need the Paths to stay in their correct X and Y positions), and then you add the Canvas as the child element of a Viewbox. The result is that you can resize the icon, and it will always look right.

The following steps show you how to import the .AI file.

1. Create a new Silverlight Application + Website solution or hide the existing layout containers you have been using in this chapter.

2. Open the File menu and select "Import Adobe Illustrator File...."

3. After Import, you see that Expression Blend has created a new Canvas element, as shown in Figure 5.22.

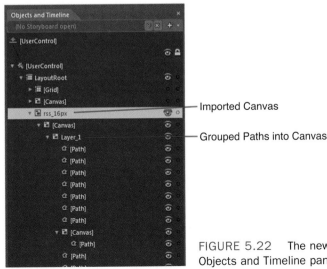

— Imported Canvas

— Grouped Paths into Canvas

FIGURE 5.22   The new element collection in the Objects and Timeline panel.

> **TIP**
>
> ### Sometimes the Imported Root Canvas Is Massive
>
> Working inside the Canvas layout created by the import is sometimes a little tricky. As expected, the imported Paths are all given fixed positions, which is sometimes a pain to try and get everything in the right place—for example, if your root Canvas element is 12000 x 12000 in size, and the vector artwork is only 16x16 and located in the center of this massive canvas.
>
> The easiest mechanism to get you on the right starting point is to select all the child Paths that you need; then right-click and group them into a Canvas element. The resulting canvas will be the right size, adjacent to the boundaries of all the child Paths you selected.
>
> You can then cut out that new Canvas element and paste it into the LayoutRoot, giving you the correct size canvas with Path elements located in the right positions.

In the example, the imported vector icon is tiny (12x15), where it really needs to be around 200 pixels high, kept in the right scale and ratio to width.

The very simple next step here is to select the root Canvas element created after import with the Paths all in the right location, and right-click on the Canvas. Select the Group Into context menu item and then select "Viewbox" from the submenu.

From here, you can hold down the Shift key as you resize the Viewbox element to keep the correct scale, and you should end up with an icon that looks like it did when you imported it, only larger. The result of this example import is shown in Figure 5.23.

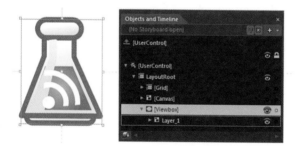

FIGURE 5.23   The scaled vector icon inside the Viewbox element.

Scaling Text

Another simple yet important feature of the Viewbox is to scale the text that is inside controls, such as the TextBox element. If you ever have the need to scale your text based on available size, this feature means that you don't have to implement some magical font size scale, as it is all handled by the Viewbox.

To try it, simply add a TextBlock element to your artboard and again right-click to group the element into the Viewbox. Try resizing the Viewbox, and you should see the text scales with it, as shown in Figure 5.24.

Figure 5.24 uses two TextBlock elements that both contain text with a FontSize property value set to 12 pixels. The second TextBlock is the child of a Viewbox element, which shows in the property panel that the FontSize is still set to 12 pixels, even though the display text is much larger than the other TextBlock.

FIGURE 5.24   A TextBlock element scaling inside a Viewbox.

StackPanel

The StackPanel has been around since the inception of WPF and is often heavily used due to its rigid functionality that provides element stacking in both Horizontal and Vertical directions (Vertical is the default). You will see a lot of the StackPanel the more you use Expression Blend, as the StackPanel is a fundamental part of the Style that is used by other controls, such as the ListBox.

The following steps demonstrate the StackPanel functionality.

1. Create a new WPF application.

2. Add a New StackPanel element.

3. Add several Button elements to the StackPanel.

Figure 5.25 shows the simple yet very useful feature of the StackPanel.

The StackPanel also allows you to see the differences between the Visibility modes of elements in WPF compared to Silverlight.

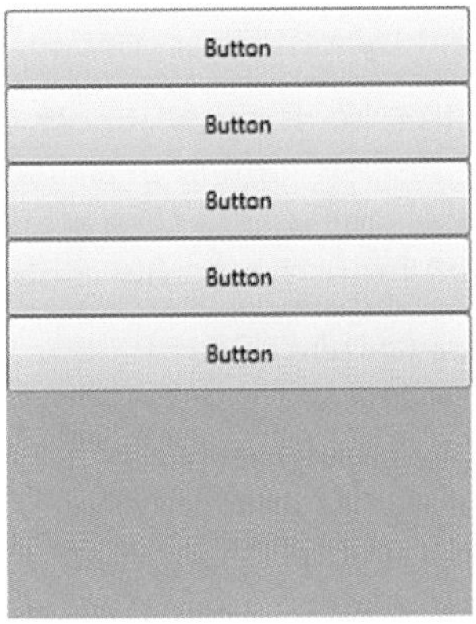

FIGURE 5.25   Several Button elements vertically "stacked" in the StackPanel control.

> **NOTE**
>
> **Silverlight Has No Hidden Property Value**
>
> Silverlight controls enable you to set a `Visibility` property value (or state) as either `Visible` or `Collapsed`, whereas WPF enables you to set one of those two values or provide a `Hidden` value as well.
>
> The StackPanel is particularly suited to this example, and following it will help you get used to the properties of the control against the platform you are working with.

The following steps demonstrate the Hidden property value.

1. Ensure you have several button elements inside your StackPanel, as shown in Figure 5.25.

2. Selecting one of the Button elements in the middle of the stack, navigate to the Appearance category of the properties panel and change the `Visibility` property to "Hidden."

You see that even though the control is indeed hidden, the real estate that the Button element normal takes up is just blank, which means that the other Button controls have not really stacked up. In order to truly hide an element in WPF, you need to set the `Visibility` property value to "Collapsed." Go ahead and try that now, and you should see the result expected of the StackPanel.

ScrollViewer

Returning to Silverlight for the last layout container of this chapter, you now look at the simple but very handy ScrollViewer container.

The job of the ScrollViewer is pretty simple. It saves you screen real estate by enabling you to embed large display content in a small contained area. The ScrollViewer, as the name suggests, enables the user to then scroll to content horizontally or vertically—most often associated with browser large file content.

The ScrollViewer is a `ContentControl`, which means that it can take only a single child element, but again like the Border control, that single child element could be a Grid (with multiple children) or anything else that takes your fancy.

The following steps help demonstrate the ScrollViewer element using large content.

> **TIP**
>
> **Work on the Content First!**
>
> As a usability tip, it's much easier to work on the content that you want to embed in the ScrollViewer before you actually go through the process of embedding it. This is because Expression Blend doesn't enable you to easily isolate the content and scroll to it at design time.

1. Open the Projects panel and right-click on your project.

2. Select "Add Existing Item..." from the context menu.

3. Find a sample images to import ensuring that it is relatively large compared to your screen. Approximately 1600x1600 is a good size.

> **Windows 7 Contains Some Great Sample Images**
>
> You will find several sample images located in the following directory in Windows 7:
>
> `C:\Users\Public\Pictures\Sample Pictures`

4. When you see the image in your file list inside the Project panel, drag the image file directly onto the artboard.

5. Right-click on the image and select "Group Into..." and then "ScrollViewer" from the submenu.

6. Give the ScrollViewer a fixed `Width` and `Height` property value of `500` pixels for each.

7. Center the ScrollViewer.

By default, the ScrollViewer doesn't enable horizontal scrolling (which could be considered strange) and the property for it is hidden inside Advanced properties of the Layout category.

As Figure 5.26 shows, changing the `HorizontalScrollBarVisibility` value to "`Visible`" fixes this.

FIGURE 5.26   How to turn on horizontal scrolling inside the ScrollViewer element.

You should now be able to run your application and scroll to your heart's content to see the full size of your image.

Summary

This chapter has shown you many different ways of controlling the layout of your elements and in detail looked at the Grid container, which you will use more than any of the others shown.

Layout can be very confusing for newcomers to Silverlight or WPF because there are so many ways to achieve different layout regimes. Most are self-explanatory, such as the simple StackPanel; however, for some (such as Grid Layout mode), handling different sizing options for rows and columns does take some time to get used to.

If your layout starts to play tricks on you and do totally weird things, remember to check all the values that apply to the constraints of the layout container. In the case of grids, first and foremost, ensure that it is in the mode that you need it to be in.

CHAPTER 6

Element Styles and Templates

Styles and templates cover a very vast array of features and functionality, not just with Expression Blend, but also within the chosen platform you are working with.

When working with elements (also known as controls) in Blend, there are three main areas of understanding that provide you with the ability to define element visuals and runtime adaptation to State changes, as follows:

▶ **Element styles and templates (this chapter).** The visual definitions used within the element(s) that make up the element.

▶ **Parts (Chapter 7, "Working with Parts").** The application and assignment of the pieces that make up the Part collection.

▶ **States (Chapter 8, "Working with States").** Assignment of property changes against the Parts to react to State changes within the element.

WARNING

This Sounds Complex?

Aside from coding the element directly, it is absolutely imperative that you consume these next three chapters with clarity in order to effectively work with Expression Blend. This understanding also enables you to work with any of the elements from the supported platforms of Blend, such as WPF or Windows Phone7.

In this chapter, you get an entry-level understanding of the makeup of a Style, how to create a new Style, and how to apply that to your chosen element.

You will work with the template that exists inside the Style, which gives you control over the makeup of the element. You will also work to understand what this template is and some of the special property settings that are applied to it.

What Is the Difference Between a Style and a Template?

Some people understand this topic without issue, whereas others struggle with it until it finally "clicks" for them. Experience has shown that the best way to explain the topic is to have people work through creating a Style and a Template with a few diagrams along the way to further impress some of the points that should be consumed.

First, you need some explanations to clarify terminology that otherwise might be confusing in the rest of this chapter.

> **NOTE**
>
> **Element = Control = Element**
>
> You will notice that I use the term "element" rather than "control" a lot in this chapter because it refers better to some of the visual language of the Blend UI and the terminology applied to some of the steps. As previously mentioned, a control is an element, and vice versa.

What Is a Style?

You would be partially correct to assume that the Style of an element would dictate the look or visual representation of an element.

It is technically more accurate to say the Style of an element contains the default pieces that determine the visual representation, but the Style also contains default settings for the properties of the element that the style is being applied to.

The following steps walk you through the Style editing process.

1. Start a new Silverlight Application + Website project.

2. Find a Button element in the Assets panel and add it to the artboard. You are seeing the default Style applied to the Button element.

3. With the Button element selected, open the Properties tab. Locate the BorderBrush property in the Brushes category and change it to a SolidColorBrush, as close to dark green color as you can using the color picker.

4. Locate the BorderThickness property in the Appearance category and set the border thicknesses for each direction to 4, as shown in Figure 6.1.

5. Locate the Foreground property in the Brushes category and change the color to a SolidColorBrush Red.

Right now you have a fairly ugly button, but what is important to note here is that you are applying property changes to the element as an instance of the Button. You are not changing the Style of the element, but in effect overriding the default Style settings applied to the Button.

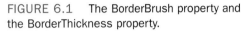

FIGURE 6.1   The BorderBrush property and the BorderThickness property.

Remember that you are now editing what is called the Instance of the button.

You can always determine which properties are overriding the default Style in your instance by the presence of a white box next to any property, as shown in Figure 6.2.

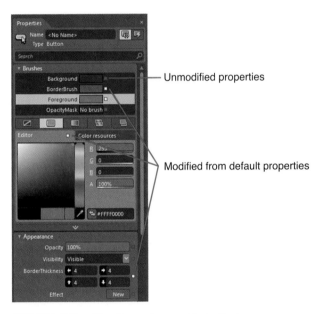

FIGURE 6.2   The Property override indicator.

If you click on the white box next to the Foreground property, you see the Advanced Options context menu, as shown in Figure 6.3. The first option is to reset the property, which returns the property to its default value—as is applied in the default Style.

Click on the Reset menu item now, and you see the Foreground property return to a Black SolidColorBrush; your Button should now show that in the artboard.

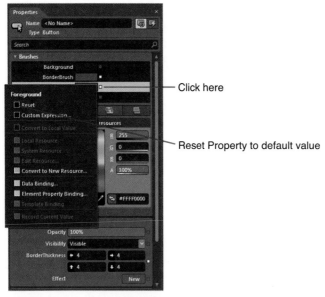

Click here

Reset Property to default value

FIGURE 6.3   The Advanced Options menu.

Where Is the Default Style?

The default Style is usually packaged up inside the element when it is first authored, but you can and will get access to it in order for you to be able to customize a version of it—in other words, use it as a blueprint to create your own as shown in the following steps.

1. Select the Button instance and then find the Object menu item at the top of Blend.

2. Locate the "Edit Style" menu item and then click on the "Edit a copy..." option.

You now see the Create Style Resource dialog, as shown in Figure 6.4. In this step, you are using the default Style as the blueprint for your own Button Style, so give the Style a meaningful name in the Name (Key) field, as also shown in Figure 6.4.

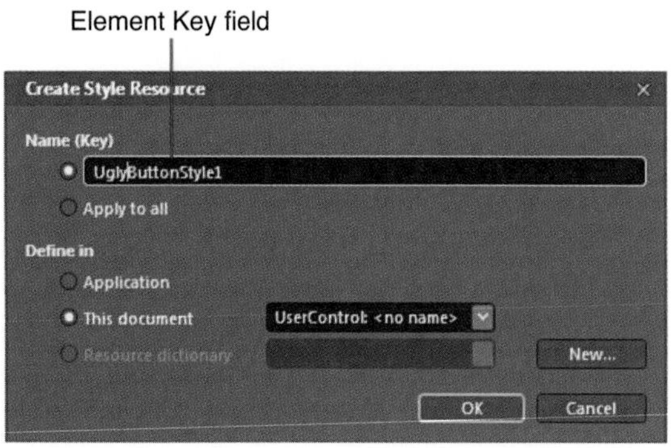

Element Key field

FIGURE 6.4   The Create Style Resource dialog box.

Not to confuse matters, but at this time, leave the other fields as shown in Figure 6.4 and click on the OK button.

Several items have now changed in the various Blend UI panels, namely the Object and Timeline tab. You might notice that the breadcrumb element on the artboard is also displaying a new icon, as shown in Figure 6.5.

This change represents that you are now editing the Style. To further indicate this, notice that you children or elements of your scene, as indicated by the solitary "Style" item shown in the Objects and Timeline tab, illustrated in Figure 6.6.

Property changes you now make are being made to the Style of the element; unless you have overridden those properties in the instance of the element, these property changes will be shown in the Button instance you were working on previously when you exit, making changes to the default Style.

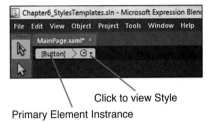

Click to view Style

Primary Element Instrance

FIGURE 6.5   The Style icon in the breadcrumb bar shows your current level in the Style hierarchy.

Single Style entry

FIGURE 6.6   The Style being edited in the Objects and Timeline tab.

The Button element is still showing on the artboard, which might be confusing, but the purpose of this is so you can visualize the changes you are making to the Style and how those property changes will look when the Style is applied to an instance of a button.

The following steps show you how to make a change to the Style.

1. Find the Text category of the Properties tab and modify the Font property by selecting a new font in the drop-down list. Figure 6.7 shows the properties selected in this sample, but you can choose whichever pleases you.

FIGURE 6.7   The Text category changes made.

FontSize Measurements

Figure 6.7 shows that the sample application is using Points (pt) as the Type Unit for fonts. You can change your this value to Pixels (px) in the options dialog by going to Tools->Options->Units.

2. Change the FontSize property.

3. Locate the Foreground property in the Brushes category and change the color to something completely different than what you currently have.

You have now made changes to the default Style, creating your own and you need to exit the Style editing process in order to work further with your Button instance and the new Style you have created.

There are a few methods to exit the Style editing process, but you are going to see the two primary mechanisms here. Figure 6.8 shows the Scope Up button in the Objects and Timeline tab (which you will learn more about shortly). Figure 6.8 also indicates that you can select the [Button] element on the breadcrumb bar to return to your instance of the button.

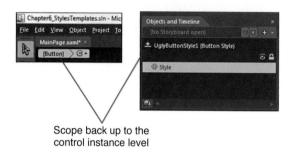

Scope back up to the
control instance level

FIGURE 6.8   Demonstrating the two methods to exit the Style editing context.

Having exited the Style editing mode, you probably haven't noticed any change to the visual representation of your Button instance. This is because the Style you just created is being applied automatically to the Button instance. To demonstrate this further, select and add an additional Button to the artboard from the toolbar.

Notice in Figure 6.9 that you have what resembles the original instance of the Button and the one that has your Style applied to it.

FIGURE 6.9   The edited Style applied to the first instance of the button and a new Button instance with a default Style applied to it.

Now to Perform Some Magic!

Select the new Button instance that you just added (you can do this in both the artboard and the Objects and Timeline tab) and right-click on it. Find the menu item "Edit Template" and then the submenu item "Apply Resource," and you should see the name of the Style you named previously, as shown in Figure 6.10.

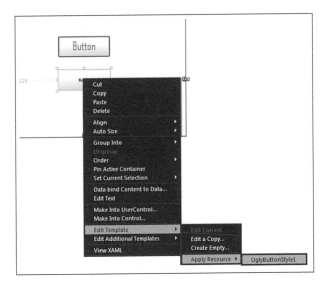

FIGURE 6.10   The context menu to find the Style.

Select the Style from the menu, and you now see your Style applied to the second Button instance, complete with the Font property values, as shown in Figure 6.11.

To verify that you have indeed worked on the Style as opposed to the Button instance, you can find the properties that you changed in the Style previously, such as the Foreground color, and you should note that there is no little white box next to the property.

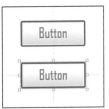

FIGURE 6.11   The Style created applied to the Button instance.

Change the Foreground color, and the white box will appear; then you can select and opt to reset the property, which returns the Foreground property to the color you selected in the Style editing process.

What is really powerful is that you can select either Button instance now, and again using the Object menu, Edit Style, you can edit the Style; you see those property changes in the Style applied to both instances of the Buttons as you make those changes.

The Style is a wrapped-up package of property settings and *Parts* that make up what appears on the screen, given a certain *State* is applied to the element. You learn more about States in Chapter 8, "Working with States," where you modify even more of your Style(s) to change, as States change in your element instances.

What Is a Template?

In this context of Styles, the Template represents a collection of "Parts" referred to in this chapter. There exist several other *types* of Template that you will be exposed to in this book, such as `DataTemplates`, `ItemTemplates`, and `ContentTemplates`, to name a few.

For the novice, this is where confusion can set in. "Parts" is an important term to take on board. In Chapter 7, "Working with Parts," you work with a *Part* editor that will be dependent on the knowledge you learn here. For now, understand that Parts are indeed elements or controls, no different from what you are already used to.

Figure 6.12 shows a diagram indicating a virtual view of a Button element instance, the Style applied to it, and inside of that Style, a ControlTemplate (which is technically a Part).

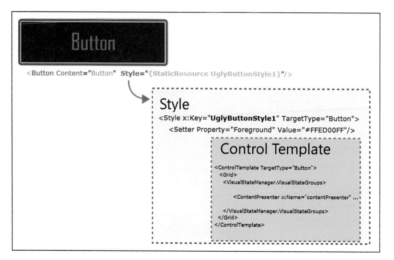

FIGURE 6.12   A virtual view of element, Style, and Template.

NOTE

Why So Complicated?

This discussion is tantamount to opening a box of worms.

You will have lots of questions, and not all will be answered in this chapter, but be patient—it will all become clear throughout your use of Styles and Templates, especially when working in a more advanced sample than a button.

It's a case of "horse before the cart," as you can't fully understand Styles without understanding Templates. Keep in the back of your mind that "yes," this is complicated, but with that comes an enormous amount of power and flexibility.

You may well be asking the question right now, "Why didn't I see any ControlTemplate when I was editing the Style?" and you would be completely justified in thinking so.

When you edited the Style previously, you only went one level down into what you see in the diagram shown in Figure 6.12. You are now going down to the next level where the Template resides. The Template is technically called a "ControlTemplate," which is an important distinction, as there are many other *types* of Templates that you will be introduced to in the remainder of this book.

1. Move one of your Button instances to the side, and the other to the center of your artboard. Select the one in the center so you can concentrate on a single instance for the moment. Before going any further, select the Background property of the Brushes category and select an arbitrary SolidColorBrush from the color picker. Figure 6.13 shows that the sample has a yellow color selected, but what is interesting to note here is that the background of the Button element hasn't really changed that much. This is really quite important to note, and you will see why this change hasn't caused an effect shortly.

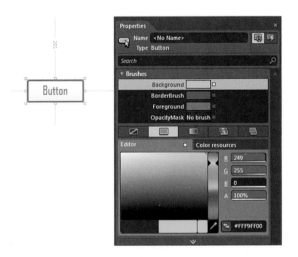

FIGURE 6.13   The Background property change and the button that it is applied against.

The following steps will show you how to edit the Template of the Button.

2. Previously when editing the Style of the Button instance, you selected the Button and went to the Object menu and selected "Edit Style." This time, select the Button instance and again go to the Object menu at the top of Blend and look for the menu item "Edit Template." It is interesting to note that the submenu appears, and this time gives you an option to "Edit Current."

3. You should immediately recognize the changes inside the Objects and Timeline panel, as shown in Figure 6.14. Note that there are vastly more elements inside the Template than what you would expect there to be inside of a Button. As you look at your Button instance, there appears to be not much more than a border and a label.

There are good reasons for this, and you will start to understand those reasons as you work at a more advanced level with Styles and Templates throughout the book.

Note that the naming convention applied to the elements inside this particular template appear to be adding to the level of confusion. You can clearly see that an element is named "Background," but as you will see in the next step, this doesn't really represent the background at all. *(Note to Microsoft....)*

4. Begin to expand the elements, exposing their children, and select the Grid element, as also shown in Figure 6.14, which is nested below the Background element.

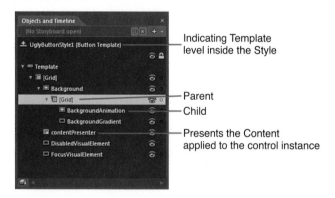

FIGURE 6.14   The ControlTemplate elements of the button Style.

5. Figure 6.15 shows the Property panel as you should also now see it, and in particular, the Background property has a golden box and the color picker also has a color box around it. This color inside the Advanced Options box indicates that this particular property is "Bound" to some other property. The binding specifically means that this property value is coming from somewhere else and that you can't directly change the property value without breaking that "binding." You can try by clicking inside the color picker, and you see that nothing happens.

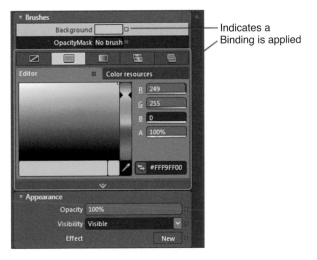

Indicates a
Binding is applied

FIGURE 6.15   The Background property with the binding indicator.

> **NOTE**
>
> **Why Is the Binding Locked?**
>
> The tricky thing to get your head around now is that the property binding can in effect be coming from anywhere. The binding could be set to take the property value from another value inside of this Template, it could be from the instance of the element the Template is applied to, it could be from a data object feeding data to this form, or it could even be from another element on your page. This sounds horrific, and you may indeed be sweating profusely at the moment, but don't despair! The point of how complex the binding could be is made for a reason; so you become very cautious about breaking bindings. Sometimes breaking a binding can render the element nonfunctional because the binding can be an integral part of the functionally that the element has.

Remember the Background property color you selected back in Step 1? The color you selected is now showing in the Background property, isn't it? You can now reliably discern that the property is indeed bound to the Background property of the Button instance. This reads a little crazy, so refer to the illustration shown in Figure 6.16 to assist you in understanding what is going on here.

6. You might have already worked out the reason why the color you selected for the Background property of the Button instance is not showing as the actual Background—select the element below the grid in the Objects and Timeline panel called the "BackgroundAnimation." Note that its properties are not bound, but what you should particularly note is that the Opacity property is set to 0. This element is not even visible at the moment; therefore, it is reasonable to assume from the name of the element and the fact that its Opacity is 0 that this particular element is used when a State change is effected to the element itself. You learn how to find which State (MouseOver or Disabled, for example) is affecting this element a little later.

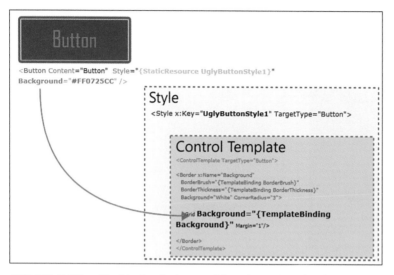

FIGURE 6.16   The binding instance of the element to the ControlTemplate property.

7. With the `BackgroundAnimation` element selected, press your `Delete` button to remove it, and you should see a pop-up from Blend indicating that an animation has now been removed because of the deletion. Figure 6.17 shows this warning, and at this stage, you should not be concerned.

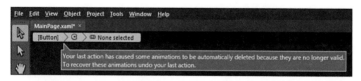

FIGURE 6.17   An animation has been deleted due to the deleted element.

8. Select the `BackgroundGradient` element that is now under the Grid element. You should note the complex gradient that has been applied to the `Fill` property, as shown in Figure 6.18.

9. This element is the sole reason you can't see the `Background` property value you set in Step 1. This element is covering up the true background, which is the `Grid` element. Delete the `BackgroundGradient` element, and again you see the warning pop-up about the animation being cancelled; what you see is that your Button instance background

> **NOTE**
>
> **Why This Property Is Now Called Fill Instead of Background**
>
> Although you would think the property *type* should be named the same, the `BackgroundGradient` element is a type of Rectangle and not a Grid or Border, as are the other elements you are working on. Notice that Shapes and Path elements have a `Fill` property rather than a `Background` property.

is now the color you would expect, as shown in Figure 6.19. The instance of the control you are not editing at the moment shows the dark Blue background color because it has the template applied to it, but you didn't change its background color like you did with the button in the center of the artboard.

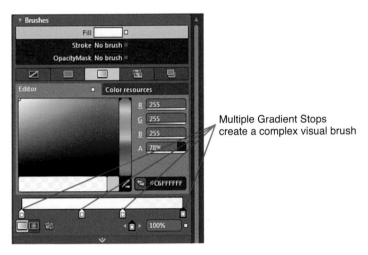

Multiple Gradient Stops create a complex visual brush

FIGURE 6.18   The complex gradient applied to the element.

10. The next element to select is the [ContentPresenter]. Take a look at the Layout and Common Properties category of the Property tab, as shown in Figure 6.20—lots of bindings to be aware of here.

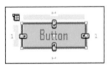

FIGURE 6.19   The button looking more like expected.

The ContentPresenter Element

If things were not complex enough for you to follow, this next part is pretty much the core of what you need to understand in order to work with Styles and Templates of content elements, such as the Button element.

What first appears to be a Label or even a form of TextBlock inside the Button Template is not either. The ContentPresenter is a special element that is bound to the Content property of the host element's Content property.

You can see the Content property binding along with several other bindings in Figure 6.20.

How or why is the Content property showing the Text "button" at the moment? The answer lies with the Content property itself being able to display a string of text *or* another element. Figure 6.21 gives a clearer example of how either text or another element can be applied to the Context property of the Button instance.

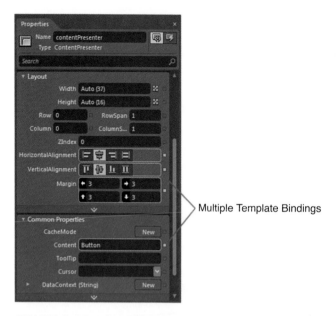

FIGURE 6.20   The bindings applied to the ContentPresenter.

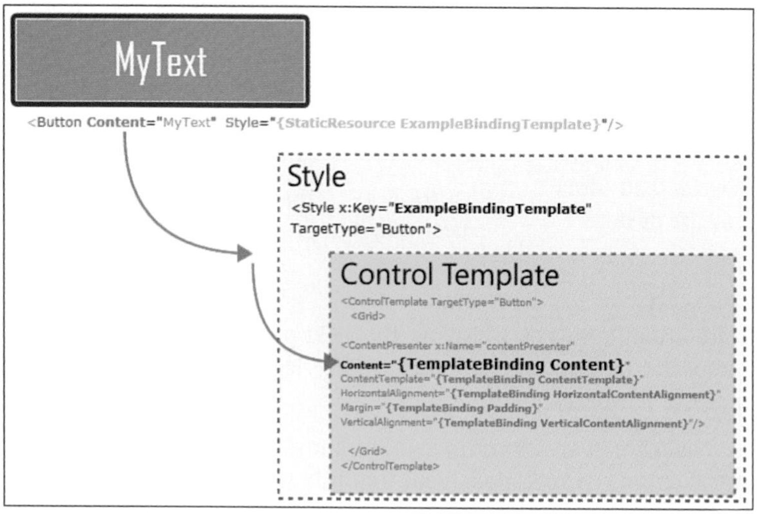

FIGURE 6.21   The concept of the ContentPresenter.

In effect, by binding to the Content property inside the ControlTemplate, the ContentPresenter element becomes a picture frame, merely displaying whatever type of content is given to it by the host element.

This form of binding is called "TemplateBinding."

To demonstrate the ContentPresenter's ability to show different element types as content, select the [Button] on the breadcrumb control, which will Scope Up back to the instance of the control, as shown in Figure 6.22. Locate the Content property in the Common Properties category of the Property tab.

FIGURE 6.22   The ever-growing breadcrumb control.

You can see that the Content property is currently showing the value "Button." This is a *string* value type applied to the property of which you can modify by typing directly in the property editor.

The following steps demonstrate the insertion of an Ellipse element as the Button content.

1. Locate an Ellipse element in the toolbox and double click to add it to the artboard.

2. Change the Fill property to a SolidColorBrush similar to Red.

3. Inside the Objects and Timeline panel, select and drag the Ellipse element, forcing it to become the child element of the Button control. It's easy to move the Ellipse element above or below the button, so pay attention to the tooltip explaining what the action will do. It doesn't quite look right, but a tooltip as shown in Figure 6.23 tells you when you are about to replace the string in the content of the button with the ellipse.

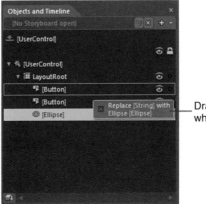

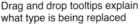

Drag and drop tooltips explain what type is being replaced

FIGURE 6.23   The tooltip when correctly dragging the ellipse as the new child element of the Button element.

4. Again, select the center Button element in the Objects and Timeline panel and locate the Content property in the Common Properties category. You see that the property value has changed to now indicate the value change to Ellipse, as shown in Figure 6.24.

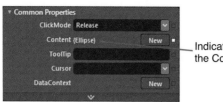

FIGURE 6.24   The TemplateBinding source value.

5. The ContentPresenter should still be present in the breadcrumb bar. Select it now, and you will again be in template editing mode.

6. Select the ContentPresenter element in the Objects and Timeline panel and inspect the properties as before, now showing the Binding value to be the same value as the element instance of Ellipse.

Depending on the array of colors you have chosen to use throughout this chapter, the chances are that you have an even uglier button than you previously thought possible to create (the Style name used in this chapter is now clear, isn't it?).

It doesn't matter, however, because you are really concerned with the conceptual understanding of the Style and Template, rather than the visuals.

Continue to play around by adding different types of child elements as the content of the Button instance and modify the ContentPresenter element to see how that affects the outcome.

Creating the Easiest Button Ever

Previously, you have been through a complex Button Style and Template, coming out the other side all smiles (hopefully). In the following steps, you are going to create a very simple Button from scratch where you can then modify the Style and ControlTemplate to suit your preference.

> **TIP**
>
> **Keeping the Ellipse Square**
>
> When drawing any of the *shapes* (Rectangle and Line also) onto the artboard, you can hold down the Shift key at the same time to ensure that the aspect ratio of the shape is maintained.

1. Remove all the Button elements from your artboard.

2. Add a new Ellipse element by double-clicking from the toolbox or drawing it directly on the artboard.

3. Color the Fill property of the shape however you please. In Figure 6.25, you can see how this sample has a RadialGradientBrush applied, along with the respective GradientBrush properties.

4. Select the Ellipse in the Objects and Timeline panel or the artboard and right-click to produce the element context menu.

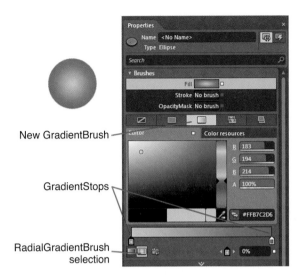

FIGURE 6.25   The RadialGradientBrush applied to the Ellipse element.

5. Select the "Make Into Control..." menu option, which then shows the Make Into Control dialog. By default, the chosen Style will be the Button. Name it as you please and leave the rest of the settings the same, as shown in Figure 6.26.

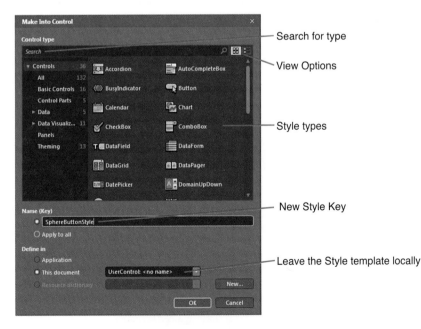

FIGURE 6.26   The Make Into Control dialog.

6. Click OK, and you find that the mode has changed directly into the Style editing mode with a vastly simplified `ControlTemplate` to what you previously worked with in this chapter.

You can now Scope Up to get back to your new `Button` instance and apply that Style directly to any Button element you add to the artboard.

How simple was that?

Add any new Button to the artboard and apply your new Style(s) to them. When you go to apply your `SphereStyle` to any new button, you will notice that the previous ugly Style is also available. Deleting an element doesn't delete the Style you created previously, and you can now apply that to any Button element.

Simple Styles

From the first versions of Expression Blend, WPF applications had a sneaky advantage when it came to editing Styles and Templates of controls. The Blend team provided a collection of "Simple Styles" and, fortunately, they are still included in Expression Blend 4.

Why this isn't the case with Silverlight isn't clear. They really make learning and using Styles very simple (as the name suggests) and it is a shame that they are not available.

The following steps show you the Simple Styles available in WPF.

1. Open Blend and create a new "WPF Application."

2. Open the Assets tab and navigate to the Style category to which you will see the Simple Styles collection inside the Styles collection, as shown in Figure 6.27.

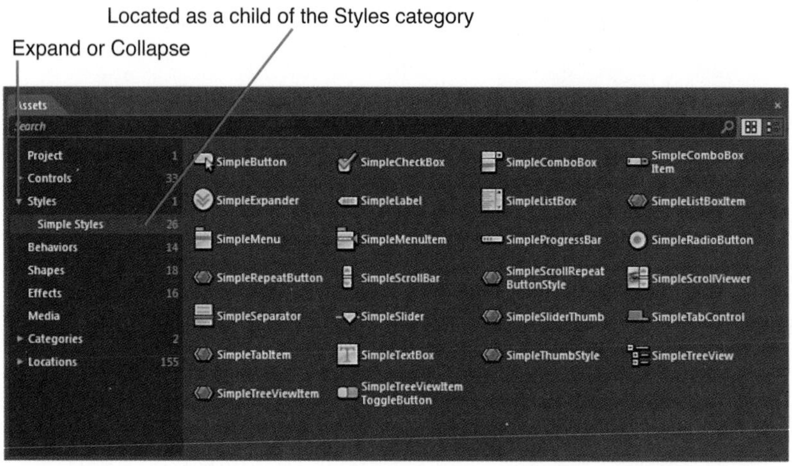

FIGURE 6.27   The pot of gold known as Simple Styles.

3. In the Assets search box, type in the word "prog," and you should be presented with two ProgressBar elements: one called "SimpleProgressBar" and the other called "ProgressBar." Add one of each element to your artboard, placing the Simple one under the standard control.

4. Right-click on the standard ProgressBar element that you added and navigate to the Edit Template menu option, noting that you will need to select "Edit a copy."

5. For this sample, keep the suggested Style name "ProgressBarStyle1" in the Create Style Resource dialog. Click OK to continue.

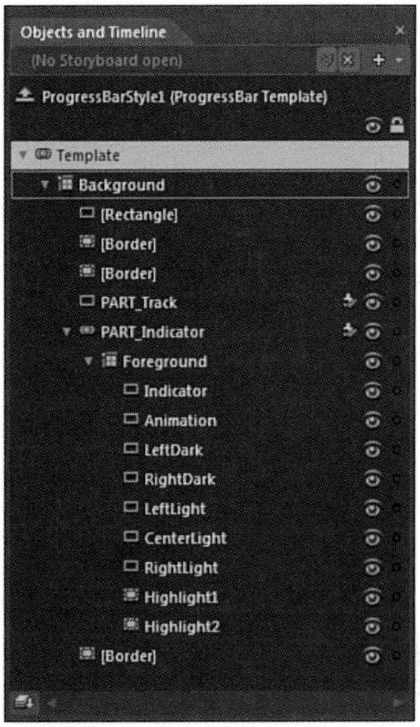

6. Note the amazing complexity of the ControlTemplate, as shown in Figure 6.28.

FIGURE 6.28   A complex ControlTemplate.

> **NOTE**
>
> **Are These Controls/Elements or Styles in the Assets Tab?**
>
> When you select any of the Styles inside the Assets tab, Blend is effectively adding an instance of the element type to the artboard for you and then applying the Style that you have selected. The short answer is therefore that you are seeing a collection of Styles rather than the elements in the Assets panel.

7. *Scope Up* to exit Template editing mode.

8. Select the SimpleProgressBar instance you added to the artboard and again right-click and navigate to the Edit Template menu option. Did you note that this time, you don't have to edit a copy? Opt to edit the current instance.

9. As Figure 6.29 shows, the ControlTemplate is vastly simplified.

FIGURE 6.29   The very simple SimpleProgressBar ControlTemplate.

When working with the Simple Styles collection, it is important to understand that if you don't create a copy of the Style, every time you add an instance of a Style (SimpleProgressBar, for example), it will show the changes that you have made to the base Style. Therefore, you are strongly advised to always make a copy of the SimpleStyle template before you begin editing it.

SimpleStyles are fantastic for understanding the ControlTemplates of some of the more complex controls, such as TreeView and TabControl, and well worth you investing some time exploring them.

> **TIP**
>
> **Why the Artboard Has Disappeared**
>
> The SimpleStyle collection of Styles resides in a file and not in the document you are editing at the present. Expression Blend changes your view because of this, which can be confusing at present. The mechanisms for understanding how to change this behavior will be explained in Chapter 13, "Skins, Themes, and Resource Dictionaries"

Summary

You have taken a lot on board with this chapter, navigating some quite complex concepts and hopefully ending with an understanding of the Style and ControlTemplate make up that is applied to an element such as the humble button.

Working with other elements, you will find varying levels of complexity with the Style and ControlTemplates available, but take comfort in knowing that the concept is the same throughout all controls and elements you will work with, regardless of the platform you are working in.

Breaking element Styles and Templates is a given, and you learn valuable lessons by doing just that. You can't break Expression Blend by breaking a control template, so don't be afraid to explore and discover. If it all breaks too severely, just start a new project!

CHAPTER 7

Working with Parts

In Chapter 6, "Element Styles and Templates," you learned how to edit a Style and `ControlTemplate`, which gives you an enormous amount of power to set about modifying controls to look the way you want when using the existing templates of the originally authored control.

There are two more important steps to learn in order to get your understanding of control styling and Behaviors to a high level: Parts and States.

In this chapter, you learn how to work with the Part editor to build up your custom control requirements by assigning Parts with your existing elements or adding new Parts. Expression Blend is not a perfect tool... yet; this chapter exposes a few of those areas that can be challenging and frustrating to new users around templates and parts, but rest assured in the end, you will approach things in a different manner.

Element Parts give you the ultimate in flexibility when modifying the collective make up of your working controls, and by the end of this chapter, you will understand how powerful this feature of Expression Blend is and the steps needed to turn any visual into any type of control Style.

NOTE

WPF Now Supports Parts

In previous versions of Expression Blend, the Parts editor was available only for the Silverlight platform. WPF controls provided in the .Net 4.0 platform now provide the platform extensions that Expression Blend needs to support Part assignment.

It's the Parts That Make Up the Whole

As you discovered in the previous chapter, the ControlTemplate is akin to a blueprint for the elements that are present during the functioning lifetime of the instance of the element.

Generically the term "Parts" was used deliberately throughout that chapter to get you prepared for this one. Technically, the term "Parts" refers to the elements inside the ControlTemplate that are referenced by code inside of the element and mostly (but not always) required to complete the function of the element.

Without the correct Parts assigned, a well-authored element won't show any errors or crash during runtime; however, it most likely won't work as desired. Therefore, it is important that you take note of the Parts when you begin editing existing elements, or you at least understand how to find the required Parts when creating controls from scratch that won't function without them.

You have probably had enough of working with Buttons for the short term, so in this chapter, you are going to work with another common control that has relatively complex Behaviors: the Slider.

The Slider is a clearly defined representation of specific interaction. You drag an element either horizontally or vertically to increase or decrease a value; this can then be applied to a property, which is normally associated with an interaction or value change, visually in another element.

The sample you work with in this chapter is very simple, so you can concentrate on the goals of this chapter, which focus on Parts and assignment in the ControlTemplate. Regardless, you need something to test your element with, as follows:

1. Create a new Silverlight Application + Website project.

2. Open the Asset Panel, and in the Search box, type the word "progress." You should see a ProgressBar control; select and draw one on your artboard, similar to Figure 7.1.

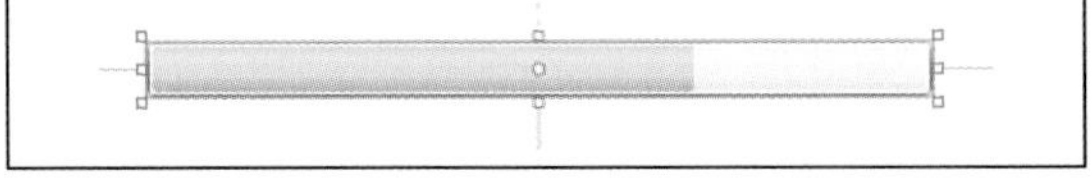

FIGURE 7.1   A ProgressBar with a value of 70 applied.

3. The property you are most interested in on the ProgressBar at present is the Value property, which is located in the Common Properties category.

4. Play with the Value property, and note the change in the visual presentation of the element. Also note that by default, the Maximum property value is 100. This is very self-explanatory, but just in case you haven't used this type of control previously,

the `Minimum` and `Maximum` property values set the boundary extents that the element will work with. `0` shows no bar and `100` (or more) shows a full bar.

5. In the Common Controls collection of the toolbox (or in the Asset Panel), find the `Slider` control and draw one underneath the `ProgressBar` element you previously added, as shown in Figure 7.2.

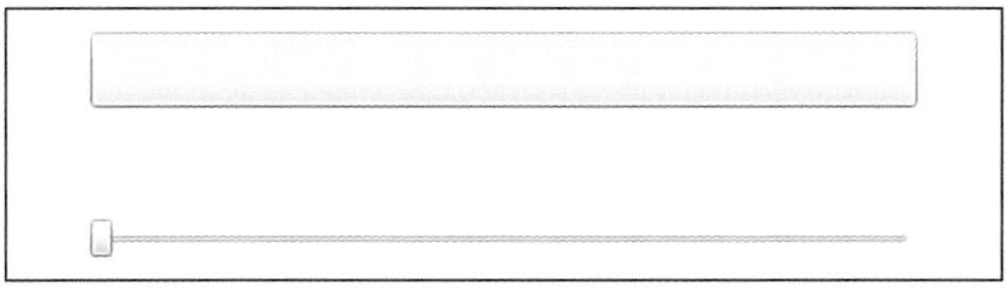

FIGURE 7.2   The reference Slider and ProgressBar elements.

The purpose of adding the Slider at the moment is twofold:

▶ It serves as a visual reference for the element you are going to try to replicate.

▶ It serves as a functional reference.

Element to Element Binding

This particular set of instructions show you how to connect or "bind" one element to another. In this case, you want to be able to drag the `Slider` element and show a corresponding value in the `ProgressBar` you just added.

> **NOTE**
>
> **Element Binding**
>
> Element binding is related to the field of data binding and will be explained in greater detail in Chapter 10, "Expression Blend Data Support."

1. Select the `ProgressBar` element on the artboard and navigate to the `Value` property.

2. Select the little box next to the property, which displays the Advanced Options context menu.

3. Find the menu option "Element Property Binding..." and select it.

4. Note that your mouse cursor has now changed to show a Target icon attached. This is called the Element Picker cursor, and you will see it often throughout the book. It simply means you can directly select or "pick" an element to work with on both the artboard and the Objects and Timeline panel.

5. Immediately select the `Slider` on the artboard, and you will be presented with the Create Data Binding dialog box, as shown in Figure 7.3.

FIGURE 7.3   The Create Data Binding dialog box and property selection.

NOTE

Your Slider Is Named

Before selecting the Slider element, when moving the mouse over the top of it, you may have noted a little tooltip telling you that the Slider will be named "slider," as shown in Figure 7.4. This occurs because the XAML needs a named reference in order to create a binding to it. If you had more than one Slider on your artboard, the compiler would not know which Slider you are referring to.

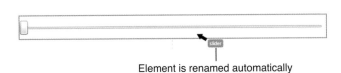

Element is renamed automatically

FIGURE 7.4   The element will be changed when selected with the Element Picker.

6. The purpose of this dialog box is to enable you to select the property to which you want to bind your ProgressBar. The dialog by default tries to match the most common property value that you are trying to bind to and a property that matches the data *type*. In this case, it is the Slider's Value property.

If not already shown, you can select the ProgressBar element and navigate back to the Value property. You should now see a gold box and rounded rectangle border around the Value property, which indicates that it is indeed the subject of a binding, the same as you learned in Chapter 6 and as shown in Figure 7.5.

For the most part, element binding is as simple as that, and you can now run the

FIGURE 7.5   The Element Binding effect on the ProgressBar Value property.

application to see how it works. Press F5, and when the application has loaded, you can drag the Slider thumb left and right, where you should see a matching ProgressBar value.

A Visual Reference

Satisfied that the Slider element is relatively simple, you should now begin to try to break down the pieces that are being used in the control.

The Slider looks like a button and a line.

The easiest way to work with an unfamiliar control Parts is to pull apart the existing reference you have added as is shown in the following steps.

> **TIP**
>
> **Visual References**
>
> I almost always prefer to have a visual reference of the control element I am about to create, even when I know that certain required functionality will almost always break my first thoughts about Parts.

1. Select the Slider element, and on the Breadcrumb control, select to edit a copy of the Slider template.

2. You are interested in the HorizontalSlider template here, so expand the element collection in the Objects and Timeline panel, as shown in Figure 7.6.

3. This looks more complicated than it really is, which is probably due to the naming convention of the Parts shown. Speaking of Parts, you should now open the Parts panel, if it is not already open, and begin inspecting the make of the panel, as detailed in Figure 7.7.

FIGURE 7.6   The element collection for the Horizontal template of the Slider.

4. Note in particular the Part assignments, as indicated by the tick icons both in the Parts panel and the Objects and Timeline panel. Note that there are only four Parts assigned for the HorizontalTemplate; the other four are for the VerticalTemplate.

5. Aside from taking note of the Parts that are assigned, select the HorizontalTemplate Grid element in the Objects and Timeline panel. Take particular note of the layout of this element on the artboard. As Figure 7.8 shows, there are several columns defined, and this is very important to replicate in your own control Style.

> **The Layout Is Extremely Important**
>
> This single piece of layout is often overlooked by novice users, and if it isn't replicated, your control won't work!

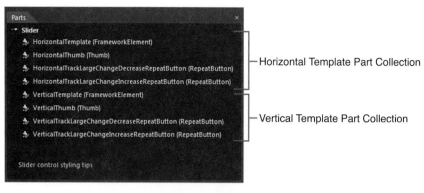

FIGURE 7.7   The Parts panel for the Slider control.

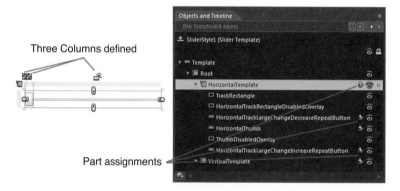

FIGURE 7.8   The layout of the HorizontalTemplate element.

You can review this Layout by typing Col into the property search box of the Objects and Timeline panel and then select the "Edit items in this collection" button, as shown in Figure 7.9.

6. Figure 7.10 shows the ColumnDefinition Collection Editor, which shows three columns in this collection. With each element selected, you can understand the value applied to each column on the right side of the dialog box. Note the Advanced Property values—in particular, the MinWidth property values set to 0

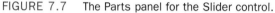

FIGURE 7.9   The ColumnDefinition property value.

for the Columns that are of *type* Auto. This means these particular columns will expand and collapse as required.

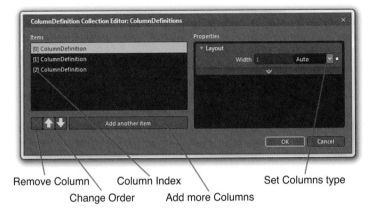

Remove Column   Column Index   Set Columns type

Change Order   Add more Columns

FIGURE 7.10   The ColumnDefinition Collection Editor dialog box.

7. You can now click Cancel to get out of this dialog and then scope up to get out of the Slider template.

You should now have a better idea of how the Slider element is constructed and as previously stated; it's of the utmost importance to replicate the layout of the Template.

You should have also noted that several other buttons and controls are present to make the Slider the control that it is. The code in the base of the Slider control is what makes the Slider slide, but because you are not modifying the functionality of the control, you needn't be concerned with the code.

Building Your Own Slider Control

You are now ready to build out your own Slider control which is detailed in the following steps.

1. Start by providing a base for your new element by using a Grid element. Draw a Grid on the artboard that could contain the width and height of the reference Slider element.

2. Give it a background color for the moment, so you can easily see the boundary of the element as you work with it.

3. With your Grid selected, find the Tools ->Make Into Control menu item and select it. You should see the Make Into Control dialog, as shown in Figure 7.11.

> **Using the Blend Part Helpers**
>
> You can continue to draw the elements into your Grid if that is how you prefer to work, but next I want you to see some of the helpers that Blend provides when trying to make a Style with Parts. This really helps a lot, and this is my preferred method of working.

4. Using the search mechanism, find the Slider element by typing "Slider" into the search box.

5. Select the Style shown and then rename it to `SimpleSlider`.

6. Leave the rest of the details in the dialog as shown and select the OK button.

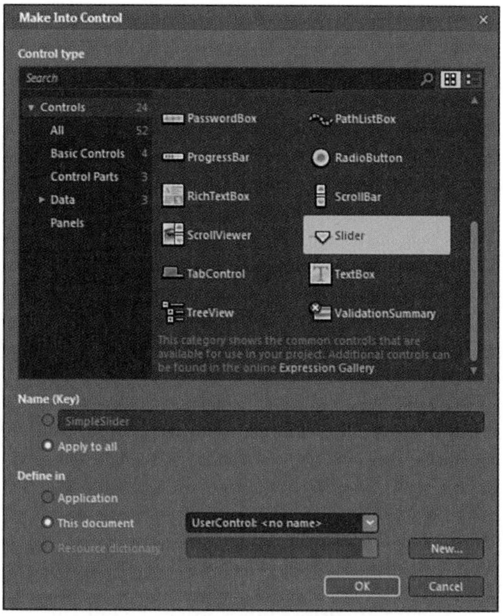

You are now directly inside the template of your Style, which should be starting to look more familiar to you now. Note the change in the Breadcrumb control, as well as the change in the Objects and Timeline panel.

Don't be overwhelmed by the collection and especially the names of these elements. Remember, you need only four of these Parts to make a functioning Slider, so you will be sticking to the easy route for the moment:

FIGURE 7.11   The Make Into Control dialog with the Slider element selected.

1. Select the `Grid` element in the Objects and Timeline panel, if not already selected.

2. As mentioned previously, you could have started drawing your own elements inside the `Grid` before making it into a `Slider` control, but this is where the Parts collection helps you out. Looking through the Parts collection, located at the top, the `HorizontalTemplate` Part and double-click it.

3. You will see that Blend inserts the Part for you as a child of your `Grid`, as shown in Figure 7.12.

4. What Blend doesn't do for you at this point is create the Column layout that was shown in the original Slider template you examined previously. If you recall, this particular grid had three columns.

    With the `HorizontalTemplate` grid element selected, open the Properties panel and search for the column editor in the properties panel by typing in "Col."

TIP

Work Faster

You can quickly drop in and out of this template and your reference template by clicking on the root element of the BreadCrumb bar.

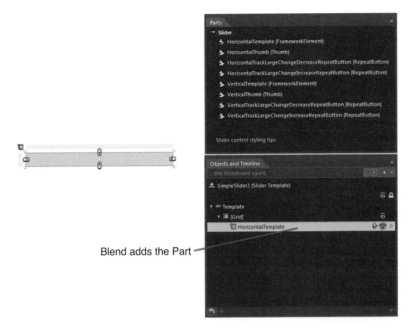

Blend adds the Part

FIGURE 7.12   The Part assignment added to your template.

5. Add three columns by clicking the "Add another item" button, setting the first two to "Auto" and ensuring that the MinWidth value is set to 0. Set the last of the columns to a Width property value of 1, Star, as shown in Figure 7.13.

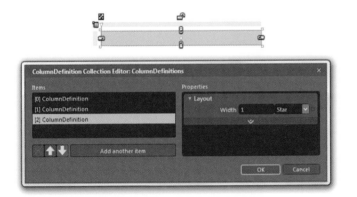

FIGURE 7.13   The Column editor with the new columns being specified.

6. You are ready to continue adding the rest of the Parts now; just remember that the rest of the Parts are child elements of the HorizontalTemplate Grid. Find the HorizontalTrackLargeChangeDecreaseRepeatButton Part and double-click to add it. Make sure that this new element has a Column property value of 0.

7. Find the `HorizontalTrackLargeChangeIncreaseRepeatButton` Part and double-click to add it. Make sure that this new element has a `Column` property value of 2.

8. Working a different way, this time add a Button from the toolbar as a child of the `HorizontalTemplate` Grid. Set its `Column` property value to 1 and ensure that its `ColumnSpan` property value is also set to 1.

9. Right-click on the Button and look for the menu option, "Make Into Part of Slider," which should open a submenu showing the Parts list. You should also note that the Parts you have already assigned are also shown with the little green tick icon. Find the `HorizontalThumb` Part and select it from this submenu, as shown in Figure 7.14.

FIGURE 7.14   The Parts submenu options.

10. This previous action will raise the Make Into Part dialog, which is actually enabling you to specify the Style of this element. Name the element `MyHorizontalThumb` and click OK.

11. You will now be inside the `Thumb` template. Scope up to exit the template, and you should now see all your Parts assigned in your Objects and Timeline Panel, as shown in Figure 7.15.

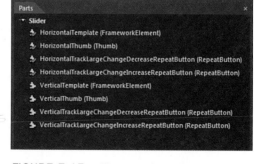

FIGURE 7.15   The completed Parts assignment.

> **WARNING**
>
> **Be Super Accurate!**
>
> It is very important to pay attention to the property values of the components that you are either adding here yourself or that the Parts editor is inserting for you. Make sure that your components are child elements of the HorizontalTemplate Grid directly and have not accidently become children of each other. You should also ensure that your controls haven't received margin values added or ColumnSpan and RowSpan properties more than 1. Remember, you can always move back and forward between a normal Slider template and the one that you are building up.

12. Keep scoping up so you get back to the very start. Your Slider looks ugly at present, but that's OK; run the application by clicking on F5.

Required Control Types

When you try to move your Slider by dragging on the button, nothing happens, does it? This is an important lesson in how you must be aware of the control *types* that the Parts should be; in this case, the Button element just doesn't cut it, and the Slider requires you to use a specific *type* of button called a Thumb control:

1. Re-enter your Slider template using the BreadCrumb control and delete the HorizontalThumb Part you added previously.

2. Search the Assets panel for a Thumb element and add it, remembering to assign the part as the HorizontalThumb again using the right-click context menus. You should ensure that the Width property of the Thumb is fixed to 20.

3. Scope up and out of the template, but before running the application, try to bind the Value property of the ProgressBar to the Value property of your new Slider, just like you did at the start of this chapter.

4. You should also set the Maximum property value of your Slider control to 100; by default, it is currently set to 10.

> **TIP**
>
> **ElementBinding Reminder**
>
> Remember that you are binding the value of the ProgressBar to the value of the Slider and not the other way around.

5. Run the application by clicking F5.

You should now have a working Slider control, as shown in Figure 7.16.

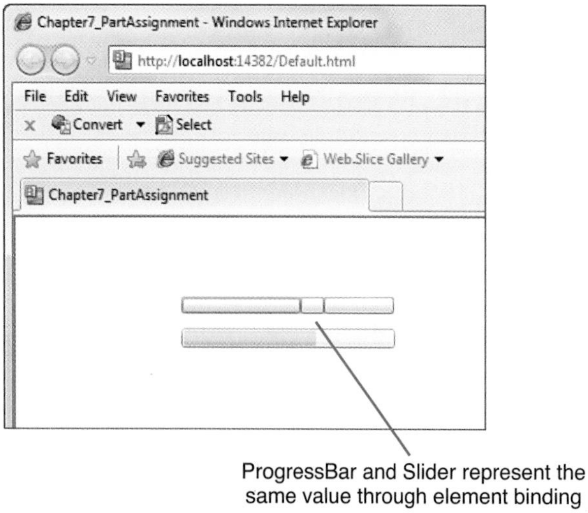

ProgressBar and Slider represent the
same value through element binding

FIGURE 7.16   The bound Slider and ProgressBar controls.

Summary

During the process of design implementation, it is often the case where the integrator or UI developer might sit with the interaction designer and mark up a design or prototype, defining the applicable controls that should be the basis for the functional implementation.

One of the primary pieces of understanding from the previous chapter on ControlTemplates and Styles was that the functionality of a control is always constant, but the Style and Template enable you to modify the visual representation of the control.

Often, it is inefficient to try to break apart an existing ControlTemplate in order to implement a required design. Parts give you the freedom to take the design and, in some cases, simply right-click and turn the designs into controls, assigning Parts to the moving pieces required by the functional specification and functional delivery of the control.

By understanding the Parts of a control, you might find that designing controls becomes easier. You now know that the Slider needs four Parts as a minimum to make it work. You can make the RepeatButton controls transparent if you want to, but don't forget that you need to have them in your ControlTemplate, or the control simply won't work.

CHAPTER 8

Working with States

In the last two chapters, you have been working within the bounds of Style templating (Parts were included in this). You have learned how to create Styles from scratch, as well as how to manipulate existing templates and make elements work as you need them to.

This chapter shows you how to make your elements respond to different State changes that occur during the lifetime of the elements in your application.

You also look at how States can be defined at a UserControl level; in other words, you will be controlling one element on the determination of the states of another element. You use Behaviors to make all this work together, and as a result, no code is required.

What Is a State?

By definition, a State is a set of conditions that are the result of logical implication.

To understand that definition, consider State another way and examine what you're doing right now.

You're reading, which could be said to be a State.

When you finish reading, you will enter another State, possibly walking or talking. If you are walking and talking, you are in another State, a multi-state to be sure, but an entirely definable State difference.

Transfer that knowledge to the elements you work with—for example, a Button element. A Button can have many states, including the following:

- ▶ Enabled

- ▶ Disabled

- ▶ MouseOver

- ▶ Pressed

- ▶ Focused

- ▶ UnFocused

The good news is that most elements you work with in Expression Blend have some form of State functionality built in. Both Silverlight and now WPF/.Net 4.0 elements support the mechanism that Expression Blend uses to expose States; this is called the Visual State Manager, or VSM for short.

Working with the VSM

The VSM replaces what was an early mechanism in WPF called Triggers. Triggers are still under the hood in reality, but both the terminology and the tooling for Triggers started to get really messy. In addition, Silverlight didn't support Triggers by design, so this new VSM mechanism was created to help you work with the replacement concept known as States.

The VSM enables you to assign State groups, which are a collection of States. You can create animations that are also called when a State is entered, so you have full control over the resulting visual exposure that you want the user to experience.

States can be applied to your entire application, but for a more direct example of how States and the VSM work, you will be editing the template of an element, examining the existing States, and modifying the properties of your element to show the State change that has occurred.

The following steps demonstrate this with a CheckBox element.

1. Create a new Silverlight Application + Website solution.

2. From either the Assets tab or the toolbox (common controls collection), find and add a CheckBox element to the artboard.

3. With the CheckBox selected, open the Properties tab and navigate to the Common Properties category. Note that by default, the property called "IsThreeState" is not checked. Check this now, as you will be creating state changes for each of the three states of the CheckBox element.

4. Edit a copy of the default template applied to the CheckBox using any mechanism you prefer (the breadcrumb control is the fastest with the fewest clicks). You should see a similar ControlTemplate as shown in the Objects and Timeline panel in Figure 8.1.

Indicates the current
Scope level

Scope up button

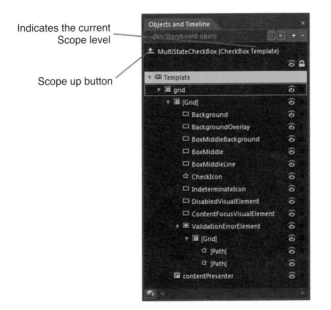

FIGURE 8.1   The complex CheckBox Control template.

5. With the Grid element expanded, note that the CheckBox template is more complex than you would reasonably assume. Don't be deterred by this apparent complexity, as the child elements of this Grid are all specifically for the "check" part of the element.

6. Open the States tab. At first glance, it might feel like you just opened Pandora's box. There are 13 States by default, but for this example, you are only interested in four of them, as highlighted in Figure 8.2. As for the rest of the Buttons and items shown in this tab, you learn what each of these provides during the progression through this chapter. For now, collapse all the State Groups to make this tab more manageable to work with.

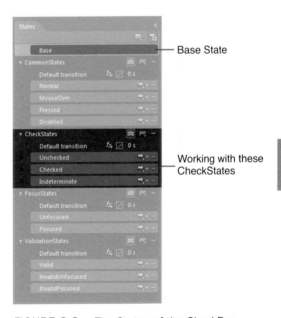

Base State

Working with these
CheckStates

8

FIGURE 8.2   The States of the CheckBox element and the four States being worked with.

The Base State

The Base State is a special State that shows your control in an idle mode scenario. This enables you to modify your control template as you might have previously done, adding and editing element Parts. You can consider the Base State as the State that your elements are always in when you are creating them or editing them in any other sense.

The workflow is therefore:

▶ Click on one of the States in the State panel

▶ Modify the properties of the elements to reflect the selected State

▶ Return to the Base State at any time by simply clicking on the "Base" entry in the State panel

The Unchecked State

Figure 8.3 shows the CheckStates Group expanded, which exposes the "Unchecked" State. Notice that the UnChecked State is selected and there is a little red dot next to the "Unchecked" label, also shown in Figure 8.3.

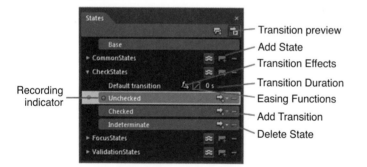

FIGURE 8.3   The Unchecked State element selected and details some of the options immediately available.

Also note the change to the design surface, as shown in Figure 8.4: a red border with the label showing "Unchecked state recording is on."

The little red dot and the big Recording dot do the same thing, and both are clickable. You can toggle recording on or off, which means that while it is on, any changes you make to any of the element properties will be recorded in this state. Remember this, as it's not unusual to forget that you are editing a State and make changes to properties that you didn't intend to.

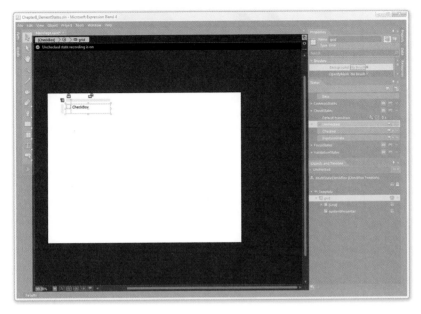

FIGURE 8.4   The Recording state the artboard is now in.

Make sure you are in the recording mode for the **Unchecked State** (select the Unchecked State in the State panel). The following steps walk you through making some property changes to indicate this State to your user.

1. Collapse the elements in the Objects and Timeline category and find the parent Grid element. Note that in the Brushes category of the Properties tab, this particular Grid element has no Background brush applied. Go ahead and make the Background property show a Red SolidColorbrush, as shown in Figure 8.5.

FIGURE 8.5   The CheckBox with its Background set to Red and the appropriate element shown in the Objects and Timeline category and the States panel.

2. Figure 8.5 also shows you that an indication is now present in the Objects and Timeline category, detailing the changes that you are applying in this State.

3. In the States tab, click back on the Base state. Don't be afraid if your Background is now black.

   No harm, no foul, though. With the Base State selected, all you need to do is set the Alpha value of the Black brush to '0,' as shown in Figure 8.6.

   To check the logic of this, now select the Unchecked State, and you should see the Red Brush applied to the Grid, and again now back to the Base State to see it return to the '0' alpha background.

> **TIP**
>
> **Why Could the Background Now Be Black in the Base State?**
>
> The answer is simple, and this exact scenario will occur a lot when editing complex states and multiple elements. Within a State (or storyboard animation), you can't add a new property value where a default is not assigned in the Base State of the element. What Blend has done for you here is pre-empt the possibility of a runtime error occurring by adding a default property value to the Background property in the Grid element. It's black because that is the default color of a SolidColorBrush.

— Modify the Alpha value here

FIGURE 8.6   The Alpha value of the Brush location is shown.

4. Enter the "Checked" State in the States panel. As expected, you see that the 'Check' mark is now present in the box on the element (note the little red dot in the icon for the Box Grid in the Objects and Timeline category).

   Again, you change the Background property value to indicate this state; make it a nice green color. If you are not seeing the green applied, this is because the alpha value is still 0, so make sure you change that back to 100%.

5. Select the "Indeterminate" State (which is the third State) and set the Background property to a random choice.

6. Toggle between the Checked, Unchecked, Indeterminate, and Base States to review the property settings you are applying to each state.

7. Press F5 to run your application.

Notice that your control is in the Unchecked State when first showing on the screen. Click repeatedly on the CheckBox element to see the changes that you specified to States. Simple, isn't it?

Control Level States

States are not just for working inside templates. You can indeed create your own StateGroups at a Global level (see Chapter 9, "Working with SketchFlow," for an example of Global States) or in this instance, at the UserControl level.

In the following steps, you are going to use the State change of the CheckBox element to control a Rectangle element.

1. Using the same CheckBox element you were working with, make sure you have Scoped-Up to the UserControl level. Figure 8.7 shows the easiest way to determine your Scope level.

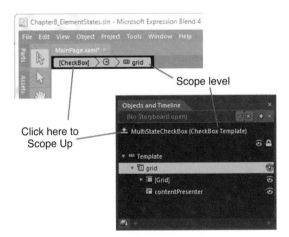

FIGURE 8.7   The current level of Scope.

2. Add a Rectangle element to the artboard, as shown in Figure 8.8.

3. Switch your view to see the States panel. Note that it is currently empty.

4. Click the "Add state group" button, as shown in Figure 8.9, and name the resulting group SimpleStates. Note that the Base State is added for you, as well as a Default transition.

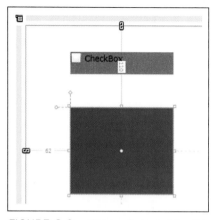

FIGURE 8.8 The basic layout for this example.

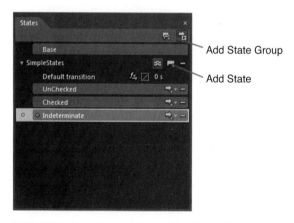

FIGURE 8.9 The creation of the State Group and child States.

5. Click the "Add state," also detailed in Figure 8.9, and name this State UnChecked.

6. Add another two States, naming them Checked and Indeterminate.

7. Select the Base State.

Now you must fire these States somehow, attaching the State Groups to an event. In this particular scenario, you want to raise these State changes with the actions of your CheckBox, and for that to occur, you need to assign the right Behaviors.

8. With the CheckBox selected in the Objects and Timeline panel, open the Assets tab and select the Behaviors category. Enter the word "go" into the Search input box as shown in Figure 8.10.

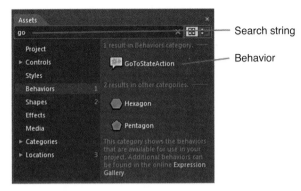

FIGURE 8.10   The Behaviors category of the Assets panel.

9. You are looking for a specific Behavior called "GoToStateAction." Drag this Behavior from the Assets panel directly on top of the CheckBox element either on the artboard or the Objects and Timeline panel.

10. You should now see the Behavior added as a child element of the CheckBox in the Objects and Timeline panel; note the change in the Properties panel, as shown in Figure 8.11.

FIGURE 8.11   The Conditional Behavior editor.

11. The Properties panel has now become a Conditional Behavior editor, enabling you to explicitly control the actions of the subscribed Behavior. In the Trigger category of the Properties panel, drop down the Event property options (which, by default,

are set to Click), and you should find an option that says `ToggleButton`. Underneath this category, you see the three events that you are interested in for this sample, as shown in Figure 8.12.

FIGURE 8.12   The event selection mechanism.

NOTE

Why Does It Say ToggleButton?

It is indeed true that a `ToggleButton` element is not defined in the `CheckBox` template that you previously edited, but what is interesting to understand is that the `CheckBox` is an element built on top of the `ToggleButton` control. This means that the `CheckBox` control uses the same functionality as a `ToggleButton` as its base of functionality, with just a simple visual Style and State modification to make the `ToggleButton` appear and function as a `CheckBox`.

WARNING

What Does Everything Else in the Conditional Editor Mean?

I have chosen not to go into detail of the Conditional Editor at this point in the book, as there are several more complex concepts that you have not been exposed to yet, such as DataBinding (see Chapter 10, "Expression Blend Data Support").

You will revisit the Conditional Editor in more detail in Chapter 9, "Working with SketchFlow."

12. In the Common Properties category of the Properties panel, you see a dropdown for the StateName property. Select this, and you see the three States that you previously defined inside the State Group. Select the UnChecked State.

13. Repeat this entire process another two times, so you have three GoToStateAction child elements of the CheckBox, each with their EventName and StateName property values aligned: Checked and Checked, Indeterminate and Indeterminate, and so on, as shown in Figure 8.13.

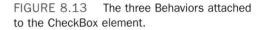

FIGURE 8.13   The three Behaviors attached to the CheckBox element.

Now that your State Group and Behavior collection is complete, you can begin modifying the properties of any of your elements to coincide with the State change raised from the interaction with the CheckBox element.

In the following steps, you are going to leave the UnChecked State as it is. This is the default starting position of the Rectangle element.

1. Select the Checked State.

2. Select the Rectangle element and drag it to the bottom-right corner of the artboard, as shown in Figure 8.14.

3. Select the Indeterminate State and notice that the Rectangle element jumps back to its original position. Move the Rectangle to the top-right corner of the artboard.

4. Toggle between your States to be sure you are happy with the placement of the Rectangle. Run the application, and click repeatedly on the CheckBox element.

Now the Rectangle moves around the screen to coincide with the CheckBox State changes, and you should also see that your CheckBox continues to show its own internal State changes that you defined within the Style.

8

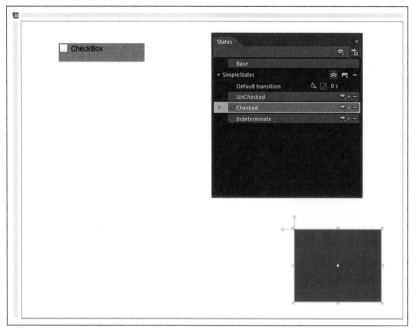

FIGURE 8.14   Your layout should be similar to what is shown.

State Transitions

This jumpy movement from one State to another is just what the doctor ordered in some scenarios, but in general, it would be a more pleasing user experience to transition from one State to another. You can use animations defined in storyboards to achieve this, but this option does add several additional levels of complexity; it also adds several levels of increased control, which you are not ready for at the present. (I sound a little like a Zen master, I know, but trust me, young grasshopper.)

Inside the State Group you defined, you might have noticed that there is a Default Transition element added by default. It is interesting to note that when you mouse over this element, you will see a weird little pop-up similar to the one shown in Figure 8.15 (Sometimes you won't see the "*" but it means the same).

> **NOTE**
>
> **What Is the Difference Between Transitions and Animations?**
>
> In the following example, you are going to look at a very simplified use of transitions in States at the UserControl level, mainly because you haven't looked at storyboards in great detail as of yet (see Chapter 11, "Animations and Transitions").
>
> State transitions are a high-level function that can be performed with pre-defined transitions. When you learn more about storyboards, you will revisit transitions inside of States to understand how you can customize these options further. Storyboards represent the greatest level of granular control over element animation.

This little pop-up is in effect telling you that it will be applied to any State transitioning to any other State. The "any" part of that statement is represented by the asterisk detailed in Figure 8.15.

Astrix denotes "any condition"

FIGURE 8.15   The Transition specification.

Forgetting the other two options on the Default Transition entry for the moment, note that the Transition duration value is by default set to "0s." Change this value to 3 either by typing in the value of dragging on the input box with your mouse.

You are now specifying that, by default, you want it to take 3 seconds for the `Rectangle` to transition from its current state to the next state. Technically, the `Rectangle` doesn't matter, because this is a State to State transition and the properties that each State changes is not a concern. It will just work.

Now you could run the application to test that your States are smoothly transitioning from one to the other, but a handy feature of Expression Blend 4 is to preview the State changes inside the editor.

For this, you need to turn on Transition preview, which is shown in Figure 8.16. You should be able to select between your different States and see the transition take place.

Transition preview

FIGURE 8.16   The Transition preview button.

This simple example shows also the reasoning behind adding the `UnChecked` State, even though you didn't modify any properties for it. Without this State, you wouldn't be able to return to your Start position, as the `Base` State is not assignable as a transition end point.

Clicking on the `Base` State snaps the `Rectangle` element back to its starting position.

WARNING

Transition Preview Button

By default, the Transition Preview button is not ON when you start Blend. So, if you close down your project and come back to applying States and transitions later, remember that you need to turn this feature back on to view everything in design time.

Transition Effects

You can apply transition effects from a generic perspective, meaning that by default, every transition also contains a specified effect, and or you can apply individual transition effects between state transitions.

Figure 8.17 shows you where the Transition Effect button is and the resulting pop-up window that enables you to select your transition of choice. Note that the pop-up changes depending on the transition effects that you select and the available options to the effect.

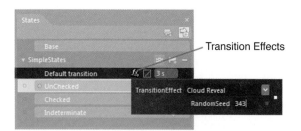

Transition Effects

FIGURE 8.17   The Transition Effect option.

To try this out, select the Transition Effect button, and from the drop-down list, choose the "Cloud Reveal" effect. You can add a value into the Random Seed property; 343 is used for this example.

You can now select between the States, and you should see that the Rectangle element transitions consistently between all of them using the magic of Cloud Reveal.

Now you are extremely happy with your default transitions, but you want to create something special for your user, specifically when going from the Checked to UnChecked State. This is where you can assign individual transitions from State to State or generic instances to and from this State, as indicated by an asterisk as mentioned previously.

Click on the Add Transition button shown in Figure 8.18. You see the array of transition options available to you, but select the second element down in the pop-up, which specifies Checked to UnChecked State.

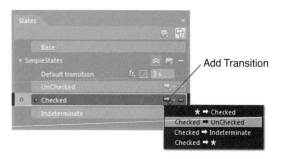

Add Transition

FIGURE 8.18   The Transition Addition options.

The transition is now added, as shown in Figure 8.19; you see that you now have the same options to modify the transition effect that is applied, as you previously set in the Default Transition.

Even though you haven't specified a transition effect using the new transition you just added, the default transition effect is no longer applied when moving from the Checked to UnChecked State. It is interesting to note that the default transition specified transition time is carried over, though.

FIGURE 8.19   The new Transition added below the State.

The following steps show you how to work with different transitions and different states at the same time.

1. Select the UnChecked State.

2. Select the Checked State. You should get the Cloud Reveal transition.

3. Select the Indeterminate State, and again you get the Reveal.

4. Select again on the Checked State.

5. Now Select the UnChecked **State** above the Checked state, and you see that the Rectangle element now glides from the Bottom of the screen to the top.

6. Select the UnChecked **Transition**.

7. Apply a new transition effect, this time selecting the Ripple effect.

8. Modify the transition apply time to 5 seconds.

9. Select the Checked **State**.

10. Select the UnChecked **State**.

> **NOTE**
>
> ### Pay Attention to the Visual Difference
>
> This is where new users can get a little confused, and it is very important to pay attention to the visual difference in the Blend UI of what is a State and what is a transition, as shown in Figure 8.19. The confusion is due to the same name being given to States and transitions.

Although the effect was present in the default you selected previously, the Ripple effect shows to greater levels that the entire UserControl takes the effect; the CheckBox element also ripples during the transition effect.

Transition Effect Priority

When dealing with complex State scenarios, animations, and effects, it is important to note what transitions have priority. I have seen users spend hours trying to figure out why their newly applied effect doesn't appear to be working, only to review the transition collection to find that priorities have not been taken into consideration. This is especially prominent when working with large teams or when multiple people are working on the same scene.

To demonstrate this, in the following steps you are going to apply transition effects where one cancels the other out.

1. Select the Checked State.

2. Add a new transition for Checked to Indeterminate.

3. Add a Blinds transition effect for the new transition, as shown in Figure 8.20.

FIGURE 8.20   The new Blend transition effect being applied.

4. Select the Indeterminate State.

5. Add a new transition for asterisk to Indeterminate.

6. Add a Wipe transition effect for the new transition, as shown in Figure 8.21.

Now you have two transitions applied for the same action: one that is to apply when moving from Checked to Indeterminate, and the other that should also cover this scenario of moving from Checked to Indeterminate, as indicated by the asterisk in the transition.

To test this, select the Checked State and then select the Indeterminate State, and you see that the priority is given to the transition applied to the Checked State.

As a general rule, try to be as explicit as possible when assigning custom transition effects to States to minimize the possibility of priority assignment issues.

FIGURE 8.21   The new Wipe transition effect being applied.

Summary

This chapter has given you a lot of control over not only the changing States of your control templates, but also the changing States of your scene; you have gone further by then applying transition effects to those changing States.

It's a lot to take in, but you are advised to review the last three chapters in unison when you need to refresh your understanding of how the Style, templating, and States of controls work. Always start simple and then modify and test as required. Sort of like shampoo—rinse and repeat!

You should also always be aware of how gratuitous your effects are to the end user. Ripple and Wave effects sound cool in a geeky type of way but can quickly become a very annoying experience if done to death. Add some sound to this, and all of a sudden you are back in the 80s.

State and transition effects can and do get more complex the deeper you go with the tool, and you will experience this in Chapter 11 where you take on data binding elements to a `ListBox` control and use the `FluidMove` feature of States.

For now, you should experiment with modifying the States of controls you are comfortable with.

CHAPTER 9

Working with SketchFlow

Expression Blend 3 launched in 2009 with an awesome new piece of functionality called SketchFlow. SketchFlow was introduced to enable users to create rapid interactive prototypes.

To work within the prototyping workflow and indeed the entire design process, Expression Blend was given additional functionality enabling users to import artwork directly from Adobe Illustrator or Photoshop.

In this chapter, you first review the user-centered design process (UCD) and how the output of a SketchFlow prototype can be used to make the bridge between designer and developer an easier one to cross.

You see how your skills have been building up to enable you to work very quickly in a prototyping scenario, and you also understand the reasoning behind specific workflows that I recommend you adopt when working with Expression Blend 4 in general.

External Files Required to Complete this Chapter

You will need to have access to several MP3 files and album image artwork during this chapter.\

The User Centered Design Process (UCD)

UCD is a process where the user takes the priority as a focal point for defining project requirements. This is not to say that business requirements are ignored, but by understanding who will be the users of a solution and or what devices they will be interacting with, you can determine the methods by which interaction is most engaging and relevant to them.

It's All About the Process

Figure 9.1 shows a very simple workflow of the UCD process stepping through and iterating on design until a functional specification and associated documentation is produced. The flow represented in Figure 9.1 is a general guide, and you should note that although several variations of the UCD process exist, they all follow a similar process of discovery, iteration, and test.

Understand Phase

The very first part of the process is collectively known as the "Understand phase." This is perhaps the most important part of setting the stage right for an outcome that will be relevant to users because it is during this phase that general concepts, requirements, and "personas" are first thought about.

> **NOTE**
>
> **You Need to Approach This Chapter with an Open Mind**
>
> The most important point to understand in this first section is that there is a clearly defined process for design and subsequently design and development collaboration.
>
> Many professional software developers haven't been directly involved with or experienced a true design process in their careers—ever.
>
> When you take that point on board, it is easy to understand why a lot of professionals believe that design is just painting pretty pictures, and that by accident an amazing UI (and somehow a magical user experience) is created.
>
> This simply is not the case; a lot of time, effort, and iterations are performed to reinforce good design practices and to expose the science of usability and interaction.

Project Initiation

Most of you have been in one of these meetings. You all get to shake hands and sit around a table, telling everyone your name and what it is that you do. It feels awkward most of the time, but a good initiation will make the difference between teams and people working well together. It should be an open, friendly, and relaxed atmosphere where everyone is free to express their ideas and what they see as the job at hand. Depending on the size and complexity of the solution, it is not unusual to already have some requirements defined from major stakeholders, which can be a good starting point to discussing what the goals and outcomes of the project are.

Requirements Gathering

This is sort of like an interview where the user experience designers (UX) tend to take the lead from the design point of view, asking as many relevant questions as possible about the solution and key objectives. Development should also be represented here to begin to get the foundation concepts together, and most importantly understand the infrastructure, communication solutions, and the cobbling together of a relevant data model to support the solution.

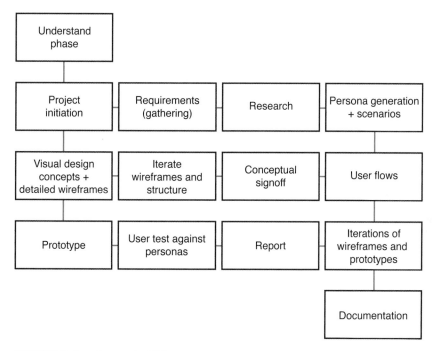

FIGURE 9.1　　A sample UCD process.

Research

Mostly the research phase is about competitive analysis, technology requirements, and perhaps the most important piece, user interviews. What is discovered here typically becomes the base by which the next section (persona generation) is created from. It is not unusual to analyze information such as web traffic reports (if appropriate) and any other areas where the solution is intended for use.

Persona Generation + Scenarios

Personas are an analytical representation of the types of users that you will be targeting and clearly defines what is important to those users in their workflows and goals.

User Flows—Hi-Level Wireframes Review

A journey that resonates with the personas goals is usually decided upon by the team and the stakeholders. This journey is then represented by low-fidelity wireframes to give all involved an understanding of the pending conceptual output. The wireframes also contain most of the large areas of functionality that need to be defined.

Conceptual Signoff

This is usually done by the client (or perhaps a steering committee) and represents a functional journey by which both parties understand how the interaction of the solution will work for the end user. It is normally just wireframes at this point, which are highly annotated and briefed to the stakeholder(s) by the UX designer(s) who created them or lead the team that did so.

Iterate Wireframes and Structure

It is unusual to strike gold on the very first pass, so more often than not, the UX designers will head back to the wireframes to fix issues that were raised in the conceptual signoff process. This iteration occurs over and over until everyone is satisfied that the skeleton of interaction is pretty close to the mark.

Visual Design Concepts and Detailed Wireframe

Wireframes are fleshed out at this point with ever more granular details that enable both a visual designer and a developer to understand how the solution flows, receiving input and presenting data back to the user.

The visual designer(s) at this stage should have a good understanding of the brand requirements that, to the uninitiated, are generally more complex than just making sure the logo and color scheme is correct. Brands rarely represent just a visual mark, moreover helping an organization to project identity and continuity between the offline and online digital worlds of a specific product and or service(s).

Prototype

The word "prototype" can be an open, endless question that is as broad as the term "designer." There are several types of prototypes, or levels of prototype, that a team might work to.

This can be as simple as a "paper prototype," using sketches and sticky notes, or it could be a full-on moving and working data-driven digital solution. Table 9.1 shows a list of the most common levels of prototyping that are undertaken in digital solutions.

TABLE 9.1   A Simple List of Prototypes to Consider

Prototype Name (Complexity Level)	Description	Approximate Time to Create*
Paper	The Paper prototype is simple and fast and typically involves the use of hand sketches, sticky notes, and cutting and pasting pieces into a storyboard-type scenario.	Several hours
Click Through	Many new tools (such as Axure) have taken the wireframe solution a little further by enabling the designer to "connect" screen to screen, defining a button object that enables the test user to click-through the storyboards defined in a wireframe. Several additional features also work to make this in essence a one-way interactive wireframe.	1–2 days

TABLE 9.1   Continued

Prototype Name (Complexity Level)	Description	Approximate Time to Create*
Golden Path	Consider a Golden Path prototype to be a more mature solution then a wireframe-based prototype. This scenario is usually created to enable a specific user journey within the proposed solution to be shown and often includes an iteration of design to give a much broader understanding to the stakeholder(s) of what it is that they are paying for.	3–8 days
Data Driven	When you think data driven, think about all those demonstrations you have seen at conferences, such as Microsoft MIX. The vast majorities of these solutions shown are indeed a data-driven "proof-of-concept" (POC) and have a defined path to demonstrate function and interaction. Unlike a wireframe-based prototype, this level usually includes a full visual representation of the solution, connected to live services such as the Web and other data stores.	5–15 days

* Approximate time must be adjusted based on complexity. The more time spent on creating an accurate prototype reveals greater levels of understanding during test which should reduce iteration time.

User Test Against Personas

A user test is a very interesting exercise in determining just how close your understanding and execution is to the requirements of the solution against the types of end users of your solution. It is most often better to get an external party to perform this function during your development process, a company that is not afraid to tell you how wrong your solution is, if that is what is needed in order to fix it. The tests usually are performed by real people who match the personas that you are building against, and to that end, the testing company will usually recruit people directly who match the persona in order to get a real understanding.

Combined with software that tracks eyes and hand movement, you start to get a picture of how well tasks such as visual signposting inside the solution have been executed. How long does it take the user to perform a task of finding something, or how intuitive is the solution?

Remember, you are never building (designing and developing) a solution that you think is cool. You are trying to create a solution that your end users will find cool and easy to use, and sometimes that can go against your every instinct; the data rarely lies.

Performing another round of user testing after fixing issues is not uncommon and will validate the first round along with the execution of functionality and design.

Report
Reporting is often overlooked (or under delivered) by many undertaking this process. The resultant reports deliver evidence for the decisions that are made when constructing the end or final design. It is very important that as much information as possible is conveyed in your reporting to the client, as this report is sometimes the only documentation that busy stakeholders will see or possibly read. The last thing you need is for the project to be put on hold while you need to go away and then come back to stakeholders, with answers to questions that arise from the high-level view that usually takes place at this point in the process.

You can also use the point to enforce major design decisions that ordinarily raise conflict between internal departments on projects. An example is when a marketing department doesn't consider the legal requirements of a compliance department and so forth. Complex transactions that need to adhere to all departmental requirements are specific areas where you can never have "too much" detail.

The report also informs the documentation stage, which many studios use to create a functional or detailed specification for the actual solution build.

Iterations of Wireframe and Prototype
I was once told by a respected designer friend of mine that "design is iteration."

For the design folks among you reading, I know I am preaching to the choir so to speak, but for those not familiar with design, rarely is a perfect or even great user experience and user interface the result of a single pass. Design takes time, and great design usually takes more time because design grows organically; ultimately, the end result being the evolutionary result of several attempts to improve upon understanding.

At this stage of the process, things are beginning to look very sharp, as rounds of user testing and iteration have informed the result.

Documentation
What makes a great functional specification or delivery document that will inform teams that need to execute against a design?

Have you ever heard the phrase "a picture is worth a thousand words"? This is particularly well suited to the task at hand in creating functional specifications and delivery documents.

Clear documentation that refers to screen shots and notations against interactions, combined with some form of detailed prototype, is the most accurate and efficient method for informing a production scenario. Removing interpretation is one of the key points of collaborative solution delivery, so the more details you have supporting the specifics of a scenario or action, the less likely it is to be misinterpreted.

> ## TIP
>
> ### The Sign That It Is All Wrong
>
> I have seen a 4,000-page functional specification for a large health insurance project I once worked on. It was one of the poorest documents I had ever attempted to imbue, which many of my colleagues flatly refused to try and do the same, simply using "their part" as a reference guide. The problem with that approach is that quite often "their part" didn't convey the entire context of responsibility, and so the resulting blocks and modules created appeared disjointed and not at all easy to use. Also, the experience and presentation mechanisms of the UI were left open to interpretation from team to team, so while one team would use a ComboBox for one task, another team would use a ListBox. The eagle-eyed among you will instantly also understand that this meant there was a considerable lack of reuse of control structures, so more and more defects were introduced as each part was tested differently, and on and on it goes.
>
> It becomes a mess, and this is unfortunately how most large consultancies actually like things to happen. This is why you quite often hear of a government project going $100m over budget. I bet you wondered how that was even possible. Now you know. It's a gold mine—or should I say, a fools-gold mine!

The prototype and visual design combination also informs the development teams that the experience and visual representations are also not open to interpretation. Pixel perfect representations of visual designs are no longer a dream, and you should advocate accuracy in any reproductions of such to hold design integrity.

Collaboration Isn't Easy

Integrating UCD processes into a test-driven development (TDD) process is not easy; it takes work, but the results and rewards are there for anyone truly dedicated to designing and developing a world-class solution, be it web, desktop, mobile, or any other solution.

Expression Blend 4, Visual Studio 2010, and various other tools will help you enable and succeed at implementing collaboration, but they won't be the golden goose that delivers a massive basket of eggs.

In development, functional specification are usually massive documents that few people read; they are referred to "after the event" when developers are in full flight, and it's only there that issues are discovered. It might appear cynical for me to say, but this is where the "Agile" methodology was born. Everything in life is about how you sell it, so for a group of people to review their work every few weeks (and call them sprints), and then to discover that things aren't quite right and adjust slightly (or in design terms—reiterate), is really just an excuse for people to admit that they didn't do the job right in the first place. Generally, it is far more inexpensive and efficient for a designer to do the reiteration piece by changing wireframes and designs than it is for a team of developers who have just dumped several thousand lines of code. The other benefit is that by reiterating in the design stage, the end clients actually get to see most of what the end product will look like, understand if the processes will conform to and implement the business rules, and can get a clear understanding of the project requirements before development starts.

When Pictures Aren't Enough

Wireframes and visual designs are fantastic tools, but they don't tell the entire story. The way that an end user works with a piece of software can be very telling and can determine if they will continue to use your software or if they will go to another company.

> **NOTE**
>
> **Lessons Learned from Industrial Design**
>
> As a human race, we have now been manufacturing products for a very long time. What industry worked out long ago was that all products need to be designed first, and then constructed using the appropriate materials and processes to maximize efficiency.
>
> The building industry itself has been using this process for an even longer time, employing architects and engineers to design and hypothesis integrity before the first brick was ever laid.
>
> In this sense, developers are the twenty-first century bricklayer and should be given a set of plans—a blueprint (a functional specification) that is 98% structurally complete, which allows them to be the most efficient when creating the product. No real excuses for needing to reiterate, and a cost estimate can realistically be very accurate based on those blueprints instead of an unknown pot of time billed against time and materials.
>
> How long would a building company last if its bricklayers had to keep tearing down the walls and rebuilding them?

Developers need to have interaction instructions—that is to say, "what is supposed to move here or display there when the user does this?." An equally important part of this collaboration is that developers need to be able to effectively architect the solution framework or skeleton that the solution hangs on. They need to design the mechanisms that transport the data, validate the inputs, and respond to certain events. They also need to advise the designer when an inordinate amount of time might pass from one interaction to another (for instance, in a web call that processes files or payments), so the user can be given a message or indicator that something is occurring. The design

> **WARNING**
>
> **Prototypes Are Not Production Pieces**
>
> It is an extremely bad idea to take the decision from the outset to make a prototype become a production solution. Prototypes are meant to be fast to put together, a fixed path in many scenarios that demonstrates functionality and interaction. It needs to be reiterated several times in order to meet requirements of stakeholders, and if you have all the production-level validation and wiring hooked up inside of your prototype, it is going to make adding changes through iterations a nightmare for you and a very time-consuming process for the people wanting to see something fast.

needs this information in order to produce a message or visual signpost that is consistent with the rest of the application, minimizing learning time and frustration of the end user.

This is the power of the interactive prototype.

> **TIP**
>
> **Leading a Horse to Water...**
>
> As the old saying goes, "you just can't make the horse drink." For those who don't want to adhere to the advice of creating a prototype and not making it a production solution, you can indeed convert a SketchFlow solution.
>
> Check the User Guide that comes with Expression Blend accessible through the Help menu; this details how to modify the project files and the correct .dll file to remove, which will remove the SketchFlow components from your solution.

Creating a Basic SketchFlow Solution

You've done the theory, so now is the time to put all this together in a very simple prototype; this will reinforce the usage of the screens, as well as get you working with shared components, some data binding, and an effective SketchFlow animation.

The brief here is to create a sample scenario for your client, showing them a new Media Player. Of course in real life, you would get very creative with this, but for the sake of simplicity (and the fact I have a maximum page count in the book), take this sample for what it is, which is a learning experience using SketchFlow.

In the following simple sample, you are going to create a SketchFlow prototype that shows the following:

▶ A user logging into a music player solution

▶ A simulated library import from a settings screen

▶ A component representing a signed in user

▶ A view change of the library

▶ A SketchFlow animation of the library

▶ A selection and playback of the music files

▶ A simple sign-out scenario

SketchFlow-Specific Screens

To begin working with the following sample, create a new Silverlight SketchFlow Application.

> **TIP**
>
> **Do You Have Some Music?**
>
> You need several MP3 files to work through this solution, as well as some album cover artwork.

Once your new SketchFlow application is created, what you will notice is that SketchFlow enables several new panels inside of Expression Blend. There are three in particular that are highlighted in Figure 9.2 that are specific to creating a prototype.

FIGURE 9.2   The new SketchFlow panels.

SketchFlow Animation Panel

This animation panel is specific to SketchFlow prototypes (different from the Objects and Timeline KeyFrame animation panel detailed in Chapter 11, "Animations and Transitions"). Although you have worked through animation already in several areas of this book, the animation you create in this panel is more about creating an animated composition to "show functionality" rather than perform some arbitrary animation of elements.

The SketchFlow animation panel enables you to capture snapshots of the entire artboard and basically create a little movie that you can run during the prototype playback. When considering how much time it might take to create the mechanics of a complex animation, this solution enables you to demonstrate what you need to show to stakeholders fast, adhering to the rapid nature of prototyping.

You work with this panel throughout this example.

SketchFlow Map Panel

The SketchFlow Map enables you to very quickly map out "screens" and "components" that you use within your prototype. You can drag new screens from existing screens and color code areas of the map to ensure that you are covering all the goals of your prototype.

This panel in particular holds the key to creating extremely rapid prototypes, and you will use this panel shortly to do just that.

SketchFlow Feedback Panel

This panel is an enabler for rapid and pronounced iteration of your prototype, as it allows your solution reviewers to post multiple versions of feedback about your prototype as you are working. You can even switch different versions of feedback as an audit trail, as well as export feedback into Visual Studio Team Foundation work items.

Mapping Out the Solution

Remember that creating a prototype is meant to be a rapid exercise, so don't spend a lot of time getting bits lined up correctly for your first iteration. You can always come back and make it so. The following steps lead you through a rough and ready solution, while at the same time giving you an introduction to the most important panels and functionality to take notice of.

> **TIP**
>
> ### The Importance of a Sketchy Style
>
> You will notice when adding new components to your prototype that they take on an almost hand-sketched appearance, which has been done not only for aesthetic reasons but also to ensure that attention is not diverted away from the functionality you are trying to demonstrate in the prototype.
>
> All too often I have seen clients get hung up on the color of a visual style instead of focusing on what is important at this stage of the solution development lifecycle. The Sketchy style eliminates this issue quickly.
>
> You can at any time change the Sketchy style into another style of your choice, the same as you would do in a normal solution.

Using the SketchFlow Map panel, you can quickly create the majority of screens that represent the flow of your prototype. The features of the SketchFlow Map panel are detailed next, as referenced in Figure 9.3.

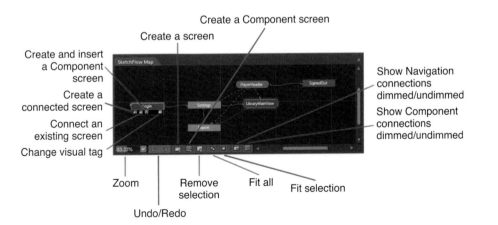

FIGURE 9.3   The extended options panel of the SketchFlow Map objects and panel features.

Zoom

Zoom the map specifically to your chosen size or fit the entire map within the current panel boundaries.

Undo/Redo
The functionality of these options is as expected.

Create a Screen
Creating a new screen (represented in the map as square-cornered rectangles) effectively creates a new user control and adds navigation connections within the SketchFlow solution. New screens can also be created as detailed in Figure 9.3 directly from an existing screen. These screens are also referred to as navigation screens.

Create a Component Screen
This is a reusable piece of functionality that can be shared between one and several other screens. Components are represented by rounded rectangles in the map panel. Their usage is visualized as a broken line, as shown in green in Figure 9.3.

Remove Selection
Selecting a screen then enables you to remove it.

Fit All
Fit all contents of the map to the existing boundaries of the panel.

Fit Selection
Select several screens from a large collection and fit only those screens to the map boundaries.

Show Navigation Connections Dimmed/Undimmed
Dim or undim the solid connecting lines between navigation screens.

Show Component Connections Dimmed/Undimmed
Dim or undim the broken connecting lines between component and navigation screens by following these steps:

1. Open Expression Blend and create a new Silverlight SketchFlow Application if you have not already done so.

2. Inside your SketchFlow application, you should see that a default "Screen 1" object has been added to the SketchFlow Map panel. Double-click on this object and change this screen to show "Login" as the title.

   When you mouse over the Login screen object in the SketchFlow Map panel, you see a small panel that animates down from the object, as detailed in Figure 9.3. This is the extended options panel for the map object.

3. Select and drag the first button from this little panel, which creates a connected screen. Drag it to the right of the Login object and a new screen will be created called New Screen.

4. Rename the New Screen to Settings.

5. Select the Change Visual Tag button on the extended options panel, as shown in Figure 9.4, and change the visual tag to Orange.

6. Mouse over the Settings object and again select the first button to drag and create a new screen to the right of the `Settings` screen. Rename this screen the `LibraryView` screen and set its visual tag to a nice violet color, as shown in Figure 9.5.

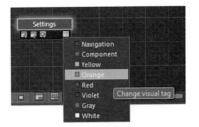

FIGURE 9.4   How to change the visual tag to Orange.

FIGURE 9.5   The current SketchFlow Map view.

7. As part of the Settings flow, you want to also demonstrate that the user could import their current media files. Again, use the extended options panel on the Settings screen to drag and create a new screen; this time place it below the `Settings` screen and call it `Import`. You should also change the visual tag to Orange to denote that that panel is part of the same flow.

8. The second button in the extended options panel enables you to connect an existing screen to another existing screen. Selecting the second button in the Import extended options panel, drag to the existing `LibraryView` screen. You should now have two connections leading to the `LibraryView` screen, as shown in Figure 9.6.

FIGURE 9.6   The current SketchFlow Map view.

You now have a very simple flow for your prototype that you can begin filling out to again quickly get to a demonstrable solution.

Building the Login Screen

The first task is to create a very fast login screen. At the end of the day, you most likely have seen many login screens before, and no doubt your client has as well, so unless you have a requirement to show a specific login scenario, you are going to put the bare minimum required to show this functionality in the following steps.

> **WARNING**
>
> **Remember to Double-Click!**
>
> Just selecting a screen in the SketchFlow Map panel will not change the current screen that you are working on. Although this becomes less of an issue when you have your screens built out, at the start of the prototype after you have simply created the screens, they all look like the same plain white screen; pay attention to what screen you actually are working on.

1. Double-click on the Login screen in the SketchFlow Map panel.

2. Drag a Grid element into the center of the artboard with enough width and height for you to add several rows and columns.

3. Add Row and Column definitions to the Grid, as shown in Figure 9.7.

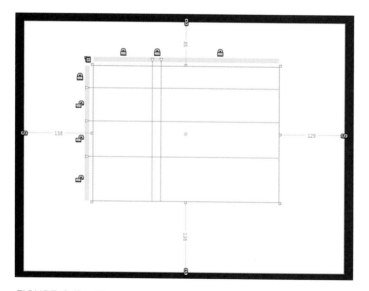

FIGURE 9.7   The simple login box grid layout.

4. Add three TextBlock elements—a TextBox, a PasswordBox, and a Button—as shown in Figure 9.8.

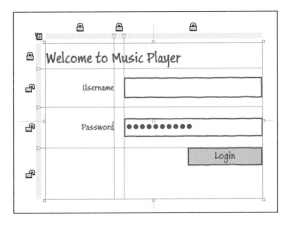

FIGURE 9.8   The general layout and details applied to the elements.

Notice that there is already a series of characters added to the PasswordBox, and this is because you shouldn't really care about what information is added to the username or password box. You are interested only in showing the process by which the user is working through the solution.

Work as Fast as Possible to Get Your Prototype Together at This Stage of the Process

I can't stress enough that this should be a very quick process—this only took me 3.5 minutes to complete. Don't get hung up on sizes and accuracy, which is the beauty of the Sketch Style to enforce this as well.

You can now connect the Login button up using the SketchFlow navigation scenarios, which will easily enable you to switch between the flow of your screens you mapped out previously.

5. Right-click on the Login button and at the bottom of the context menu, you will see an option called Navigate to, as shown in Figure 9.9. You then see the Screens automatically appear in the subsequent menu, and in this case, you want the user to move to the Settings screen. Select it.

Building the Settings Screen

Again, the settings screen is an indication of the solution process, where you will offer the user the ability to import media or go straight to playing music. In this screen, you also build a simple shared component that other screens will also share. The component screen enables you to create once and share as demonstrated in the following steps.

1. From within the SketchFlow Map panel, double-click on the Settings screen.

2. As shown in Figure 9.10, create a new row in the LayoutRoot element and fix its size as an estimate. Inside the row, add a new Grid element and set it to have a light gray background.

9

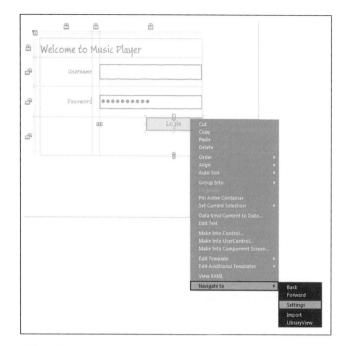

FIGURE 9.9   How to hook up the automatic navigation inside SketchFlow screens.

FIGURE 9.10   The new layout of the Settings screen.

3. Add a TextBlock to the new Grid, as well as an additional Grid containing a TextBlock and Button, as shown in Figure 9.11.

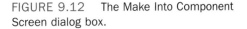

FIGURE 9.11   The additional elements added to the new Grid element.

4. Selecting the `Grid` that was placed in the first row, as also shown in Figure 9.11, right-click on the `Grid` and select the option "Make Into Component Screen."

You should now be presented with the Make Into Component Screen dialog, where you should give the new component an explanatory name, as shown in Figure 9.12.

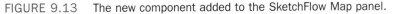

5. You now see that the component is created as its own composition, and you should see that the `Component` element has been added to the SketchFlow Map panel, as shown in Figure 9.13. Note the connection between the `Component` and the `Settings` screen.

FIGURE 9.12   The Make Into Component Screen dialog box.

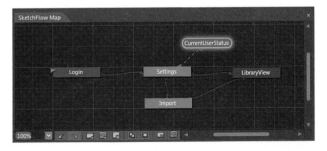

FIGURE 9.13   The new component added to the SketchFlow Map panel.

6. Create a new `Connected` screen from the `CurrentUserStatus` Component called `SignedOut`.

7. Change the `SignedOut` screens visual tag to Red.

8. Double-click on the `Settings` screen again in the SketchFlow Map panel to return to the previous view.

9. Add some `TextBlocks` and `Button` elements, as shown in Figure 9.14.

FIGURE 9.14   The details of the Settings screen.

10. You should be able to right-click on the buttons and select the correct navigation options to both the Import Screen and the LibraryView Screen.

Building the Import Screen

In this simple screen, you are mocking the process of performing an import function, not that you are going to make that actually work. You use a simple animation to depict the import process; follow these steps:

1. Double-click on the Import Screen in the SketchFlow Map panel.

2. The first task here is to add the Component screen you previously created to indicate the user status. With the SketchFlow Map panel open, hover over the CurrentUserStatus component element to display the drop down options. As Figure 9.15 shows, the third option enables you to drag and insert the selected component into a new screen.

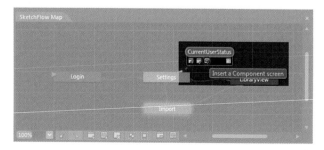

FIGURE 9.15   The third option to insert your component into another screen.

In this case, you should drag the option down to the `Import` screen, where you will see a white line and arrow snap and connect to the screen resulting in a dashed lined, as shown in Figure 9.16.

SketchFlow Map
CurrentUserStatus
Login
Settings
LibraryView
Import
100%

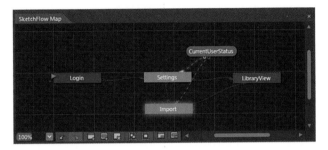

FIGURE 9.16 The result of the connection in the SketchFlow Map, as well as the inserted panel into the Import screen.

3. Seeing that the `Component` screen has a fixed height, you should also now create a `RowDefinition` on the `LayoutRoot` element to solidify the positioning of the `Component` so it remains in the same position throughout the journey of the prototype.
4. Add the collection of elements, as shown in Figure 9.17, paying attention to the `ProgressBar` that is in the middle of the screen with a value of `0`. You will need to find the `ProgressBar—Sketch` in the Assets panel.

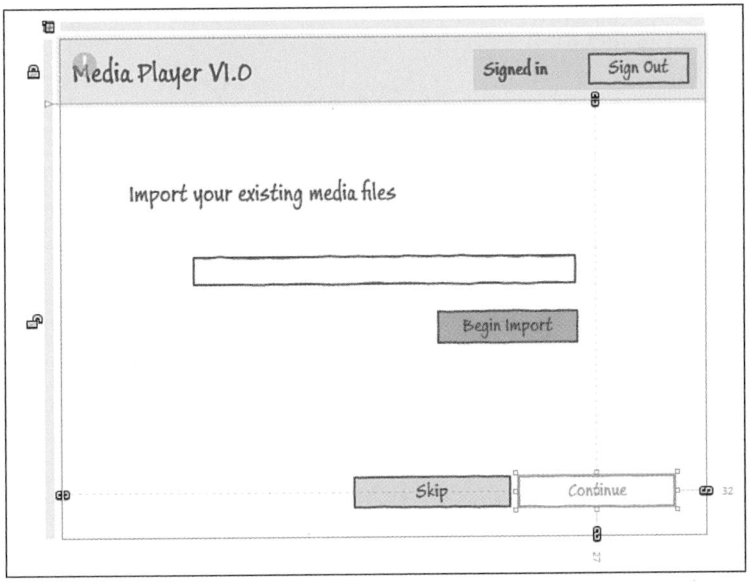

Media Player V1.0
Signed in
Sign Out
Import your existing media files
Begin Import
Skip
Continue

FIGURE 9.17 The new elements of the Import screen.

The Continue button also has a background color of light green, the same as the Begin Import button; after setting the background color, you should set the IsEnabled property to false for the button.

The Skip button should have its navigation set to go straight to the LibraryView Screen, the same as the Continue button.

An effective method of conveying actions is to use the storyboards to change property values. In this particular scenario, when the user clicks on the Begin Import button, you want to show the progress bar becoming 100% over a period of time, and when that occurs, you want to disable the Skip button and enable the Continue button.

5. Create a new storyboard called BeginImport.

6. At Playhead position 0.000, set both the Begin Import and Skip button IsEnabled property values to false.

7. At Playhead position 3.00, set the ProgressBar element to a value of 100.

8. Select the KeyFrame recorded at position 3.000 and set the EasingFunction-InOut value to Quintic. This will give the impression of fast start and slow to end the import.

9. Move the Playhead to position 4.000 and set the Continue button IsEnabled property to True.

10. Close the Storyboard editor.

11. Select the Begin Import button and then open the Assets panel to the Behaviors category.

12. Find the Behavior "ControlStoryboardAction" and drag it onto the Begin Import Button, setting the Storyboard property to the BeginImport storyboard you just created, as shown in Figure 9.18.

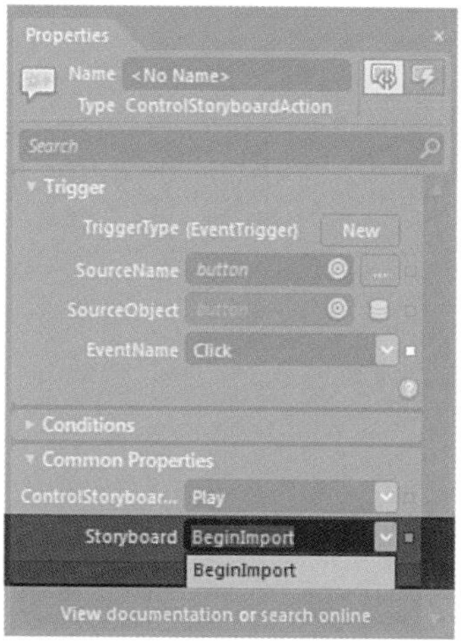

FIGURE 9.18   The ControlStoryboardAction Behavior added to the Begin Import button.

Building the LibraryView Screen

In this screen, you are going to create a sample data source that represents the music collection of the user, which you will need to have a few MP3 files and Album cover artwork available. You will also create another animated view of the library using the SketchFlow Animation solution.

The following steps show simple use of data to give some depth to your prototype.

1. As with the previous screens you build, open the SketchFlow Map panel and insert the CurrentUserStatus component into the LibraryView Screen.

2. Create a RowDefinition in the LayoutRoot element to fix the position of the inserted component.

3. In the Projects panel, right-click on the SketchFlow project and select to Add Existing Item.

4. Navigate to your MP3 files and select them all to insert. For the moment, this is just the music files and not the album cover art.

5. Open the Data panel.

6. Create a new Sample Data set, as shown in Figure 9.19.

NOTE

A Data Source Sounds Complicated!

Don't be too concerned with the details of the Data panel at the moment, as this will be covered in detail in Chapter 10, "Expression Blend Data Support."

TIP

Being Organized Helps!

For this sample, I created a separate folder with the five music files and associated album covers in it, which makes finding things a lot easier as well as distributing becomes less of a problem.

FIGURE 9.19   How to create a new Sample Data set.

7. In the New Sample Data dialog, rename the data source to MyMusicStore.

By default, this will create a simple data store that contains two properties. You are going to modify those properties now with the addition of a third property. This isn't always required as the sample data store provides sample data, but for this example, we want to drive home the solution experience, and this shows that you can make your prototype as simple or as complex as you need to.

8. Add a new Simple Property to the collection, as shown in Figure 9.20. Don't worry about the property type at the moment, as you will fix that in the next step.

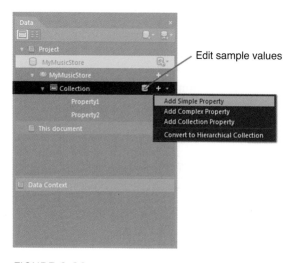

FIGURE 9.20   How to add another property to the collection.

9. You can now edit the sample property values by clicking on the Edit Sample Values button, as also shown in Figure 9.20.

This presents the Edit Sample Values dialog box, as detailed in Figure 9.21, which looks to be filled with nothing but crazy values at the present.

10. Reduce the number of records to 5 or to the number of music files you imported previously.

Property1 is of *type* String, which is exactly what you need; in order to understand which values should be entered into the properties, you should import the album art first so you can match the correct titles with the correct images.

11. Change the property *type* to Image for Property2, as shown in Figure 9.22. You should then use the Browse button and navigate to your album cover art folder. This is significantly easier to do if you have a separate folder for it, as stated previously.

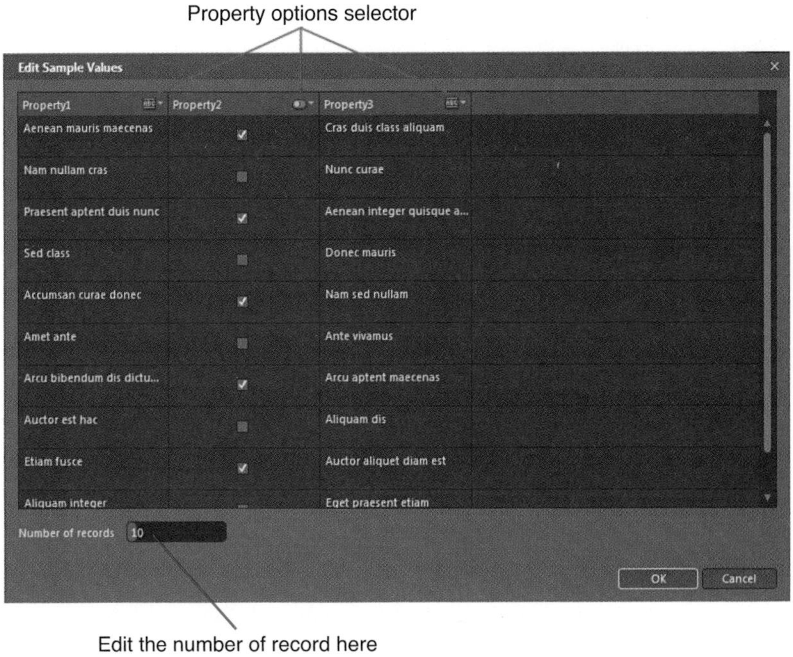

Property options selector

FIGURE 9.21   The Edit Sample Values dialog box.

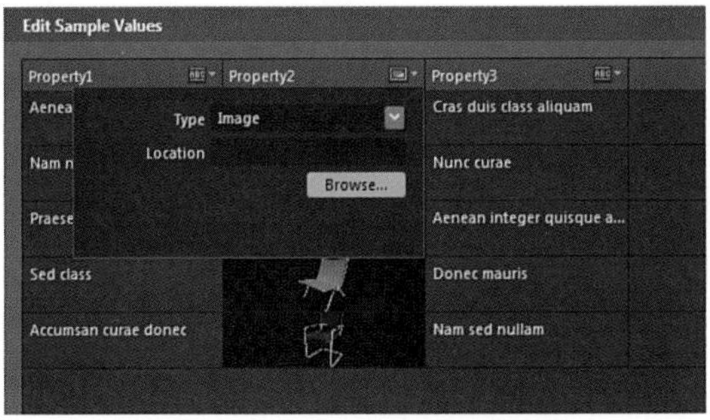

FIGURE 9.22   How to change the property type for Property2.

You should end up with a property collection similar to Figure 9.23.

12. You can now double-click on each of the property values for Property1 to edit them, giving each entry the correct artist or album name.

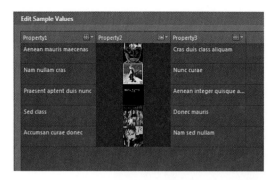

FIGURE 9.23   The new image collection imported to fill the property.

13. `Property3` should already be of *type* `String`. You should change it if this isn't the case. Work through each value of `Property3` to enter the media file import path.

An example is that I have the Black Eyed Peas as the first entry, and the associated MP3 file is imported into my solution as bep.mp3. I need to add the value "/bep.mp3" to the matching property entry. Don't forget the forward slash!

Figure 9.24 shows my completed property collection against the Project tab.

FIGURE 9.24   The completed edited collection.

14. Press the OK button to close the Edit Sample Values dialog.

15. Add a new `RowDefinition` to the `LayoutRoot` with a fixed height of approximately 50 pixels.

16. Add a `Grid` to the new row and set its `Background` color to a dark gray.

17. Add two new buttons to the `Grid`, one with the content set to Details and the other set to Collection, as shown in Figure 9.25.

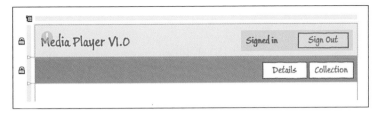

FIGURE 9.25   The new button elements.

Building the Details Grid

You are now deep into your prototype, and you are about to build a data bound list of all the media you just added to your sample data store. There is an element of data binding being used in the following steps, but don't get overwhelmed with the details of it all at the moment. The goal here is to create a list containing all the album names, and when each album is selected in the list, the appropriate album cover will show in an image. You also add a Play button, so you can play the appropriate media file from the selected album:

1. Add a new Grid element to the body of the LibraryView screen and name it gridListView.

2. Open the Data panel again and ensure that you are in List Mode, as shown in Figure 9.26.

3. Drag the "Collection" element (directly under MyMusicStore) onto the artboard. You should be presented with a Sketch style ListBox, complete with album cover artwork and album names, as shown in Figure 9.27.

   You also see in the Data panel that the entire store is now data bound to this panel, as indicated by the orange border also shown in Figure 9.27.

FIGURE 9.26   Where to select List Mode and the Collection element.

A topic you look at in further detail in Chapter 10 is data templates. Just as you defined a Style and ControlTemplate for the functionality and appearance of a Button previously, a DataTemplate defines how data is represented in various controls, such as the ListBox.

In the following steps, you will quickly edit the ListBox ItemTemplate, which is contained inside the DataTemplate.

FIGURE 9.27   The new bound ListBox element and the Data panel.

TIP

Template Inside a Template?

If you remember back to when you edited the template of a `Button` element, the `ControlTemplate` is located inside of the `Style` template. This is no different in theory. Each item in your data collection is represented in the `ListBox`, but you see that each item appears exactly the same in terms of the make-up of the item. The band name is followed by the album cover image and then followed by the location of the media file.

These three elements make up a single item, which has a template that defines this.

---

1. Right-click on the `ListBox`, selecting Edit Additional Templates, then Edit Generated Items, and then the Edit Current. This sequence is shown in Figure 9.28.

   You should now see the Objects and Timeline panel composition change to show the components that are inside this `ItemTemplate`, as shown in Figure 9.29.

2. Delete the `Image` element and the `TextBlock` element below it from the `ItemTemplate`.

   Your `ListBox` should look similar to that shown in Figure 9.30.

FIGURE 9.28   How to edit the Item Template.

FIGURE 9.29   The ItemTemplate represented in the ListBox.

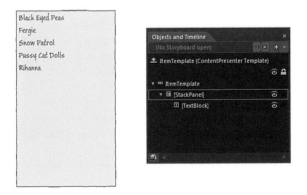

FIGURE 9.30   The new ItemTemplate representation.

3. Scope up inside the Objects and
    Timeline panel, so you can once
    again see the elements you are
    working with on the artboard.

    Everything appears to be working
    just as you would want it to at this
    stage, but importantly, there are
    several data-binding issues that we
    will not be dealing with in this
    chapter and without fixing these,
    your prototype won't work as
    expected.

    One of these issues is that your
    ListBox is data bound to your
    sample data store, but the
    DataContext of the ListBox is not
    correctly set, which you will now
    fix with a shortcut.

4. Locate the DataContext property
    inside the Common Properties
    category and click on the
    Advanced Options box to the right
    of the property, selecting the
    Custom Expression menu item, as
    shown in Figure 9.31.

FIGURE 9.31   The location of the Custom
Expression option in the Advanced Options
menu.

NOTE

Is This All Just Some Sort of Voodoo?

In Chapter 10, you learn the rest of the data-binding procedure in this type of scenario, but
that procedure is out of scope for this chapter.

What you are doing here is adding the XAML code directly to the properties to enable the
data binding of the album image as the source of an image element, as well as the source of
the media that you will also play shortly. Without doing these steps, every time your user
selected a new album in the ListBox, nothing would change or update on the screen, and
effectively you would just see a single (the first) album cover and only be able to play the first
elements media also.

This might all appear very confusing at this point, and there is admittedly a little bit of magic
going on, but for now, just accept that this is a shortcut and one that in time you yourself will
come to use.

5. You now see the Custom Expression dialog box, which might have some text already in it. Enter "{Binding Source={StaticResource MyMusicStore}}" into the box (without the quotes), overwriting what was previously present

6. With the `ListBox` element remaining selected, name the element "ListBox."

7. Select the `gridListView` element.

8. Locate the `DataContext` property in the Common Properties category and again select the Custom Expression option inside the Advanced Options menu.

9. Replace the current value with "{Binding SelectedItem, ElementName=listBox}".

10. Open the Data Panel, change it to Details Mode and then drag `Property2` directly onto the artboard to the right of the `ListBox`.

    A new `Grid` containing an image element will be automatically added for you because that is the property *type*. Resize the `Grid` and the `Image` element on the artboard, as shown in Figure 9.32.

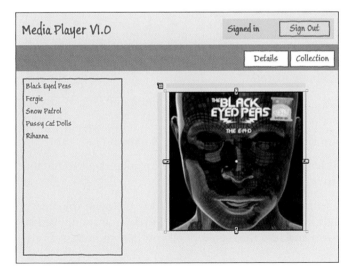

FIGURE 9.32   The location and approximate size of the Image element added to the scene.

11. Add a new `Button` element directly underneath the `Image`, but most importantly, make sure that the new `Button` element is also a child of the same grid that contains the image.

12. Change the content label to "Play."

13. Open the Assets panel again, locating the `PlaySoundAction` Behavior in the Behaviors category.

14. Drag the Behavior onto the `Play` button element and expand the Objects and Timeline panel, so you can see the Behavior.

15. Open the Data panel again and drag `Property3` directly onto the Behavior in the Objects and Timeline panel under the `Play` button element. This raises the Create Data Binding dialog box, where you should select "`Source`" as the value of the `PlaySoundAction`, if it is not already done so by default.

Your details view is now complete with only one action left to perform, which is quite subtle but an important element to note.

When you add collections of items to elements such as `ListBox` or `ComboBox` elements, by default the initially selected item is -1, which translates to no items being selected. In this prototype, you want the very first album to be selected by default, so you should select the `ListBox` element, find the `SelectedIndex` property in the Common Properties category of the Properties panel, and set the value to `0`, which represents the first element in the collection you created.

In preparation for the next set of steps, you should select the `gridListView` element inside the Objects and Timeline panel and hide it using the "eye" icon.

Building the Collection Grid

This `Grid` is really quite easy to build, but to add to the overall functionality of your prototype, you use the special SketchFlow animation functionality to create a very simple yet very effective carousel of the album artwork:

1. Create a new `Grid` in the body of the `LibraryView` screen and name it `gridCollectionView`.

2. Set the `Background` color similar to the `gridListView` you worked on previously.

3. Add a 300 x 300 size `Image` element to the middle of the `Grid`, aligning it to the top and adjusting the margin so it sits slightly off center.

4. As you have been working with your data store in this particular screen, the bindings of all your album images are automatically available to you. You should be able to select the `Source` dropdown and find the names of all your album images, as also shown in Figure 9.33.

5. Duplicate your `Image` five times and change each image element source property to one of the album images. The most accurate way to do this is to copy and paste directly.

6. Add a new `Button` element below the images and change its `Content` property value to "View Library."

Creating a Simple SketchFlow Animation

You are now ready to create a SketchFlow animation sequence, which is different from other types of animations you might have worked on previously in this book, while keeping some of the same core concepts available, such as Transitions and Easing functions.

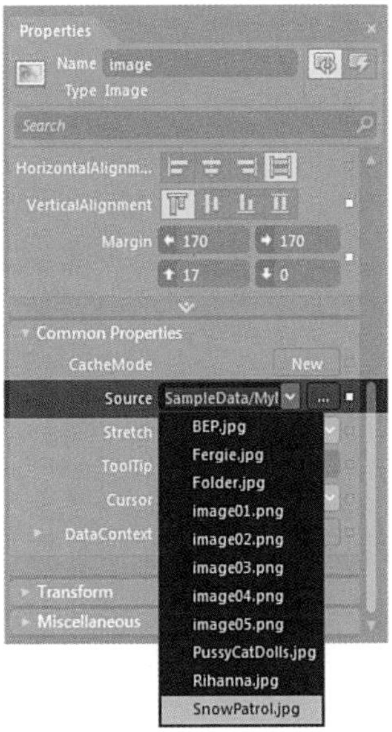

It must be said that initially the SketchFlow Animation panel adds a massive amount of confusion to new users and some experienced ones alike, as it is assumed that you should work with it in the same way as creating Keyframe animation in the Storyboard editor. You certainly still work within the Storyboard editor, but it is the combination of both these panels that makes the entire experience disjointed and a poor user experience. I believe that this panel will change in coming versions of Expression Blend because of this very reason.

FIGURE 9.33   The new image element and the Source bindings already available.

Using the panel, you need to remember one very basic rule. You are essentially capturing screenshots—or snapshots, to be more accurate—of the current state of your scene. This is akin to keyframes, but on a scene globally rather than a single property change that you would normally be making; you are creating frames.

To this end, you will be simply modifying the scene to show a new album cover and taking a snapshot of the entire screen in a frame. Then, modify again and continue on until all the albums have been shown in the cycle.

You also need to work sequentially in how your animation is going to work, and the magic at the end of this is that SketchFlow will implicitly tween between each frame, applying any Easing functions and Transition effects that you have added along the way.

There are several basic controls that are part of the SketchFlow Animation panel that are detailed next and referenced in Figure 9.34.

Add a Frame

Add a new frame to the start of the composition or after/before other frames.

You can also right-click on any frame to insert new or copy the properties from one frame to another.

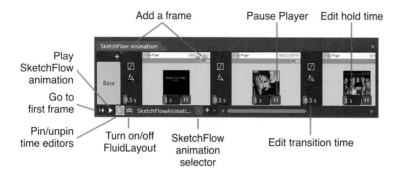

FIGURE 9.34   The SketchFlow Animation panel.

Go to First Frame
When creating particularly complex SketchFlow animations, this enables you to quickly return to the starting frame before playback.

Play SketchFlow Animation
Preview and play back the SketchFlow animation.

Pin/Unpin Time Editors
In Figure 9.34, the time editors are pinned to show which is particularly handy if you need to individually time frame playback, as well as control the playback of the animation when running the prototype.

Turn On/Off FluidLayout
Refers to animated layout changes. See Chapter 11 for more details on FluidLayout.

SketchFlow Animation Selector
You can create multiple SketchFlow animation per screen. This set of tools allows you to select, create new, and delete existing SketchFlow animations.

Pause Player
This is used for when you play back your SketchFlow animation in the SketchFlow Player. Occasionally, you might want or need your animation to pause at a particular junction of the animation, and this functionality enables you to control that on a frame-by-frame basis. You can restart the animation inside the SketchFlow Player again by clicking on the animation name inside the Player navigation window, which will be discussed shortly.

Edit Hold Time
This is different from transition time, as you might need a particular frame to stay in place for x number of seconds and then the transition speed to occur the same as all other transitions.

Edit Transition Time

This enables you to set the amount of time it takes to transition from one frame to another.

Before you begin creating your animation in this instance, you should prepare your scene by making changes to default property values as you need them to be. Just like when you used the State panel, you need to return to Base to make changes to your default element properties as shown in the following steps.

1. Click on the '+' symbol next to the Base Frame in the SketchFlow Animation panel. This will also create a new SketchFlow animation, and by default, name it SketchFlowAnimation. You can change the name by double-clicking on the animation name label.

   You should also have noticed that your artboard has a familiar red border around it, notifying you that recording for this frame is now on.

2. You are now in Frame1 recording and see that the Objects and Timeline panel has changed slightly to show you the Storyboard editor is now active, as shown in Figure 9.35.

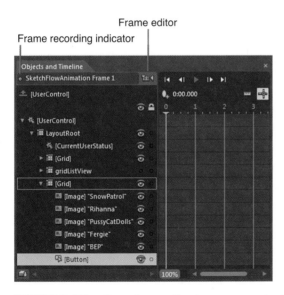

FIGURE 9.35   Frame1 recording is now on and a Storyboard editor is now available.

3. Select all your images and set their Opacity property to 0. Do this for all except the first image that will be shown by default.

4. Move your mouse to the top-right corner of Frame1, and you should see a very faint—and + symbol. Click on the + symbol to create a new frame after Frame1.

   You should now be in Frame2 recording.

5. Select the first image in the Objects and Timeline panel.

6. Open the Transform category of the Properties panel and then find the `Scale` tab.

7. Set both the `X` and `Y` property value to `1.5`.

8. Locate and set the `Opacity` property to `0`.

9. Find the second image and set its `Opacity` value to `100`.

10. Add a new frame from the top right of `Frame2` in the SketchFlow Animation panel.

11. Repeat the image property settings for all the five images, creating a new frame each time.

12. On the second last frame, set the first image `Scale` X and Y values back to `1`, but don't set the `Opacity` yet.

13. On the last frame, set the `Opacity` property back to `100`, which gives the appearance of the carousel returning to the start.

    You should be able to use the SketchFlow Animation panel Playback functionality to view the simple effect created.

14. Open the Behavior category of the Assets panel and locate the `PlaySketchFlowAnimation` Behavior.

15. Drag it directly onto the `View Library` button element.

16. Select the appropriate animation in the `SketchFlowAnimation` property of the Behavior.

    You are almost complete and only need create some simple States to transfer between one view and the other.

17. Select the `gridCollectionView` and set its `Visibility` property to `Collapsed`.

18. Open the States panel.

19. Add a new State group.

20. Add two new States: one called `Details` and the other called `Collection`.

21. With the Details State selected, also select the `gridListView` in the Objects and Timeline panel and record its current `Visibility` property value from the Advanced Options menu.

22. Select the `gridCollectionView` in the Objects and Timeline panel and also record its current `Visibility` property value.

23. Select the `Collection` state.

24. Again select both the `gridListView` and `gridCollectionView` elements individually, and this time simply change their respective `Visibility` properties to record new values in the state.

25. Drag a new `GoToStateAction` Behavior onto each of the `Details` and `Collection` button elements in your scene and set each one's `StateName` property to the correct State that you just created.

Building the SignedOut Screen

The last part of the prototype build is the `SignedOut` screen you created earlier. This adds closure to your demonstration and allows you to return to the beginning by adding simple navigation between the screens.

The following steps detail the build of the `SignedOut` screen.

1. Double-click on the `SignedOut` screen inside the SketchFlow Map panel.

2. Add a new `TextBlock` and `Button` element, as shown in Figure 9.36.

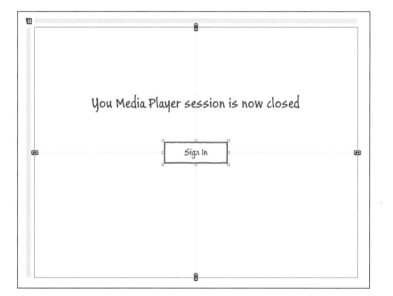

FIGURE 9.36   The simple SignedOut screen elements.

3. Right-click on the new Button, and at the bottom of the Content menu, you see the Navigation options. Select the `Login` screen, and you see that the SketchFlow Map panel automatically creates the link for you.

4. Open the `CurrentUserStatus` Component and set the navigation state of the "Sign Out" button element to the `SignedOut` screen.

Your SketchFlow Map panel should look similar to Figure 9.37, if all has gone well.

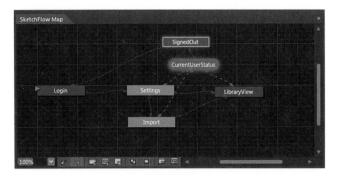

FIGURE 9.37   The end visual of the SketchFlow Map panel.

Using the SketchFlow Prototype Player

You should now run your prototype for the first time.

Unlike a standard Silverlight or WPF application, the SketchFlow prototype comes packaged with its own "player" to assist you and others with navigating through it, as shown in Figure 9.38.

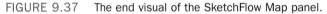

FIGURE 9.38   The login screen and the SketchFlow Player.

The Player Navigation by default is docked to the left of the web browser window but can be "floated" to enable you to move the control around inside the browser window. The core parts of the Navigation panel are detailed next and referenced in Figure 9.39.

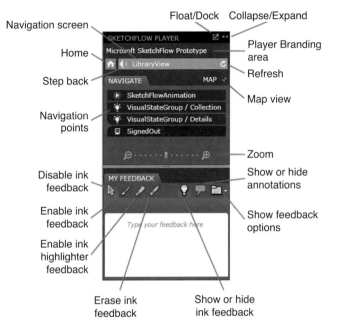

FIGURE 9.39   The SketchFlow Navigation panel.

Float/Dock
This enables you to float or dock the Navigation panel inside the browser window for Silverlight applications or outside the Player window completely in WPF prototypes.

Collapse/Expand
This collapses the Navigation panel away and allows you to expand it back out again.

Player Branding Area
Currently shown as a simple line of text, this value can be changed from within the SketchFlow Project Settings dialog box, which is detailed shortly. Furthermore, you can also add a logo and revision information about your prototype with a little more work. See the User Guide that comes with Expression Blend to understand the requirements and instructions on how to perform these operations.

Home
This returns you to the start of the prototype.

Step Back

This enables you to step back through the journey that has been taken throughout the prototype.

Navigation Screen

This is the current screen being shown in the player.

Refresh

If your prototype is data driven, the refresh button allows that screen instance to start again and refresh any and all content areas.

Map View

Display an overlay of the SketchFlow Map panel into the prototype. This enables you to click on screens and jump navigation to suit.

Navigation Points

Figure 9.39 represents the user currently in the `LibraryView` screen; as you will recall, you have two states inside that screen to switch between the `Details` and `Collection` view, as well as the SketchFlow animation that you created to show the collection carousel. You can click on any of the items here to fire the correct state or action required.

Zoom

This zooms the prototype within the SketchFlow Player screen.

Disable Ink Feedback

When ink feedback is turned on, the prototype effectively becomes frozen to enable the drawing of feedback directly over the screen. You need to click on this button to enable the functionality of the prototype to continue.

Enable Ink Feedback

Ink feedback enables you or the user to select a color brush and brush size to draw directly onto the artboard, as shown in Figure 9.40. You also see in Figure 9.40 that feedback has been typed directly into the feedback panel. You should note that any feedback added is done so on a per-screen basis, so when you navigate between screens, you will see the ink and typed feedback disappear.

Enable Highlighter Feedback

Referenced in Figure 9.40, the highlighter is another form of ink feedback.

Erase Ink Feedback

Erase parts of the ink feedback.

Show or Hide Ink Feedback

Toggle the display of ink feedback on or off.

Highlighter feedback

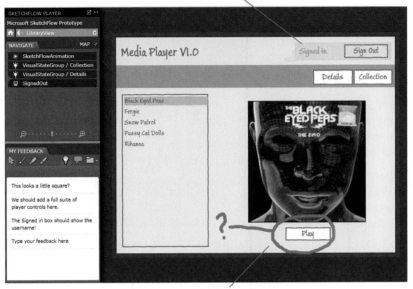

Ink feedback

FIGURE 9.40   Ink feedback in action.

Show or Hide Annotations
Annotations are often added to prototypes as more revisions continue. This button toggles those annotations on or off.

Show Feedback Options
This enables you to export all the comments and feedback that have been added to the prototype, into a file. This feedback can be imported back inside of Expression Blend after the revision.

Importing the SketchFlow Feedback
Your stakeholders can add feedback directly to your prototype, or you could make notes along the way by working with the ink and typing feedback features of the SketchFlow Player.

When you have added all your feedback, be sure to select the "Show feedback options" button and then export your feedback into a file (somewhere you can easily remember the location).

> **NOTE**
>
> **Add Some Feedback Yourself**
>
> Before working through the following steps, you should run your prototype and add some feedback with the ink, and type into the feedback input box at various steps of the playback screens, so you have some feedback items to work within the next steps.

The following steps show you how to view the feedback added to the prototype.

1. Inside of Blend, open the SketchFlow Feedback panel, which is detailed in Figure 9.41.

2. Click on the Add button in the SketchFlow Feedback panel and navigate to the exported feedback file you created.

3. Navigate within the SketchFlow Map panel to the different screens where you added feedback to see those feedback items.

FIGURE 9.41   The SketchFlow Feedback panel with feedback imported back into the project.

Adding Annotations

Now that you have feedback, you can go ahead and action those feedback items or add some annotations that explain what you have done, as follows:

1. Select the element in the Objects and Timeline panel to which you want to link an annotation.

2. From the Tools menu, select Create Annotation.

3. Add the information you want to show, as shown in Figure 9.42.

> **TIP**
>
> **Team Foundation Work Items**
>
> If you have connected Expression Blend to work with Team Foundation, you can right-click on any of the feedback items and convert them to Team Foundation work orders. See the Expression Blend User Guide for information on working with source control mechanisms.

Exporting and Packaging the SketchFlow Prototype

From the File menu, you have several options to package and export your prototype, although they mean two different things. Packaging your prototype allows you to distribute it to people who done have Expression Blend installed, as well as distributing the package via Microsoft SharePoint if you have those facilities available.

Exporting the prototype enables you to create a word document that breaks down your prototype map and includes feedback information and annotations for each of the screens and is commonly used to provide developers with a clear road map of what it is that they have to build. You can try this feature by selecting the Export to Microsoft Word feature from the File menu.

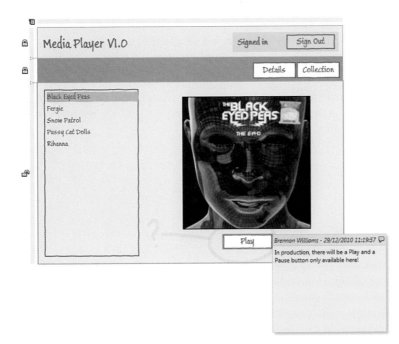

FIGURE 9.42   A new annotation attached to the Play button.

Summary

In this chapter, you have learned the importance of working rapidly to create a vision of the solution you intend to build. Prototypes are not about accuracy to a large degree, but more about getting concepts and ideas across to the stakeholders who will make the decisions around you moving into production.

You have worked with specific SketchFlow functionality, such as the SketchFlow animation solution, that is confusing at first, but simple to implement once you get used to working with it.

You also got a very quick look at the power of sample data usage in Expression Blend, which when used correctly, can greatly speed up your time to produce a prototype, without having to wait for developers to hook up complicated data access layers or connections to servers.

And finally, you got to work with the feedback mechanisms that make the iterative process of building successful prototypes simple within SketchFlow.

On the whole, SketchFlow represents fantastic functionality within the Expression Blend product, but unfortunately all too often users have opened the functionality and became either confused or frustrated at the proposition that it represents.

As discussed at the start of this chapter, creating prototypes is also about workflow, and making the prototype work as part of the workflow is where a tremendous amount of value can be taken from it, not to mention the outputs of the prototype into work items and documentation.

I hope the Expression Blend teams are allowed to progress the SketchFlow functionality within the product and work to make it an even tighter integration into the normal user experience of the rest of the product.

CHAPTER 10

Expression Blend Data Support

Although you might continue to simply design user interfaces based on assumptions and specifications, there is nothing quite like working with interactive pieces of a puzzle.

Depending on the complexity of what you are choosing to tackle, Expression Blend 4 has a rich interactive data function that enables you to effectively mock both simple and complex types within your design time solution, as seen briefly in Chapter 9, "Working with SketchFlow." You can also work directly with live data sources such as XML in WPF projects or data that is provided from code-based objects.

As forewarning, there is a little bit of code in this chapter, but nothing too hard core, and the code is simplistic in concept, as you will see.

In this chapter, you create a sample dataset in Expression Blend to define your user interface and then you switch from this sample data to a mock "live" data source that you are going to write in code.

Designing Sample Data

Expression Blend 4 has a robust set of data tools available to the user to enable rich design time data support that can, with a little planning, be compatible with live data at run time. The concept here is that you can create templates for use with controls that represent the desired visualization of data for a specific scenario.

Sometimes in the designer/development process, data is not available at the time that will suit you best. This could be for a number of reasons, such as the backend of an application not being ready; maybe a web service is not available due to technical difficulties, or even something as a database administrator sleeping through his alarm.

Defining sample data is a process that, as you worked with in Chapter 9, is quite easy, but you should still have some solid thought behind the *types* of data you will be working with, by discussing such data requirements with your development team.

Thinking About the Data

When thinking about a user interface, you need to think about the interaction of the end user in order to design the components correctly. The same applies to data; you need to design the types and think about what is going to be visualized when considering the UI. This is another reason why using a user-centered design process can make the creation of such data schemas easier in the planning stages.

What are the types and values that you would expect to get from a weather report? You could reasonably expect the following as an example:

- ▶ Location name
- ▶ High temperature
- ▶ Low temperature
- ▶ Wind speed
- ▶ Wind direction
- ▶ General report

Now that you know the information, you can reasonably look at the *types* of data that would fit. Table 10.1 shows the heading defined and what we would expect as the matching data types.

TABLE 10.1   Defined Data Types That Fit with the Type of Data Required

Description	Data Field Name	Data Type	Sample
Location	PostName	String	A string is a collection of characters (or chars). For example, "Heavy snow can be expected today." or "Black run 1."
High temperature	HighTemperature	Int	An int is representative of a whole number, such as 2, 55, or 108.
Low temperature	LowTemperature	Int	
Wind speed	WindSpeed	Int	
Wind direction	WindDirection	Int	Direction will be represented as a degree value.
General report	GeneralReport	String	

Defining Sample Data

Now that you have the list shown in Table 10.1, you can easily begin creating a matching sample dataset.

Figure 10.1 gives a general overview of the Data panel that you will be working with in this chapter. You should have a quick review of this and note the difference between creating a new data source and creating sample data buttons.

List Mode

List mode gives you the ability to drag a collection of data items onto the artboard and automatically fill an element, such as a `ListBox`.

> **NOTE**
>
> **No Spaces**
>
> Note how in Table 10.1, the data field names have no spaces and use a camel case (for example, WindDirection) with capitalization of the first letter of each word. The camel casing is not a requirement, but will make it easier for other designers or developer working on your solution to determine what you are doing. Spaces—or lack thereof—as a rule should be adhered to when giving names to elements and fields. In some special cases, it is a requirement to have no spaces, so getting used to it now should stop you from having issues in the future.

Details Mode

Details mode gives you access to all the properties of the data collection as they are being selected from a list.

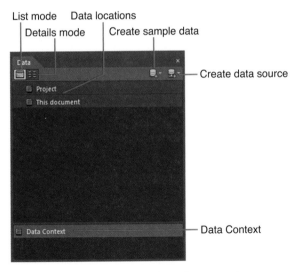

FIGURE 10.1   Overview of the Data panel.

Create Sample Data

You can create sample data directly from within Expression Blend or use existing data schemas that are defined within an XML document or a .Net code object.

10

Create Data Source

You can create a data store to enable your application internally to track data in a simple field-based scenario or from a .Net code-based object. XML data sources are available, but only in WPF applications.

Data Locations

You can provide data to the entirety of your project or specific to the document that you are working in.

Data Context

The data context indicates what data source is supplying data to the currently selected element or entire document. It is important to know what data is available to you by looking at the data context, as follows:

1. Create a new Silverlight Application + Website solution.

2. Locate the Data panel inside Blend.

3. Select the Create sample data button. You see the three options you presented, but for this sample, select "New sample data...."

4. As shown in Figure 10.2, the New Sample Data dialog box is shown, asking you to specify a name for the new data source. Give it a name such as "WeatherDataSample." Note that there are no spaces in this name.

> **TIP**
>
> **Running with Sample Data**
>
> You should note in Figure 10.2 that the CheckBox "Enable sample data when application is running" remains checked. This informs your application that you will treat this sample data as a live source during run time, which you can change at any stage. Without this option selected, you wouldn't expect to see data when you run your application.

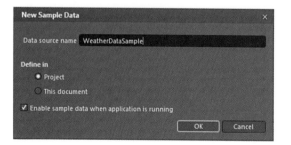

FIGURE 10.2   The New Data Source dialog options.

5. Leave the "Define in" Project radio button selected and click OK to close the New Sample Data dialog box.

The location of the data becomes important when working with larger solutions.

6. Figure 10.3 now shows you the sample data collection that you have created, clearly defining two default properties: `Property1` and `Property2`. `Property1` is of *type* `String` and `Property2` is of *type* `Boolean`. You also see the button options that enable you to create additional properties, as will be required shortly.

Referring to Table 10.1, you should create matching property names and types. It is important that you name your properties exactly as the data schema defines them in Table 10.1.

FIGURE 10.3   The WeatherDataSample created inside the Data panel.

7. Rename `Property1` to `GeneralReport` by double-clicking on the property name to enable editing mode. This property is already of *type* `String`.

8. Rename `Property2` to `HighTemperature`.

9. You can select the Change property type button and then change the property to that of `Number`, as shown in Figure 10.4.

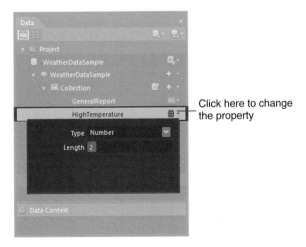

Click here to change the property

FIGURE 10.4   How to change the property type.

10. Add the rest of the properties that are defined in the data schema of Table 10.1. Your sample data collection should then resemble Figure 10.5.

11. Figure 10.3 detailed where the "Edit Sample Values" data button is located, which you should click on now to see the Edit Sample Values dialog box, as shown in Figure 10.6.

Property Name

This represents the name of the property.

Change Property Type

Changing the property *type* to another of the basic property *types* displays a simple options dialog that is contextual to the property type being referenced, as shown in Figure 10.7, which shows the String property *type* options.

FIGURE 10.5   The new properties added to the sample data source.

FIGURE 10.6   The Edit Sample Values dialog box.

Sample Data

This is sample data that matched the property *type* selected.

Number of Records

Working with various numbers of records is always helpful to understand how your user experience might need to change to handle large and small collections alike.

What you can see in the Edit Sample Values dialog box is that Expression Blend creates completely random values that match the Property *types* of the created sample set. You have a degree of control over the sample values as well, and by selecting the "Change Property type..." button for Property1, you see that you can indeed change the format from Lorem ipsum to addresses, phone numbers, or one of many choices, as shown in Figure 10.8. You can also limit the word count and word size in terms of character count.

The following steps walk you through changing some of the property values in the Edit Sample Values dialog.

1. Click on the Change property type for the GeneralReport property and set the String property Max word count value to 25, with a Max word length value of 8.

2. Click on the Change property type for the PostName property and set the String property Max word count value to 3, with a Max word length value of 8.

3. Change the Number of records value to 5.

4. Click OK to close the Edit Sample Values dialog.

   You could take the time to edit the sample values to more realistic values, as you did previously in Chapter 9, but at the moment, you don't really care about this data. It's for display purposes only, and the live data connection later in the chapter will give more meaningful results.

FIGURE 10.7   The String property type options.

FIGURE 10.8   The Format options for the String type.

5. Drag the collection from the Data panel to a new `ListBox` element, as shown in Figure 10.9.

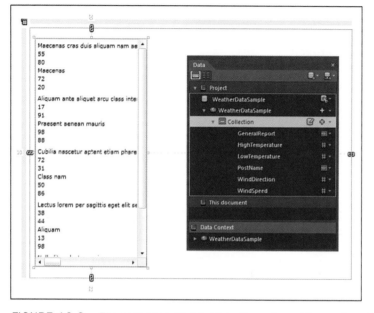

FIGURE 10.9   The collection dragged into the artboard to create a ListBox containing the sample data.

Editing the Data Template

Similar to a `ControlTemplate` that is used in a Style, the `DataTemplate` is referenced by the control and is commonly referred to as the `ItemTemplate`.

The purpose of the `DataTempate` is to define what data is provided to the control by the data context that is assigned to it, by assigning controls (such as `TextBox`, `CheckBox`, and so on) to display the data.

If you select the `ListBox` element, you should be able to locate the `DataContext` property in the Common Properties category of the Properties panel. You see that the `DataContext` is shown as the `WeatherDataSample`, as shown in Figure 10.10. Notice that the `ItemSource` is showing an active binding as well, which was created automatically for you when you dragged the collection to the artboard from the Data panel.

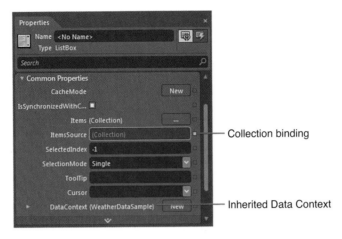

FIGURE 10.10   The DataContext setting and ItemSource binding.

You will now edit the `ItemTemplate` to ensure that only the data you want is displayed, as follows:

1. Right-click on the `ListBox` element and select Edit Additional Templates -> Edit Generated Items (ItemTemplate)->Edit current, as shown in Figure 10.11.

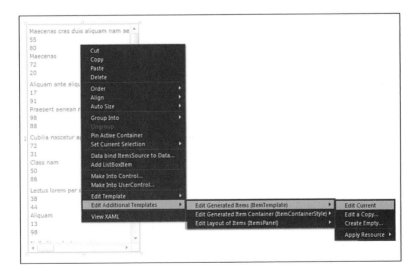

FIGURE 10.11   How to edit the ItemTemplate.

The Objects and Timeline panel changes to show the context of the `ItemTemplate`, as shown in Figure 10.12. As you can see, Blend has determined that a `StackPanel` containing a `TextBlock` control for each data property should be shown.

10

Remember that this is just a default `ItemTemplate`, and you can modify this to suit your needs. In this sample, you want to see only the `PostName` and `HighTemperature` fields in this list.

2. Select the first `TextBlock` element under the `StackPanel` element in the Objects and Timeline panel.

3. Locate the `Text` property inside the Properties panel.

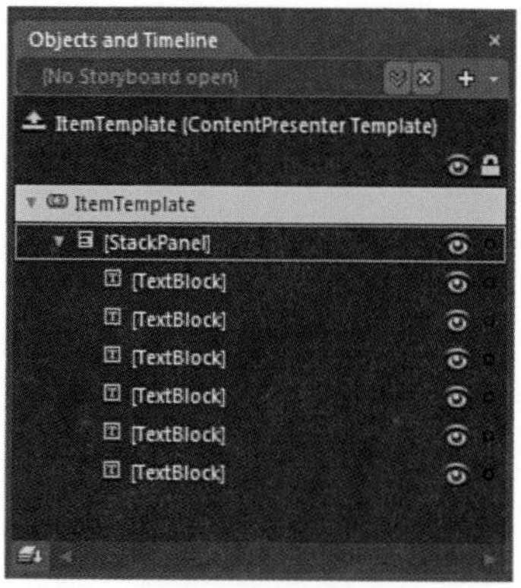

FIGURE 10.12   The context of the Objects and Timeline panel changed to reflect the ItemTemplate.

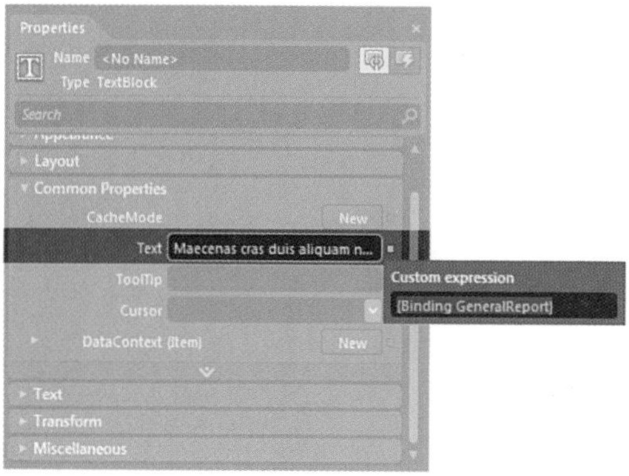

You can see that the `Text` property is bound to data by the orange border that is around the control; however, because you are using sample data, you don't really have any immediate indication as to what field this element is bound to, so you might delete the wrong element.

The easiest method to determine this is to select the Advanced Options button and then view the Custom expression value, as shown in Figure 10.13, which clearly shows that this property is bound to the `GeneralReport` field.

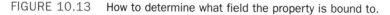

FIGURE 10.13   How to determine what field the property is bound to.

4. Delete the selected `TextBlock` element.

5. Continue through all the `TextBlock` elements until only the `PostName` and `HighTemperature` elements are remaining.

6. Change the `StackPanel` `Orientation` property to `Horizontal`.

7. Switch the order of the `TextBlock` elements in the `StackPanel` by dragging the bottom one to the top inside the Objects and Timeline panel.

8. Right-click on the StackPanel inside the Objects and Timeline panel and select Change Layout Type to Grid.

9. Adjust the Width of the Grid to almost the entire width of the ListBox. You know if you have gone too wide as the HorizontalScrollBar will appear in the ListBox.

10. Select the TextBlock element containing the HighTemperature field and change the FontSize to 20.

11. Open the Paragraph tab of the Text category in the Properties panel and set the TextAlignment property to Center. If your numbers are no longer shown, you need to select the parent Grid element and set the Height property to Auto.

12. You are now able to add a ColumnDefinition to the parent Grid element to ensure that both the TextBlock elements remaining in their own space.

13. Select the TextBlock element containing the PostName field and change the FontSize to 11 and set it to Bold. Ensure that this element also has a ColumnSpan property value of 1.

14. Set the Width and Height properties of the HighTemperature TextBlock element to Auto.

15. Set the HorizontalAlignment and VerticalAlignment properties to Stretch.

16. Set the Margin properties values to 0.

17. Set the Width and Height properties of the PostName TextBlock element to Auto.

18. Set the HorizontalAlignment property to Stretch.

19. Set the VerticalAlignment property to Center.

20. Set the Margin properties values to 0.

21. Set the PostName element TextWrapping property value to Wrap.

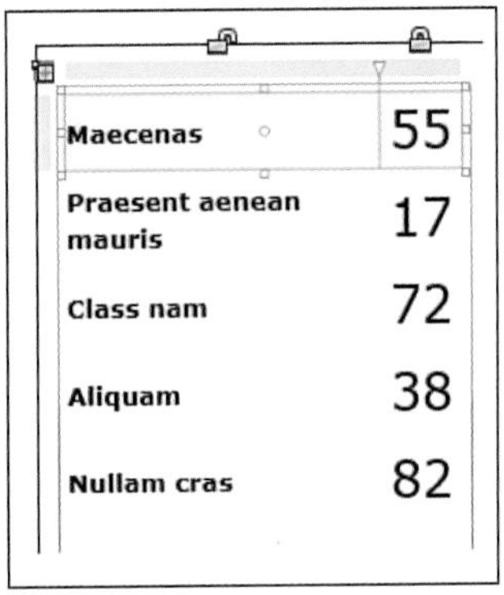

FIGURE 10.14   The modified ItemTemplate.

You should now have an ItemTemplate that looks similar to that of Figure 10.14.

You can now scope-up out of the ItemTemplate back to the root scene.

Editing the ItemContainerStyle

The ItemContainerStyle is part of the Style of the element that references it, which in this case is a ListBox. Because you have bound a data collection to the ListBox, a ListBoxItem element has been created for each item of data in the data source that the

ListBox is bound to. For each instance ListBoxItem created, an instance of the ItemTemplate you just modified is applied.

You can edit the ItemContainerStyle to change the visual representation of the container that each instance resides in, as follows:

1. Select the ListBox element.

2. Locate the SelectedIndex property and change it to 0. You can see that by default, it's a pretty dull blue color. You want to change this to a combination of yellow and orange to add some warmth representing temperature.

3. Right-click on the ListBox element and select to Edit Additional Templates->Edit Generated Item Container (ItemContainerStyle)->Edit a Copy..., as shown in Figure 10.15.

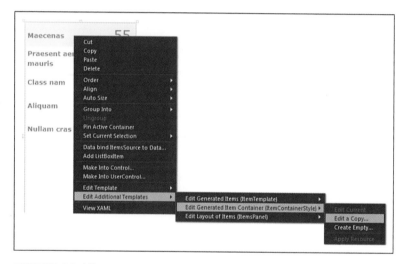

FIGURE 10.15   How to edit the ItemContainerStyle.

4. You are now presented with the Create Style Resource, which you can keep exactly as it shows and click on the OK button to begin editing the ItemContainerStyle. This again changes the Objects and Timeline panel to show the context of the template, as shown in Figure 10.16.

Using States to Help with Template Editing

The elements that are shown in the Objects and Timeline panel let you change the visual of the container at runtime when the item is selected or has focus or is disabled, for example.

When you edit the template directly as you are currently doing, it doesn't help that you can't see the effects of the changes you make to the Container style directly in the ListBox. To help you do this, you need to open the States panel, which enables you to select through the States defined to get a better understanding of what each element is actually being used for.

In this example, there are two `FillColor` elements that are shown, and ordinarily you would be confused as to what each one is used for. When you open the States panel, select the `MouseOver` state and then open the Timeline inside of the Objects and Timeline panel. This shows you that the first `FillColor` element is being used to show this value.

Select through the States and change the colors of the elements to suit. In this case, I am changing the mouseover to show a sunburned type of effect with a `GradientColorBrush` applied to the `FillColor` element. I applied a lighter version of that `GradientColorBrush` to the `FillColor2` element in the `Selected` state.

Change these properties to your own style. Figure 10.17 shows the results of my editing of the `ItemContainerStyle` and returning back to the root level of the control.

Now that you have finished with the `ListBoxItem` styling, you should select the `ListBox` element again locating the `SelectedIndex` property and return its value back to `-1`.

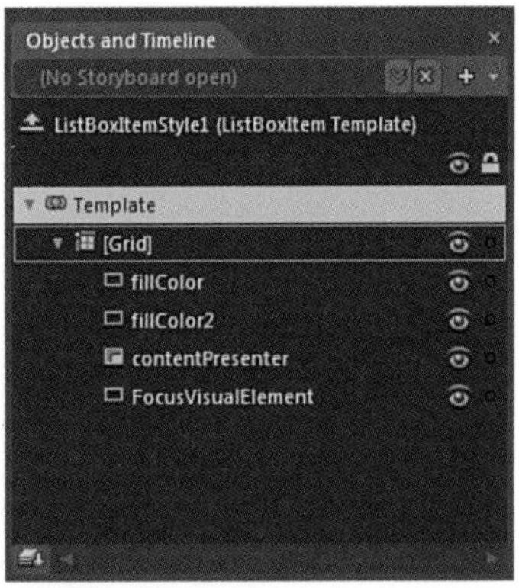

FIGURE 10.16   The ItemContainerStyle template context.

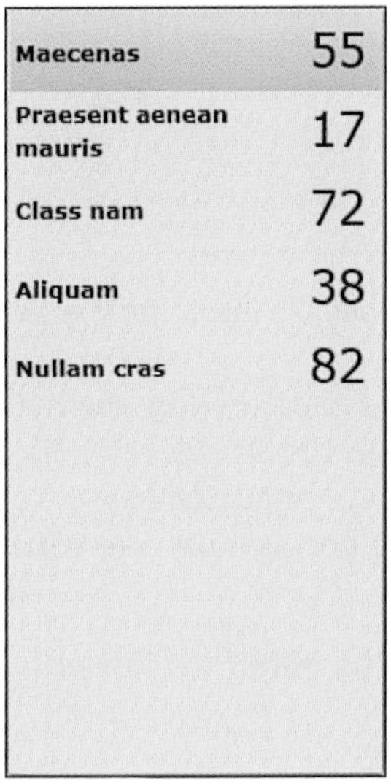

FIGURE 10.17   An example of the ItemContainerStyle I created.

Working with the Details

You will now work with the `DataContext` scenario to power several elements inside a `Grid` element. The secret here is to set the `DataContext` of the parent element (`Grid`) and then simply bind each of the elements to the correct field name from the data source.

In the following step, you add the `Grid` which represents the parent element to which the `DataContext` is assigned to.

1. Add a new `Grid` element to the artboard that is the same height as the `ListBox` element, taking the remaining size of the scene.

The elements and layout shown in Figure 10.18 are what I put together for the sample solution in this chapter, but by now you are most likely able to decide this for yourself.

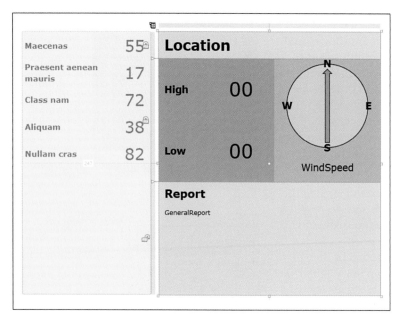

FIGURE 10.18   The sample layout for the details data presentation.

The WindDirection is represented by the makeshift compass control, which is a simple Arrow element found in the Shapes category of the Assets panel sitting on top of an Ellipse element. A word of advice here is to set both the Arrow and the Ellipse element as center aligned both horizontally and vertically, because you will need to rotate the arrow shortly.

Go ahead and create the rest of the layout to suit.

Binding the Elements

After you have completed the creation of the details panel, you can begin to data bind the elements to the corresponding data source fields, following these steps:

1 Select the Location TextBlock element.

2. Locate the Text property and open the Advanced Options menu.

3. Select the Data Binding... menu item, as shown in Figure 10.19.

Data Context Binding

You should now be presented with the Data Context tab of the Create Data Binding dialog, as detailed in Figure 10.20.

FIGURE 10.19   The location of the Data Binding menu option.

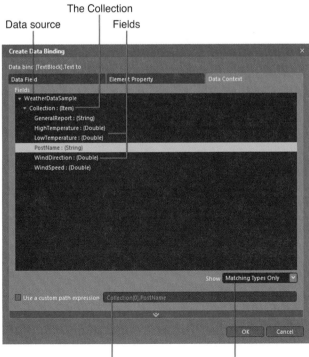

FIGURE 10.20   The Data Context tab of the Create Data Binding dialog box.

Data Source

The data source represents the current data source from which the element is receiving data context. In this scenario, it is the sample data you previously created.

Collection

The collection represents all the items that are available from the data source.

Fields

The fields are what each data item contains and is defined by the data schema you created earlier in the sample data source editor.

Show Options

This enables you to specify which fields should be shown from the data source. In this instance, because you have basic property *types* (strings and numbers) in your data source, all fields can be shown inside a `TextBlock` and are therefore shown as an optional source. In more advanced scenarios, you might not want to see data fields that are irrelevant to the element property *type* you are trying to bind to.

Custom Path Expression

In various data sources (XML and CLR), you might want to define your own path expression in order to retrieve the correct data values from your source. This can also assist with retrieving data from sources which have a data structure that Blend doesn't recognize.

Details Bindings

You see in Figure 10.20 that the `PostName` field is selected, which represents the location value you want to bind to. You can click on OK when you have selected the `PostName` field to complete the binding.

Unfortunately, this is a direct binding to the data collection, which is not what you need at this point and, inevitably, confusion sets in as to what you are supposed to be binding to.

To verify it is indeed a direct binding, select the `Text` property of the Location `TextBlock` and view the Custom expression value from the Advanced Options menu, as shown in Figure 10.21.

You can tell that this binding is direct due to the "Collection[0]" shown before the field name.

The first task is to change the parent `Grid` binding instruction to take its data context from the `ListBox` element, as follows:

1. Select the parent `Grid` of the details elements.

2. Locate the `DataContext` property and open the Advanced Options menu, again selecting the Data Binding menu item.

3. Of the three tabs in the Create Data Binding dialog, select the middle one named Element Property.

FIGURE 10.21   The current binding expression for the Location TextBlock.

Element Property Binding

The tab shown in Figure 10.22 shows the Element Property binding solution inside of Expression Blend. This tab enables you to locate an element in your current scene, select it, and then bind to one of the properties of that selected element.

FIGURE 10.22   The Element Property tab.

In the following steps, you will bind to the ListBox element.

1. As shown in Figure 10.22, you need to locate the ListBox element in the collection of Scene elements in the lefthand list and the scroll to find the SelectedItem : (Object) property in the Properties list on the righthand side.

2. Click OK to close the Create Data Binding dialog.

3. Selecting the Location `TextBlock`, again open the Custom Expression option of the Advanced Options menu.

4. Remove the 'Collection[0].' from the input, as shown in Figure 10.23.

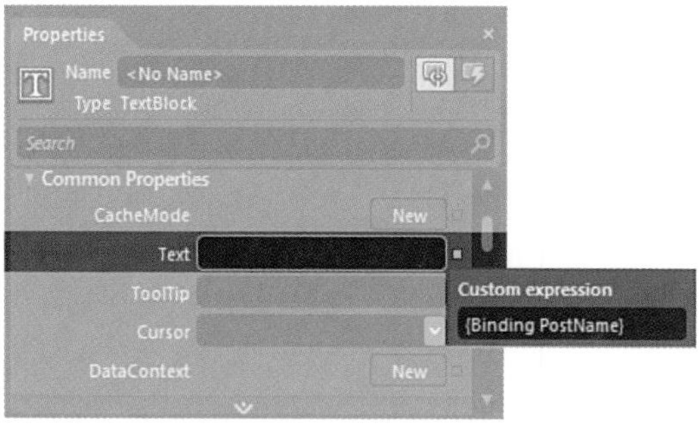

FIGURE 10.23   The Custom Expression and how it should now be.

5. Press F5 to run the solution.

You should now be able select different items in the lefthand `ListBox` element, and you should find that the Location value now changes and is shown as you change your selection.

You can now do the same for each of the elements representing the remainder of the fields in the solution.

Binding the WindDirection Field

The WindDirection field is represented by the makeshift compass that by default points to 0 degrees when referring to a rotation value. The following steps show you how set the compass rotation value.

1. Select the `Arrow` element and locate the `Rotation` property inside the Transform category of the Properties panel.

2. Bind the `Angle` property using the Data Binding dialog to the `WindDirection` field, as you previously did for the location and temperature fields.

The ValueConverter Solution

The `WindSpeed` value is showing as you would expect as just a number, which really isn't telling your users too much or at the very least asking them to make a giant assumption that this is, in fact, a wind speed value.

One of the issues here is that the number value provided in the data set is exactly that—a number and not a string value that can show a figure and then an abbreviation after it, such as "mph" or "km/h" depending on what side of the pond you are from.

This is an example of when a ValueConverter can help you continue to work seamlessly with data without having to add additional elements to fulfill a design requirement.

In the following example, you are going to write a ValueConverter class in code that takes the number parsed in through the data binding, append the correct abbreviation to it, and then return the entire value as a string back out to the binding:

1. Open the Projects panel and right-click on the Silverlight C# project, selecting Add new item from the menu options.

2. Add a new class and name it WindSpeedConverter, as shown in Figure 10.24.

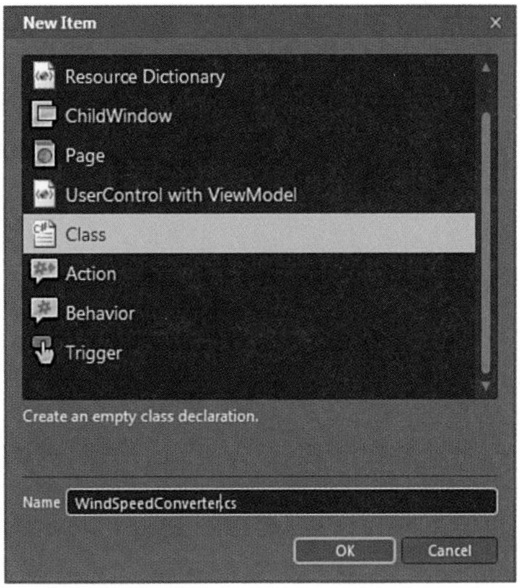

FIGURE 10.24   How to create a new class in the solution.

TIP

Visual Studio Makes This an Easier Process

The use of Visual Studio to create value converters is significantly easier, as the Intellisense it provides enables you to automatically create the required code methods. If you don't have access to Visual Studio, ensure that you copy the code in the following listings exactly.

WARNING

Code Syntax Is Beyond the Scope of This Book

You are about to enter some code into your solution. Some of you might not be familiar with C# code, and it is beyond the scope of this book to explain to you the very detailed and often complex subject of writing code. There are many fine texts available that can show you easily how to become a competent coder with the .Net Framework, and it is my advice that you refer to such texts should you wish to fully understand the code that is being shown.

3. Your new class now needs to implement the IValueConverter interface. Begin by modifying the class declaration, as shown in Listing 10.1.

LISTING 10.1   Adding the IValueConverter to the Class Declaration

```
public class WindSpeedConverter : IValueConverter
```

The IValueConverter requires that two specific methods are added to the class, regardless of if you intend to use those methods.

4. Inside the class, add the code as shown in Listing 10.2.

LISTING 10.2   Creating the Two Required Methods for the IValueConverter Interface

```
public class WindSpeedConverter : IValueConverter
{
        public WindSpeedConverter()
        {
                // Insert code required on object creation below this point.
        }

        public object Convert(object value, Type targetType, object parameter,
System.Globalization.CultureInfo culture)
        {

        }

        public object ConvertBack(object value, Type targetType, object parameter,
System.Globalization.CultureInfo culture)
        {

        }
}
```

The Convert method is what you are interested in this scenario. Its job is to take a value that is parsed into the method (the first parameter called value, which is of *type* object) and to return a value.

5. Add the code shown in Listing 10.3 to the Convert method you have just created.

LISTING 10.3   Appending the Abbreviation to the Value Parsed into the Method

```
return value.ToString() + " mph";
```

Because each method expects a return object, you should add the code line shown in Listing 10.4 to the ConvertBack method.

LISTING 10.4   Returning Nothing in This Scenario

```
return null;
```

6. Close the code file.

7. From the Project menu at the top of the screen, select the Build Project option to ensure that your solution still compiles. If it doesn't, review the code you just added to ensure that you haven't added or missed anything inadvertently. Even a period ('.') can break your code!

Applying the ValueConverter

The following steps show you how to now apply your ValueConverter.

1. Select the WindSpeed `TextBlock` element and again open the Data Binding dialog by using the Advanced Options menu from the `Text` property.

2. Open the Advanced Properties extension located at the bottom of the Create Data Binding dialog, as detailed in Figure 10.25.

> ### TIP
>
> #### Using IValueConverter in More Complex Scenarios
>
> The `IValueConverter` is an extremely helpful interface to enable you to convert from one property type to another and back again in more complex data scenarios. It is beyond the scope of this book to explain the `IValueConverter` in any more detail than has been shown here. I advise you to research the interface if you wish to fully understand the usage of parameter conversion and other usages should you need this functionality.

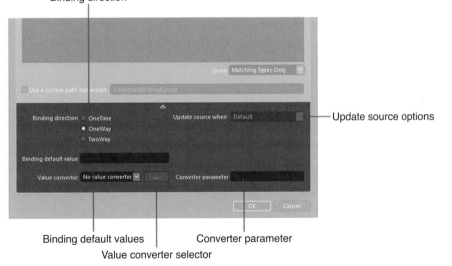

Binding direction

Update source options

Binding default values   Converter parameter

Value converter selector

FIGURE 10.25   The Advanced Properties of the Create Data Binding dialog.

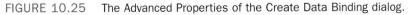

Binding Direction

The binding direction enables you to control how data is provided to or from your scene or both directions. The default is `OneWay` and the following list details the options available to you.

▶ **OneTime.** Takes the value once on instantiation of the scene and binds to the element property.

▶ **OneWay.** Data is provided from a source to the scene elements.

▶ **TwoWay.** Data is provided to the scene, and changes in the data are also given back to the data source.

▶ **OneWayToSource (WPF only).** Enables you to update the source from changes in the scene. This is the opposite of the OneWay binding direction.

Update Source When

This option is available only when you are using TwoWay data binding, and you want to update the source with changes that have been made in the scene. By default, changes will be applied as they are made by the user, but you can also expressly opt for explicit updating, where you need to accept the changes made in code.

Binding Default Value

This enables you to specify a default value for the binding.

Value Converter

This enables you to specify or find the .Net class that will convert from one value to another.

Converter Parameter

Specify any parameters that should be parsed to the IValueConverter interface, as follows:

1. Select the Add new value converter button as indicated in Figure 10.25, which opens the Add Value Convert dialog shown in Figure 10.26.

2. You see in Figure 10.26 that you can type the name of the converter class you just created into the dialog and then are able to select the converter to use.

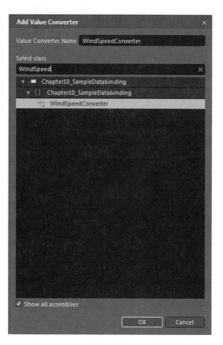

FIGURE 10.26   The Add Value Converter dialog.

3. Click OK to close the Add Value Converter dialog and then again click OK on the Create Data Binding dialog.

You should now see that your WindSpeed TextBlock shows the correct appendage of "mph" to the speed, as shown in Figure 10.27.

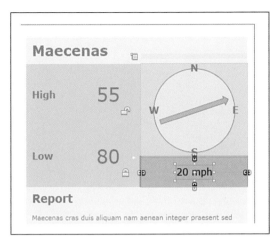

FIGURE 10.27   The application of the value converter to the WindSpeed TextBlock.

Run your solution now, and you should see that selecting the different list items displays the details of the sample data.

Switching to Live Data

In this scenario, you have completed your concept that demonstrates the desired functionality, but your development team is now in the position to provide live data to the application—or, at the very least, the data objects in code that your solution will map to.

It would always be easier if the development team had created the data objects for binding first, as you can import that and refer the sample data schema from it, but life isn't always that straightforward.

In the following sample, you are going to create the code for the data objects. This isn't going to be explained in detail, so be sure to accurately match the code listings:

1. From the Project tab, right-click on the Silverlight project and opt to add a new class item.

2. Call the new class WeatherDataItem.

    You are now going to add Properties to the class, which represent the same data as you created in the sample data previously in this chapter. What is important here is that you name the properties exactly as they are in the sample data, as well as give them the same Property *type*.

    You can open the Data panel and look into the collection as a reference when creating these properties, as shown in Figure 10.28.

FIGURE 10.28   The data collection field names.

NOTE

Auto Property Types

You are going to be creating auto properties in this sample, which are very simple types of properties and not at all recommended as the correct property *type* for every solution. Again, you should research development methods and concepts to understand when you should and shouldn't use these types of properties. You are using them here for the sake of simplicity.

---

3. Inside the newly created class, replicate the code shown in Listing 10.5.

LISTING 10.5   The Auto Properties Added to the Class

```csharp
public class WeatherDataItem
{
    public WeatherDataItem()
    {
    }

    public string GeneralReport { get; set; }
    public double HighTemperature { get; set; }
    public double LowTemperature { get; set; }
    public string PostName { get; set; }
    public double WindDirection { get; set; }
    public double WindSpeed { get; set; }

}
```

The `WeatherDataItem` represents a single weather entry that is shown in the `ListBox` element when your application runs.

You now need to create another class that contains the collection of data items that will be shown.

4. Right-click on the Silverlight project in the Project tab and create another new class item.

5. Name this class "WeatherDataCollection."

6. Before changing the code in this new class, you need to include a specific .Net library class that provides the functionality of the collection. At the top of the new class, you should see several lines of code that each begin with the term "using," which is the instruction. Add the single line of code shown in Listing 10.6 underneath all the existing using statements.

LISTING 10.6   The New Using Statement to Add to the Class

```
using System.Collections.ObjectModel;
```

7. Duplicate the code shown in Listing 10.7 exactly into your class.

LISTING 10.7   A Code Listing That Creates Sample Data and Builds Your Live Data Collection

```
public class WeatherDataCollection : ObservableCollection<WeatherDataItem>
{
    public WeatherDataCollection()
    {
        this.GenerateSampleData();
    }

    private Random RND = new Random(DateTime.Now.Second);

    private void MakeTemperatures(ref double High, ref double Low)
    {
        High = Convert.ToDouble(RND.Next(10, 40));
        Low = Convert.ToDouble(RND.Next(10, Convert.ToInt32(High)));
    }

    private double MakeWindSpeed()
    {
        return Convert.ToDouble(RND.Next(2, 25));
    }

    private double MakeWindDirection()
    {
```

10

```
        return Convert.ToDouble(RND.Next(0, 360));
    }

    private void GenerateSampleData()
    {
        for (int i = 0; i < 10; i++)
        {
            WeatherDataItem WDI = new WeatherDataItem();
            string PreText = "ITEM " + i.ToString();
            WDI.GeneralReport = PreText + ": This is a sample weather report
which can contain a lot of text as you would expect a weather report to contain.";

            double ReturnedHigh = double.NaN;
            double ReturnedLow = double.NaN;

            this.MakeTemperatures(ref ReturnedHigh , ref ReturnedLow );
            WDI.HighTemperature = ReturnedHigh;
            WDI.LowTemperature = ReturnedLow;

            WDI.PostName  = "Location " + i.ToString();
            WDI.WindDirection = this.MakeWindDirection();
            WDI.WindSpeed = this.MakeWindSpeed();

            this.Add(WDI);
        }
    }

}
```

8. Build the solution to ensure that your code compiles.

Changing the Live Binding Quickly

You now need to create a data source in Blend that is connected to your live code collection. Follow these steps:

1. Open the Data panel and select to create a new Object data source, as shown in Figure 10.29.

2. You should now be presented with the Create Object Data Source dialog, as shown in Figure 10.30. As you also see in Figure 10.30, you only need to type the word "Collection" into the Search input box, and you should find the name of the class you just created, WeatherDataCollection.

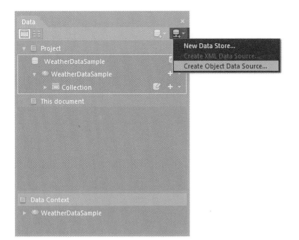

FIGURE 10.29   How to create a new Object data source.

FIGURE 10.30   The object collection selection in the Create Object Data Source dialog.

3. Select WeatherDataCollection and click OK to close the dialog.

You should now see in the Data panel that your data source has been created. Pay attention to the Data Context tab at the bottom of the Data panel, which still shows that your scene is bound to the sample data source, as shown in Figure 10.31.

Data Field Binding

You can now actively work with this data source to power all the fields you previously connected to the sample data source, by following these steps:

1. Select the LayoutRoot element in the Objects and Timeline panel.

2. Location the DataContext property in the Properties panel.

3. Open the Data Binding dialog from the Advanced Option menu.

4. Navigate to the first tab in the Create Data Binding dialog, the Data Field tab, as shown in Figure 10.32.

5. Select the WeatherDataCollection DataSource, as shown in Figure 10.32.

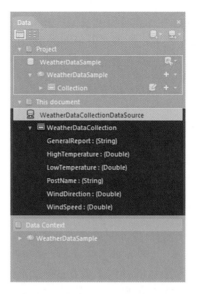

FIGURE 10.31   The new object data source created in the Data panel.

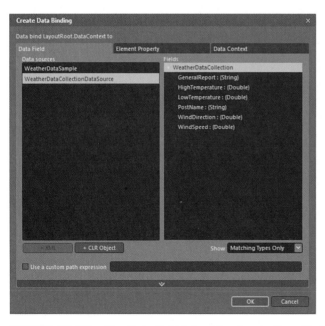

FIGURE 10.32   The Data Field tab of the Create Data Binding dialog.

You should now see inside the Data panel that the binding has changed to show the live data source is in use; the data context should also have changed to the collection.

The last change you need to now make is the binding of the ListBox to the correct collection name from the data source. Currently, it is still bound to the "Collection" of the sample data source.

6. Select the ListBox element in the Objects and Timeline panel.

7. Locate the ItemsSource property.

8. Open the Advanced Options menu and select the Data Binding option once again.

9. You should now see the Data Context tab, as shown in Figure 10.33. Select the Fields value of WeatherDataCollection and click OK to close the Create Data Binding dialog.

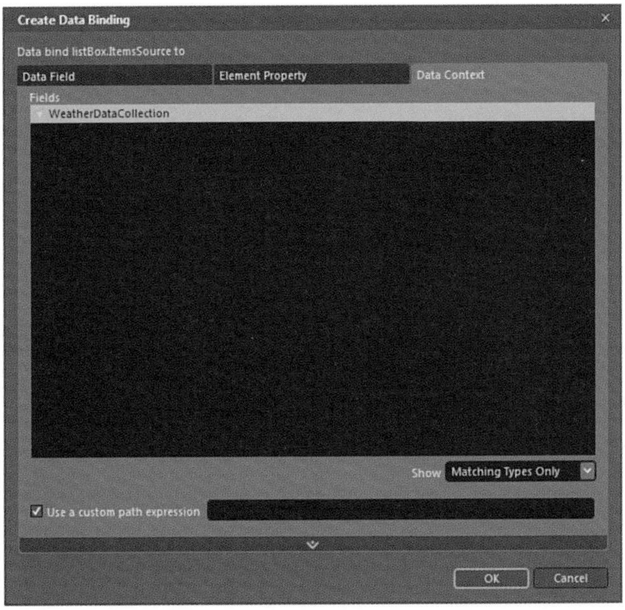

FIGURE 10.33   The new collection available in the Data Context tab.

You should be able to run your solution now and see 10 items listed, as shown in Figure 10.34, which have more meaningful information in them.

Of course, until such time as your developers actually hook up the class to a weather service and retrieve the information, it still might not be that realistic. That is a problem for them to solve now that you have created the user interface to display the data.

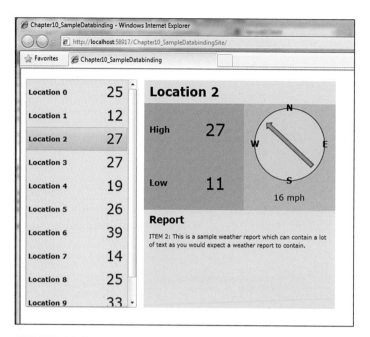

FIGURE 10.34   The completed solution bound to the live data.

Summary

Data binding is one of those topics that can frighten new users of the platform types that Expression Blend supports, such as Silverlight and WPF. Hopefully, you have seen in this chapter how simple it is to work with not only simple sample data, but relatively complex data also.

Expression Blend does a great job at hiding a lot of the complexities for the designer with simple drag-and-drop scenarios and very straightforward explanations of the data collections you are working with. The only area to keep an eye on is the data context. There will be several times when working within Blend that you bind your controls to a data source, and no data will show up either in design time or at run time. For the most part, this is either because of an incorrect binding to the proper data context or, in the case of Details binding, you are still binding directly to the collection instead of taking the context from the Items binding. This was represented by the ListBox element in this chapter.

If you are going to work with data that is reasonably more complex in terms of how it reacts with your solution, you are pretty close to having to work exclusively in code. Don't be afraid to ask questions of your developers to understand how the data is being pushed into the solution and how best to represent that data in your user interface.

CHAPTER 11

Animations and Transitions

Throughout this book, you have been exposed to storyboards, transitions, and animations at a very light level to this point, enabling you to move components around the screen with no real depth of understanding or accuracy.

There are several locations within Expression Blend where you have the opportunity to create and apply animations, such as when using the State editor, or even straight out of the box directly at the UserControl or scene level.

In this chapter, you look at the storyboard and animation mechanisms used within Expression Blend within the Storyboard editor, as well as the State management of those storyboards to obtain full control of your creative requirements. Transitions are simple implementations of state change, but created right, they add a genuinely nice quality to your end user's experience. As with all things with such nature, balance is the key to getting it right.

The Storyboard Editor

The Storyboard editor is where all the action happens in terms of controlling the elements and applying various effects that can change the rate of transition applied to your chosen element properties.

Storyboards are really a timed method of incrementing or decrementing a property value. The value change that occurs between your start and end points is referred to as interpolation, which can also be customized to speed up or slow down.

Figure 11.1 shows an example of the Storyboard editor with a selection of simple controls that have animations applied. You see that every property that is animated gets its own line as a child element within the Storyboard editor. These entries are called "timelines." This makes it very easy to understand what you are animating and when.

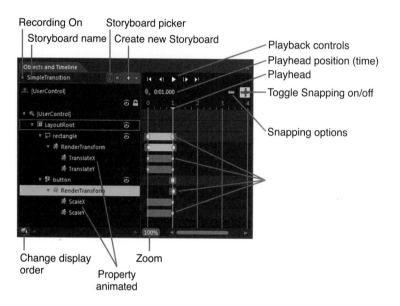

FIGURE 11.1   The Storyboard editor.

The following example walks you through the usage of the Storyboard editor, opening up the most common requirements and usage:

1. Create a new Silverlight Application + Website solution.

2. Add a new `Ellipse` element to your artboard and set the background (`Fill` property) to a solid color of your choosing.

3. Specifically set the `Width` and `Height` properties to `150`, as shown in Figure 11.2. Also, take note of the `Margin` values being set to 25 Left and 25 Top, as well as the `HorizontalAlignment` and `VerticalAlignment` properties set to both `Left` and `Top`, respectively.

4. Add a new storyboard by selecting the New option in the Storyboard menu located on the Objects and Timeline panel, as shown in Figure 11.3.

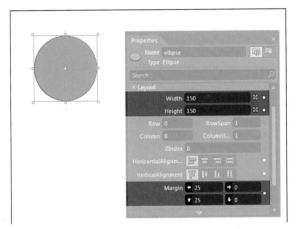

FIGURE 11.2   The new Ellipse element set up for this example.

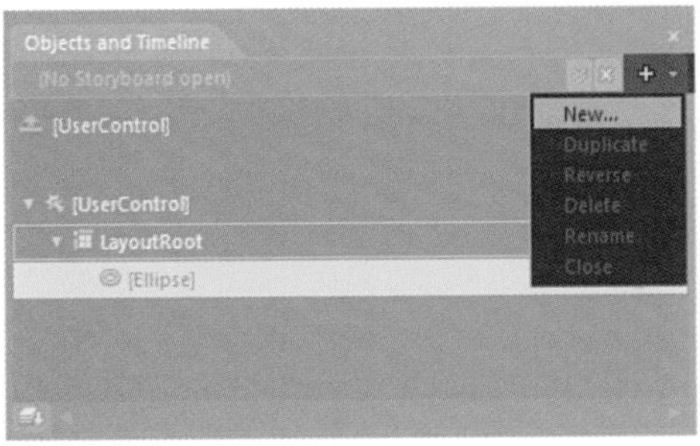

FIGURE 11.3   Where the Storyboard menu is located on the Objects and Timeline panel.

5. This opens the Create Storyboard Resource dialog, as shown in Figure 11.4. Name this storyboard "GlideDownRight."

FIGURE 11.4   The Create Storyboard Resource dialog.

6. You are now in Storyboard mode, as indicated in both the artboard signposting (shown in Figure 11.5) and the changes present in the Objects and Timeline panel, which is shown in Figure 11.6.

Storyboard mode has some pretty unique scenarios to be aware of, which can and will at some stage trip you up. Chief among these is the fact that almost any property change you make while in this mode will be recorded as a new animation keyframe, which might lead to unintended consequences.

Best to pay attention!

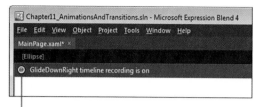

Toggle recording on/off

FIGURE 11.5   The artboard signposting, indicating that you are in Storyboard mode.

FIGURE 11.6   The new changes in the Objects and Timeline panel.

Animation Keyframes

Keyframes are a way to ensure specific property values are enforced at a specific point in time. A keyframe can and often contains a collection of singular keyframes that range in values that you add to the storyboard during the recording mode.

How to Record a Keyframe

One of the easiest methods is to simply start messing around with your elements in place on the artboard, and if you do that, Expression Blend will automatically start adding keyframes and their values to the storyboard.

Often you want to be more accurate than that, though, so each property that can be recorded as a Keyframe value has a handy Advanced Options context menu item that enables you to record that value specifically. This is shown in Figure 11.7 and explained in Step 7, as follows:

1. At the start of this animation, you want to instruct the storyboard to ensure that the Ellipse has the fixed Width and Height value of 150 px. Ensuring that the Playhead position in the Storyboard editor is at 0.000, click on the Advanced Options button next to the Width property and find the Record Current Value menu option, as shown in Figure 11.7. Do the same for the Height property.

   Your values are now fixed and, as shown in Figure 11.8, the keyframes have been recorded as separate timelines in the Objects and Timeline editor.

2. Move the Playhead position to the 1.000 mark by dragging the orange guide.

3. On the artboard, drag the Ellipse to the bottom-right corner.

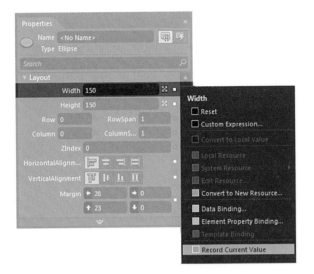

FIGURE 11.7   The location of the Record Current Value option.

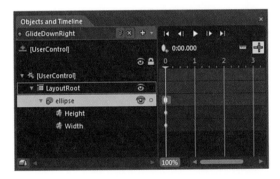

FIGURE 11.8   The new Recorded values as timelines in the Objects and Timeline panel.

Transformations

You should now see the changes to the Objects and Timeline panel. Notice that a new timeline collection called RenderTransform has been added to the Storyboard editor, as shown in Figure 11.9.

Transformations are used to apply various visual changes to elements. You can rotate an element, for example, or change the scale of an element. You can do this as part of your initial property definition or animate the transformation values to apply different effects, such as changing the location of an element such as what you have just done.

You can view the Transformation options available to you by opening the Transform category of the Property panel, as shown in Figure 11.10.

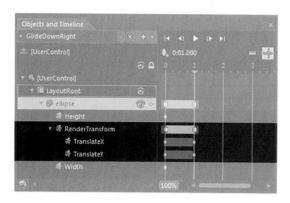

FIGURE 11.9   The new RenderTransform timeline collection added to the Objects and Timeline panel.

Concentrating on the top half of the Transform category at the moment (as the bottom half is platform specific), you see that there are six different transformations that can be accessed by the tabs.

In the following continuation of the example, you apply a different transformation at each 1.000 second interval in the storyboard to understand the usage of each of the transforms.

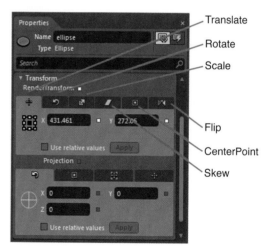

FIGURE 11.10   The RenderTransforms available.

Translate

To translate an element is to move an element by a specified X and Y incremental value, which is relational to the original location of the element. This means that instead of moving an element relative to its position on a Canvas, for example, translating an element in the X axis by 25 pixels will always move the element 25 pixels from its current position, rather than to the location of 25 px on the X axis of a panel as a location point.

Take a look at the Margin values of the Ellipse element. If you remember when you first created the Ellipse, you set the Margin values to 25 Left and 25 Top. Those Margin property values shouldn't have changed, even after the Ellipse has moved position in this animation as proven in the following steps:

1. To prove the point, close the storyboard and set the Left Margin value of the ellipse to 300.

2. Open the storyboard and now move the Playhead position to 1.000. You see that the Ellipse now animates on the same trajectory but completely off the screen, as shown in Figure 11.11.

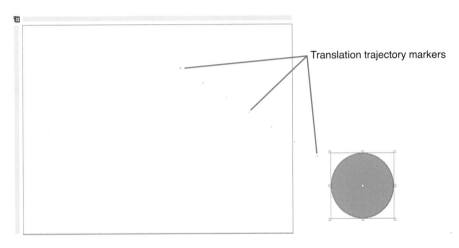

Translation trajectory markers

FIGURE 11.11   The Translate effect on the element.

3. Close the storyboard.

4. Return the Left Margin value of the ellipse to 25.

Rotate

The name of this transform is pretty self-describing. Specifically, it controls the amount of rotation applied to an element around a center point.

Center Point Change

The CenterPoint property enables you to set an offset for the rotation. This will be covered shortly in the following sections.

The following demonstrates element rotation.

1. In order to see the rotation that is occurring, change the Fill property of the Ellipse to a LinearGradient before opening the storyboard, as shown in Figure 11.12.

2. Open the storyboard and move the Playhead position to 1.000 and record the current Rotation value, as shown in Figure 11.12. You should see that a Rotation timeline has been added as a child to the RenderTransform timeline collection in the Storyboard editor.

3. Move the Playhead position to 2.000.

4. Change the rotation value to 180.

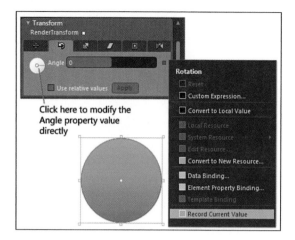

FIGURE 11.12   The addition of the Rotation value and Ellipse Fill property change.

That really can't be any easier. You should also note that you can control the rotation by holding your left mouse button down on the Rotation display element, also pointed out in Figure 11.12.

Scale

Scale enables you to modify the `Scale X` and `Scale Y` values of an element independently of each other or to the same value. Again, this being a transformation, once it is applied, you should note that the actual size of the element does not change, similar to the `Margin` property values reviewed previously.

The following steps demonstrate applying Scale to an element.

1. Move the Playhead position to `3.000`.

2. Inside the Scale Transformation category, change only the `Scale Y` property to `1.5`.

The value applied in this property is a relative value to the initial size of the element; a value of `1.5` is specifying that your element should now become 50% larger in the `Y` axis only.

Run the animation from inside the Storyboard editor, and you should now see that your `Ellipse` takes on an egg-like shape.

In Figure 11.13, it is interesting to compare the original `Ellipse` bounding box to what is now the Transformed element box. Still, the existing element is officially the same size and at the same location.

Original bounding box of the Elipse

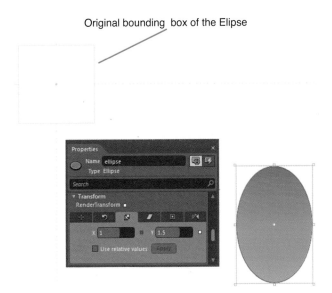

FIGURE 11.13   The transformed ellipse and the original bounding box of the ellipse.

Skew

Similar to the Scale Transform, Skew enables you to independently modify both the X and Y Skew values to an element. Skewing pushes an element on an axis to another point on the same axis, which gives the appearance of the element being stretched.

The following steps demonstrate the application of Skew to an element.

1. Move the Playhead position to 4.000.

2. Modify the X axis Skew value by applying a value of 15, as shown in Figure 11.14.

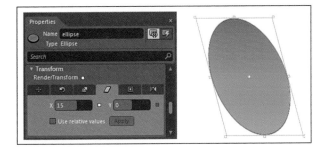

FIGURE 11.14   The X axis Skew applied to the element.

You can obviously get some interesting shapes if you play around with Skew in both the X and Y axis, changing the entire appearance of the original element.

CenterPoint

The CenterPoint transformation is interesting as it really needs to be used in conjunction with a second transformation to see any real effect, but it is one of those properties that can't be animated; thus, any change made to the property values is applied globally.

By default, the CenterPoint X and Y axis values are set to 0.5. This translates to mean the center point is 50% positive in the X and Y axis, resulting in the center point being located at the exact center of the element regardless of its shape or transformed appearance.

The following steps demonstrate how to modify the CenterPoint of an element.

1. Play back the animation using the Storyboard controls. Take very careful note of how all the current transformation are applied as the animation plays out.

2. Move the Playhead position to 5.000.

3. Change the CenterPoint X and Y values to 0, as shown in Figure 11.15.

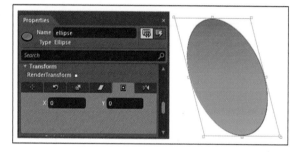

FIGURE 11.15   The values applied to the CenterPoint transformation.

You should immediately notice two important things here. First, the Ellipse should have changed position on your artboard dramatically, and second, no keyframe has been recorded at position 5.000.

Run the animation now, and you should see a completely different rotation effect applied to the element, as it is now effectively rotating around the very top-left point of the element.

Flip

The Flip transformation is perhaps the most confusing of all. This is because the Flip transformation effectively applies a Scale transformation to your element, reversing its current value from the positive to the negative, or vice

> **TIP**
>
> **Where Is the CenterPoint?**
>
> As mentioned previously, the CenterPoint is applied globally to the element, and just because you were in the Storyboard editor at the time you changed it doesn't mean that when you close the storyboard, it all goes back to the way it was. Close the storyboard now, and with the Ellipse selected, you see that the CenterPoint indeed has been changed permanently, as shown in Figure 11.16.

versa; for an example, if your element currently has a ScaleX value of (positive) 3, applying a Horizontal Flip transformation will make the ScaleX value -3. This isn't very clear, and it's easy to get confused when first working with this.

You might also expect that a simple Horizontal Flip would mean that the element would simply change across the axis it's being flipped on, but as will be shown in the following steps, because

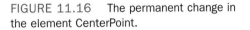
New CenterPoint location

FIGURE 11.16   The permanent change in the element CenterPoint.

you have applied a rotation transform and skew, the animation is probably completely unexpected. The Flip is applied against all transformations currently applied to the element, except for translations.

Study Figure 11.17 for a moment and notice that there is Rotation, ScaleY, SkewX, and Translate X and Y applied.

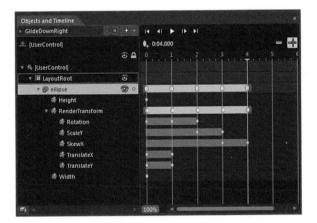

FIGURE 11.17   The current transforms applied to the Ellipse element.

The following steps detail how to apply a Flip transformation to an element.

1. Move the Playhead position to 5.000.

2. With the Ellipse selected, find the Flip category of the transformation category and click on the FlipX button, as shown in Figure 11.18.

Study Figure 11.19 and notice how a new transformation timeline has been added to flip the element against a ScaleX. ScaleY has been left untouched, as has the Translation values, but the Skew and Rotation transformations have also been extended.

FIGURE 11.18   The Flip options in the Transformation category.

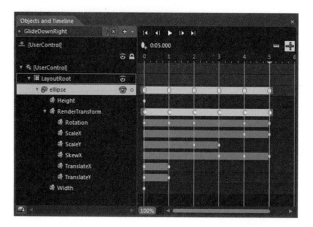

FIGURE 11.19   The change in the animation transformations.

Move the Playhead manually very slowly from position 4.000 to 5.000 and watch the craziness unfold as the `Ellipse` rotates and flips.

Aside from the later part of the transformation samples you have created, most are very easy to use. Practicing the use of transformations is a worthy cause, as more complex animations require you to understand fully what is happening at every point. Certainly when and if you ever need to reference and modify an animation in code and at runtime, you will need to query the transformations in order to apply logic to the element, which has its own pitfalls to be sure. Remember that the center point is very important, and if animations are not performing in the way you expect, the center point is the first place to look to verify that it is where it should be.

Plane Projections

In Figure 11.18, you see that there is a FlipZ button, which is available only when working with elements that are present in 3D space. Currently (and I say "currently" as my bet is that Silverlight will also support full 3D very shortly), only WPF supports full 3D, whereas Silverlight works with what is known as 2.5D.

2.5D in reality is a system of mathematical transformations through plane projections that give the appearance of 3D in some scenarios (or elements inside a 3D Canvas). Nevertheless, 2.5D is an effective transformation set that can, if applied sparingly, add a really nice effect of depth in your animations.

The following sample runs you through a quick example to drive home the effects in discussion:

1. In a new Silverlight Application + Website or in the same sample application, add a new Rectangle element.

2. Apply to the Fill property a GradientColor Brush of your choosing.

3. Create a new storyboard.

4. Open the Transformation category of the Property panel and navigate to the lower part of the category to the PlaneProjection section, which is detailed in Figure 11.20.

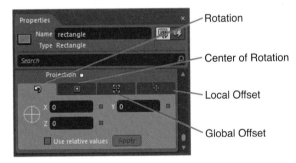

FIGURE 11.20   The Tab options of the PlaneProjection section.

5. Inside the Storyboard editor, move the Playhead position to 1.000.

6. Enter the value 90 into the YAngle property in the Rotation tab of the PlaneProjection section.

You can now play the animation, and you will find a very convincing 3D-like transformation of the Rectangle element.

The additional options in this section enable you to modify the center point of the rotation in much the same way as you previously performed with 2D transformations. You can also offset the location of the transformed object relative to the screen or relative to the 3D space that the element resides in. The difference is the actual location space (move the element across/up the physical screen) compared to 3D space where the element will take on depth—for example, if you move the element deeper into the screen along the Z axis.

Take some time to play with the projections, and you will find an endless array of fun you can have applying these simple effects.

Easing Functions

Easing functions enable you to control the speed at which values are applied to properties heading into or out of a keyframe. For example, you can make an animation appear to start slow and then speed up toward the end, which gives an animation a much more natural appearance of acceleration.

The functionality has always been available in Expression Blend for both WPF and Silverlight, but quick access easing functionality was introduced in Expression Blend 3 for Silverlight and is now supported in WPF solutions as well. This lets you simply select from a preexisting list of easing scenarios, such as Springs, Bouncing, or even Sine wave type effects to animations.

The easiest way to understand Easing functionality is to apply it, as you soon get the hang of the usefulness of the mechanism.

In the previous example, you rotated a `Rectangle` element in 3D space along its `YAxis`, which was all very nice, but the animation doesn't really have any emotion in it at all. The following continuation of the example demonstrates the usage of the quick selection Easing functions to give that little edge to your animation:

1. To view the Easing Function dropdown, you need to select and isolate a keyframe to apply the easing to. Figure 11.21 indicates this with the keyframe selection and the Properties panel now showing the default Easing function ("None") in the dropdown.

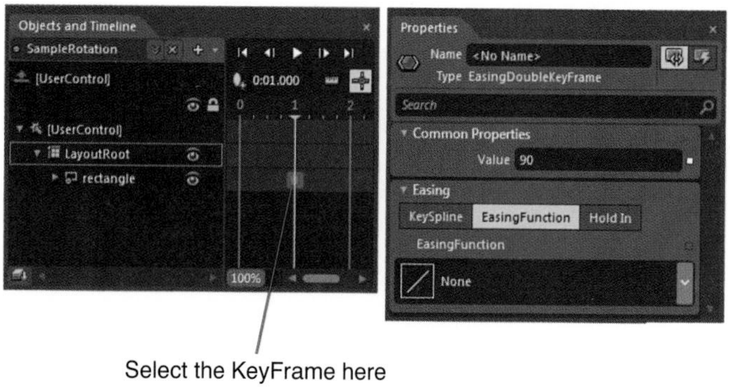

Select the KeyFrame here

FIGURE 11.21   The Easing category of the Property panel.

2. Select the Cubic "`In`" option, as shown in Figure 11.22.

When you now run this animation, what you see is that the rectangle slowly starts its turn and then speeds up at the end, giving an almost "closed door" effect.

In's, Out's, and In's 'n' Out's

You might be wondering what the difference is between the three columns shown in the Easing Function dropdown.

The "In" column enables you to specify that the Easing function should be applied to the animation as the animation approaches the selected keyframe.

The "Out" column enables you to specify that the Easing function should be applied to the animation after the animation passes the selected keyframe.

The "InOut" column enables you to specify that the Easing function should be applied coming into the keyframe and after passing by the selected keyframe, as you might have well guessed.

HoldIn

The HoldIn option enables you to effect an instantaneous change in a property value with no interpolation between the keyframes occurring as detailed in the following steps.

FIGURE 11.22   The correct Easing function to select.

1. Select the keyframe at position 1.000.

2. Click on the HoldIn option in the Easing category.

3. Change the Common Property value to 45.

Run the animation, and you now see that the Rectangle does nothing until it hits the 1.000 keyframe, where the Rectangle instantly changes to the 45-degree angle.

The Spline Editor

The Easing functions you have just played with are very easy to work with, but essentially they are a form of preset value for a more complex customization of a KeySpline. You have the option to manually create your own KeySpline at any time, as you will do in this section.

The Spline editor enables you to manually control the amount and or level of interpolation between one value and the next (values applied by two keyframes) over a specified period of time.

A KeySpline is a mathematical formula that controls the speed at which a value interpolates over a period of time. Figure 11.23 explains this concept clearly as the value against time.

The following steps show you how to create a KeySpline manually.

1. With the storyboard open in the Objects and Timeline category, select the keyframes located at position 1.000.

2. The Property panel changes to the now-familiar contextual view of Common Properties and Easing; you should now select the KeySpline option, as shown in Figure 11.24.

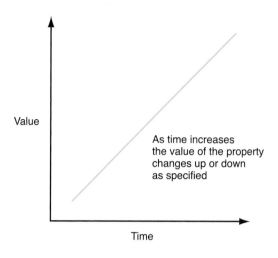

As time increases the value of the property changes up or down as specified

FIGURE 11.23   The creation of a KeySpline.

The orange "handles" enable you to drag the positions of the spline around the Grid while the four properties of X1, Y1, X2, and Y2 allow you to add accurate spline details, should you need to.

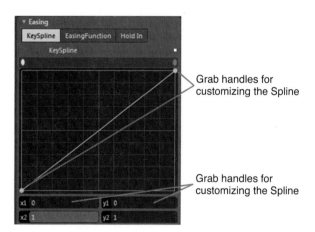

Grab handles for customizing the Spline

Grab handles for customizing the Spline

FIGURE 11.24   The KeySpline editor.

3. Drag the handle at the bottom left of the grid all the way over to the right of the Grid. This handle represents the X1 and Y1 property values.

4. Drag the handle at the top right of the grid all the way over to the left of the Grid. This handle represents the X2 and Y2 property values.

You should now have a custom KeySpline, similar to what is shown in Figure 11.25. Run the animation now and see the effect that you have just created.

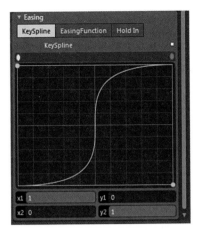

FIGURE 11.25   The new custom KeySpline created.

Repeating the Animation

Some confusion exists for new users trying to repeat an animation once applied to elements. The trick here is to understand that there are in fact two different types of "Repeat." One type enables you to control and repeat the individual parts (`timelines`) of an animation, and the other allows the entire storyboard to be repeated.

Timeline Repeating

The following steps demonstrate how to apply a repeating instruction to a specific timeline.

1. Using the same sample solution, create a new storyboard and call it "Repeating."

2. Move the Playhead position to the `2.000` position.

3. Drag the `Rectangle` element from its current position to a new position on the artboard; the opposite diagonal is a good location.

4. Open the Transform category of the Properties panel and apply a rotation of `180` degrees.

5. Play back the storyboard, and it should appear that the `Rectangle` is tumbling downwards.

6. Again with the Playhead at location `2.000`, open the Objects and Timeline panel and drill down into the `Rectangle` element to expose specifically the Rotation Timeline for the storyboard, as shown in Figure 11.26.

7. What you see in Figure 11.26 is the small context menu item called "Edit Repeat Count." You raise this context menu by right-clicking on the specific animation timeline, which in this case is the Rotation timeline.

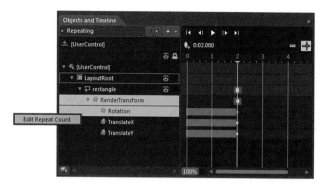

FIGURE 11.26   The Edit Repeat Count context menu applied against the Rotation element.

When you enter the Edit Repeat Mode item, the small Edit Repeat dialog appears that enables you to specify the number of repeats or to set it to "forever," as detailed in Figure 11.27.

FIGURE 11.27   The Edit Repeat dialog.

8. Set the Repeat Count value to 5.

9. Add a new Button element to your artboard.

10. Change the Content property value of the Button to "Play Repeating."

11. Open the Assets panel and navigate to the Behaviors category.

12. Drag the "ControlStoryboardAction" into the Objects and Timeline panel or onto the artboard, directly onto the new Button element you just added.

13. In the Properties panel, select the Repeating storyboard, as shown in Figure 11.28.

You now need to hit F5 to run the application and view your repeating rotation.

> ### NOTE
>
> **Preview Doesn't Show Repeats**
>
> You need to be aware that the Storyboard preview inside the editor doesn't show you the effect that your timeline repeat has.

FIGURE 11.28   Where to set the storyboard action inside the Common Properties category of the Properties panel.

Storyboard Repeating

To repeat the entire storyboard, you need select the storyboard inside the Objects and Timeline panel, as shown in Figure 11.29.

You should now see that the Properties panel has changed contextually to provide you with options relating directly to the storyboard, as shown in Figure 11.30.

The following steps demonstrate how to set a Storyboard to repeat.

14. Select the Repeating storyboard, as shown in Figure 11.29.

15. Select the RepeatBehavior drop-down menu and set it to 3x.

16. Click F5 to run the application.

It is interesting to note that when you now run the application (you need to click on your Button again to make the animation run), you see that the Rectangle moves to the position and rotates but continues from that point to stay in the same place and just continue to rotate. You might have expected the Rectangle to return to the start position for the animation to repeat.

If you remember back to Step 2 of this sample, you moved the Playhead position straight to position 2.000 and didn't create a keyframe for position 0.000. This means that the Rectangle is in the correct position when the animation repeats, as it remains there from the previous instance of the animation.

To make the Rectangle return to the start position, you should open the repeating storyboard and add a keyframe at position 0.000. You can then run the animation again, and this time you see that the repeating rotation must complete first before the entire animation is repeated.

Reversing the Timeline

You might have noticed when you selected the storyboard in the Object and Timeline panel that you also had an option to AutoReverse the storyboard. This functionality plays your storyboard in reverse when it reaches the end of the normal playback functionality.

Select here to view the Repeat options for the Storyboard

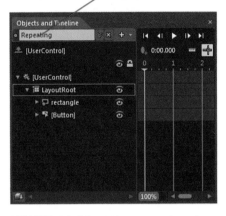

FIGURE 11.29 Where to select the storyboard.

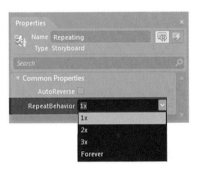

FIGURE 11.30 The repeat option for the storyboard.

You can try out this functionality with these simple sample steps:

1. Create a new storyboard called AutoReverse.

2. Move the Playhead position to 1.000.

3. Drag the Rectangle element to an arbitrary point on the artboard.

4. Select the storyboard in the Objects and Timeline panel.

5. Check on the AutoReverse checkbox.

6. Create a new Button element and change the content to "Play AutoReverse."

7. Open the Assets panel and drag a new ControlStoryboardAction Behavior onto the button.

8. Select the AutoReverse storyboard in the Storyboard property of the Common Properties category.

9. Run the application by clicking F5.

Duplicate and Reverse the Storyboard

The Storyboard picker has a nice little feature that lets you select an existing storyboard and perform various actions on the instance. One of the features you will most likely need at some point is to reverse the movements or translations of a complex storyboard, which is different to letting the storyboard run and then reversing it.

You can select any storyboard in the Storyboard picker and then, as Figure 11.31 shows, you have several options you can perform on the selected storyboard.

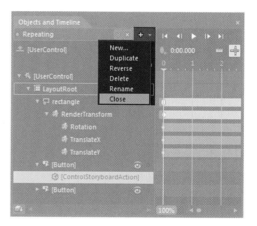

FIGURE 11.31   The storyboard action menu options.

In order to reverse the transition of a storyboard, you should duplicate it first, as shown in the following steps:

1. Select the repeating storyboard in the Storyboard picker.

2. From the Storyboard actions menu, select to duplicate the storyboard.

3. You see that automatically, the new storyboard instance is named Repeating_Copy1; you can double-click in the Storyboard label and rename to Repeating_Reverse.

4. From the Storyboard actions menu, select the Reverse option.

5. Close the storyboard.

6. Add a new button to your artboard and connect up a Behavior to call the Repeating_Reverse animation.

7. Change the Content property of the new Button to Play Repeating_Reverse.

8. Run your application.

TIP

Work Faster with Copy and Paste

There is no reason for you not to simply select an existing Button element on either the artboard or the Objects and Timeline panel and copy and paste it. The advantage with using this method is that you also get a copy of the Behavior attached to the Button, and you can simply modify the storyboard being called in the Property panel.

HandOff Animation

Handoff animation occurs when you attempt to animate the same property of the same element in two different storyboards that are running at the same time. Expression Blend fully supports this scenario as long as you *don't* define a keyframe at position 0.000 in either storyboard for the property.

The animation engine effectively works out how to interpolate between the values being applied so the result is that you have a nice smooth animation from one storyboard to the other.

The following example walks you through a simple demonstration of HandOff animation:

1. Use the same solution as previously used in this chapter or create a new Silverlight Application + Website solution.

   If you have created a new solution, add a similar Rectangle to the top left of the artboard.

2. Create a new storyboard called HandoffPart1.

3. Move the Storyboard Playhead to position 2.000.

   It is imperative that you remember not to create a keyframe at position 0.000.

4. Drag the Rectangle element from the top left to the top right of the artboard.

5. Close the storyboard.

6. Create a new storyboard called HandOffPart2.

7. Move the Playhead position to 2.000, as you did previously.

8. Drag the Rectangle element to the bottom-right corner of the artboard.

9. Add two new `Button` elements to your solution, changing the content of one to "Play HandOff 1" and the other to "Play HandOff 2."

10. Connect up `ControlStoryboardAction` behaviors to the respective storyboards.

When you run the solution now, click on the first `Button` element to begin playing part 1 of the HandOff animation sample. When the animation is about halfway through playing, click on the second `Button` to begin part 2 of the sample. You should see a nice smooth transition that changes the course of the `Rectangle` element to the bottom-right corner of the artboard.

Managing State Animations with Storyboards

You have already used States throughout this book with simple changes to element properties in Chapter 8, "Working with States." Now, with your newfound skills in working with the storyboard; you visit two State scenarios that will make more sense than if previously explained.

There are several reasons why you would use States to fire an animation rather than calling a storyboard directly. The only problem is that you can't call a storyboard directly from a State change.

I know what you are thinking right now: "When I modify a State, doesn't it create a Storyboard by default?" The answer is yes it does, but it is a special storyboard that works on only the first keyframe position of `0.000`. In other words, the timeline has no effect against the transition time of the State and a collection of keyframes will be ignored, limiting what can be animated.

The following steps demonstrate a particular solution around this concept:

1. Create a new Silverlight Application + Website solution.

2. Add a new `Rectangle` element to the top left of the artboard.

3. Set the size of the rectangle to approximately `150 x 150`.

4. Open the States panel.

5. Create a new State called State1.

6. Ensure that Transition preview is turned ON, as shown in Figure 11.32.

7. Set the default transition to `0.1` second.

8. Select `State1` in the States panel to begin recording.

> **TIP**
>
> **Why Record a Property That Won't Change?**
>
> You need to have a recorded value in the State Storyboard for it to be created and therefore able to fire the Completed event, which you will use shortly. In the case of States, Storyboards are not created by default until you modify an element property and Blend creates the Storyboard for you attached to the State.
>
> You also need a Transition time specified in order for the Storyboard to run.

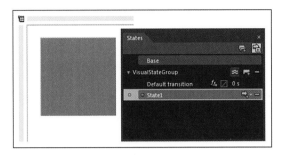

FIGURE 11.32   The new State against the new Rectangle element.

9. With the `Rectangle` element selected, open the Properties panel. Record the current value of the `Visibility` property.

10. Select the `Base` state.

11. Open the Objects and Timeline panel.

12. Create a new storyboard named StateFired.

13. Move the Playhead to `2.000`.

14. Drag the `Rectangle` element to the top right of the artboard, and just for fun, change the `Y` value of the Rotation Projection property located in the Transform category.

15. Run the animation to make sure it works.

16. Add a new `Button` element to the artboard and change its content to Play.

17. Open the Behaviors category of the Assets panel.

18. Find and drag the `GoToStateAction` behavior onto the `Button`.

19. Set the `StateName` property to `State1`, as you are calling the state in this sample and not the storyboard.

20. Open the code-behind file for `MainPage.xaml` either in Visual Studio or directly in Expression Blend.

21. Write the code in Listing 11.1 directly into the constructor, as highlighted in Figure 11.33.

LISTING 11.1   The State Storyboard Completed Event Calling the Normal Storyboard.Begin() Method

```
public partial class MainPage : UserControl
{
        public MainPage()
        {
                // Required to initialize variables
                InitializeComponent();
```

LISTING 11.1   Continued

```
         State1.Storyboard.Completed += delegate(object sender, EventArgs e)
{ StateFired.Begin(); };
      }
      }
```

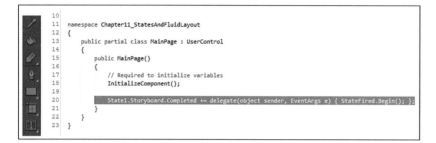

FIGURE 11.33   The code entry into the code-behind file.

You will be surprised how often a little challenge like that comes up when you start working with complex State solutions combined with animated events.

This type of challenge leads this section into another common issue when animating elements inside of fixed layout scenarios, such as a Grid.

The following steps show you how to apply FluidLayout to an animation.

1. In the same sample solution you were previously using, add a new Grid element to the rest of the body of the artboard.

2. Change the Background color to an arbitrary color.

3. Add three row and three column definitions.

4. Add a new Button element into row 0, column 0, as shown in Figure 11.34.

   You see in Figure 11.34 that the row and column definitions are purposely not spaced evenly. You should try to approximate the same dimensions in your sample. The Button is also set to stretch both horizontally and vertically, with Margin property settings of 15,15,15,15.

5. Create a new storyboard.

6. Move the Playhead to position 2.000.

7. Locate the Row and Column properties of the Button element inside the Grid and change both to 1, as shown in Figure 11.35.

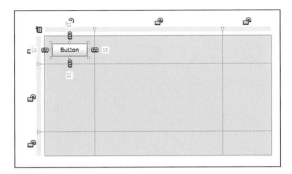

FIGURE 11.34   The sample setup with the grid and the Button element.

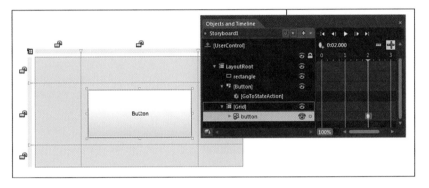

FIGURE 11.35   The storyboard with the button location change.

8. Run the animation.

   You see that the Button element doesn't move until the 2.000 position, when it suddenly jumps to the new position.

   There are quite a few properties, such as the row and column definition properties, that can't be animated for various reasons. The solution is to use a State to make this animation occur smoothly.

9. Open the State panel and create a new State called State2.

10. Turn on FluidLayout, as shown in Figure 11.36.

11. Add a * to State2 Transition and set the transition time to 2 seconds, as also shown in Figure 11.36.

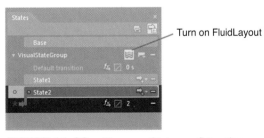

Turn on FluidLayout

FIGURE 11.36   The new State configuration.

12. With the Button element inside the grid selected, again change the Row and Column values to 1 inside the Properties panel.

13. Switch back to Base.

14. Attach a GoToStateAction Behavior to the Button element inside the Grid and set the StateName value to State2.

15. Run the application and click on the Button element inside the Grid.

You should now find a smooth animation of the Button element to the new location inside the Grid.

FluidLayout is a very elegant solution to this common problem; combining it with the storyboard call enables you to really take control of layout-based animations that require some special treatment.

Summary

You have learned a lot about animation and storyboards in a short space of time, including the secrets of working with custom splines in the Spline editor and the simple, yet visually pleasing, aspects of the Projection transforms.

Storyboards can get very complex, and you should as much as possible try to break it up into small chunks of animations, using the principles of the HandOff animation solution, and simply chain animations together for maximum flexibility.

When you combine States with storyboards and Behaviors, you can achieve pretty much any scenario that can be envisioned in a 2D or 3D environment.

CHAPTER 12

Shapes, Paths, and Effects

Expression Blend 4 sees the inclusion of a Shape library and more effects than shared in previous versions.

In total, there are 18 shapes and 15 effects available now, which enable you to work effectively with customization of imagery in the case of clip masking as well as path creation.

In this chapter, you learn how to work with shapes and effects inside of Blend, taking advantage of the tooling built in. You also work with a very exciting new Silverlight 4 control called the `PathListBox`, which enables some pretty cool usage scenarios with extremely little effort.

Taking Shape

Ok, that sub-heading is a little cheesy, but I needed to start the chapter somehow.

This chapter will not cover every one of the 18 new Shape elements here. That would result in a lot of trees being culled just for the sake of pointing out the obvious, which is that once you learn how to work with a few of the core shapes, the others will become self-explanatory.

Before you skip ahead because shapes are not really that exciting, there are some handy workflow scenarios here to look at, especially for the Shaped challenged. Making a 10-point star is simple, fast, and flexible.

Some of the shapes are not actually shapes. Let me clarify that by saying, they are not shapes technically.

Shapes are a *type* in the .Net Framework. They should not be confused with the `Path` *type* or any other `control` *type*. The distinction is important because this "*type*" fact determines if you can modify the shape by converting to a `Path`; it also comes into play if you ever need to generate one of these shapes dynamically, because you need to know the `Class` family in order to reference a `Shape` object in code.

How can you tell? Figure 12.1 shows the MouseOver details for a `Hexagon`, which points out the `Class` family and gives you the definition of the control *type*.

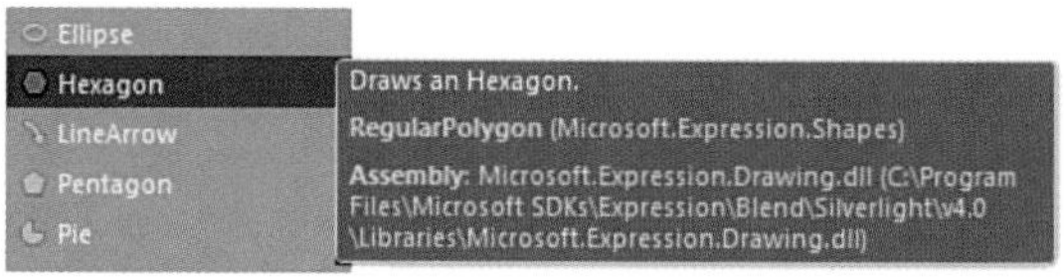

FIGURE 12.1   The MouseOver information for the hexagon shape.

The following shapes are of *type* `Shape`:

- ▶ Arcs
- ▶ All Block Arrows
- ▶ Rectangle
- ▶ Hexagon
- ▶ Line Arrow
- ▶ Pentagon
- ▶ Pie
- ▶ Ring
- ▶ Star
- ▶ Triangle

Is it a Path or a Line?

Confusing as this question appears, there is such an object specifically named as a "line" and also a tool panel item that is titled "line" but generates a "Path" element.

If you select the Line tool from the Tools panel, as shown in Figure 12.2, and draw it on the artboard, the Properties panel informs you that this is indeed a `Path` element, also shown in Figure 12.2.

In the Shapes class, an object called 'line' is also present, but this isn't represented in and easy to use drawing tool.

Element 'type'

FIGURE 12.2   A Line element from the Tools panel is indeed a type of Path element.

You never know when you might need to understand the difference, so the following will demonstrate this:

1. Create a new Silverlight Application + Website project named **"Chapter12_ShapesAndEffects"**.

2. Select the Line tool from the Tools panel and draw a `line` on the artboard of an arbitrary length. The piece you should note here is the properties, specifically in the Appearance category. Note the property *type* as a `Path` element as well.

3. Remove the `line`.

4. Enter Split Screen mode on the artboard by clicking on the Split button, as shown in Figure 12.3.

5. Modify your XAML so it resembles that shown in Figure 12.4.

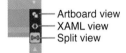

Artboard view
XAML view
Split view

FIGURE 12.3   The Split button function.

```
1  <UserControl
2      xmlns="http://schemas.microsoft.com/winfx/2006/xaml/presentation"
3      xmlns:x="http://schemas.microsoft.com/winfx/2006/xaml"
4      xmlns:ed="http://schemas.microsoft.com/expression/2010/drawing"
5      x:Class="Chapter12_ShapesAndEffects.MainPage"
6      Width="640" Height="480">
7
8      <Grid x:Name="LayoutRoot" Background="White">
9          <Line />
10     </Grid>
11  </UserControl>
```

FIGURE 12.4   The XAML to replicate.

6. You won't be able to see anything yet, so don't be alarmed. You should be able to see the element in the Objects and Timeline panel, so ensure that you have it selected. Note the Properties panel is now showing a property *type* of `Line`.

7. Open the Properties panel, and you should immediately see the difference of the Appearance category, which contains X1, X2, Y1, and Y2 properties, as shown in Figure 12.5.

8. These property values are key, but first you need to set the `Width` and `Height` properties in order to create a Shape `Viewport`. Set the `HorizontalAlignment` and `VerticalAlignment` properties both to `Center`.

FIGURE 12.5   The Appearance category properties for the Line element.

9. Set the Width and Height properties to 200 each.

10. Ensure that your Margin values are all set to 0.

11. You should now see the Viewport in the center of your artboard, but still no line.

12. Set the Fill color property to a bright red and set the Stroke property to a bright blue.

13. Set the **X**1 and **Y**1 property values to 100 in the Appearance category.

14. You should now see a line appear in the Viewport, as shown in Figure 12.6.

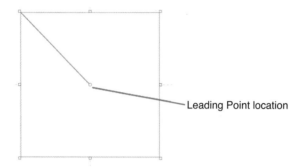

FIGURE 12.6   The line and the leading point location.

15. Essentially, the X and Y properties represent vector values that determine both the length of the line and the location. X1 and Y1 determine the leading point location of the line, as also indicated in Figure 12.6, whereas X2, Y2 determine the trailing point location. To demonstrate this, change the **X**2 and **Y**2 values to 50, which shows a shorter Line object, as shown in Figure 12.7.

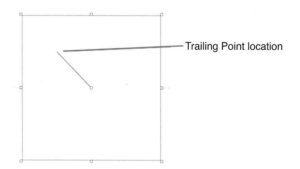

FIGURE 12.7   The new locations of the leading and trailing points that result in the new Line representation.

You can now adjust the Viewport width and height so that the line will adapt to the Viewport bounds.

Altogether, you can probably understand why the Expression team chose to enable you to create a Path element from selecting the Line tool from the Tools panel—after all, the Line element is not very intuitive and the vast majority of times that you actually want to draw a line on the artboard, you will just want to draw a line without having to consider the additional properties that must be set.

The point here is to show you that there are a lot of hidden elements and objects in the .Net Framework that are not tooled in the Blend UI. It doesn't mean you can't work with those objects, but you need to be aware that they will not always be intuitive to use.

Converting Shapes to Paths

As previously mentioned, elements that belong to the Shape family are essentially path-based elements; the line is no exception.

The requirement to modify a shape appears frequently when quickly building out proto-types or having to knock up a UI on the fly. Although for almost all the Shape elements, the properties enable you a fantastic amount of control, sometimes you need to be able to go that little bit further in customization as shown in the following steps.

1. Add a hexagon shape to your artboard and note the object *type*, as shown in Figure 12.8.

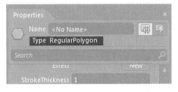

2. Open the Properties panel and find the Appearance category property called PointCount and set it to 10.

FIGURE 12.8   The RegularPolygon property type.

3. Right-click on the Hexagon and find the Path menu; then select the Convert to Path submenu item.

4. You see that nothing much has changed except for the *type* shown in the Properties panel. Select the **Direct Selection** tool on the Tools panel, and you should now see all the anchor points of the polygon path, as shown in Figure 12.9.

FIGURE 12.9   The points on the polygon path.

You are now free to modify the points of the path as you see fit. The easiest way to do this is with the Pan tool from the Tools panel.

5. Select the Pen tool from the Tools panel.

6. Move the Pen tool cursor directly over the top of any of the Polygon points, and you see that the cursor changes to show a small minus or negative sign, allowing you to delete the point. You can also move the cursor on top of any line segment and add a new point. Try to modify your polygon to look like Figure 12.10.

Table 12.1 shows the cursor modifications that occur while using the Pen tool, and Table 12.2 shows the functions of the Direct Selection tools. Some of these are available with key modifiers and represent mechanisms, enabling you to create tangents and curves against paths. It's worth you having to play around to understand the usage, especially with Alt and Shift key variants.

FIGURE 12.10   A modified polygon.

TABLE 12.1   Path Modification Cursors Using the Pen Tool

Cursor	Name	Description	Key Modifier
	Pen adjust pointer	Allows you to: ▶ Create sharp corners without smoothing. ▶ Move the tangent end point in 15-degree increments.	Alt key Shift + Alt key
	Pen insert pointer	Allows you to: ▶ Add a new point to an existing path.	
	Pen delete pointer	Allows you to: ▶ Delete an existing point from a path.	
	Pen close pointer	Allows you to: ▶ Close a path.	
	Pen join pointer	Allows you to: ▶ Create a sharp or smooth corner when joining two points on a path.	
	Pen start pointer	Allows you to: ▶ Create a new path.	Ctrl key

TABLE 12.2   Path Modification Cursors Using the Direct Selection Tool

Cursor	Name	Description	Key Modifier
	Convert point pointer	Allows you to: ▶ Make a point into a sharp corner. ▶ Make a sharp corner smooth.	Alt key
	Curve pointer	Allows you to: ▶ Create a new tangent curve with a point.	
	Convert segment pointer	Allow you to: ▶ Change curved segments to straight lines. ▶ Bend a segment into a curve.	Alt key

Combine Functions

Expression Blend provides for several Path Combine functions that are applicable only when working with two or more Path elements selected at the same time. The functions are accessed by either selecting the Object->Combine menu items or by right-clicking on multiple selected Path elements, as shown in Figure 12.11.

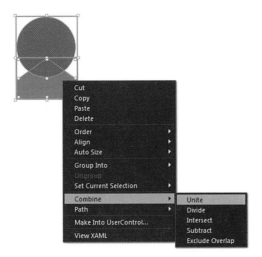

FIGURE 12.11   The Combine context menu on two elements selected.

Table 12.3 represents these functions with an example of the result applied to the same two path elements. Note that I have increased the Stroke size of the two elements to accentuate the example results.

WARNING

Does It Matter Which Element Is Selected First?

Yes. Table 12.3 shows the difference that is the result depending on the order of the Path elements selected. Sometimes, the result is merely a color change taken from the last selected element, but as Intersect shows, it can dramatically change the result.

TABLE 12.3   Path Combine Functions

Combine Function Name	Example (Path 1 Selected First)	Example (Path 2 Selected First)
Unite		
Divide		

TABLE 12.3   Continued

Combine Function Name	Example (Path 1 Selected First)	Example (Path 2 Selected First)
Intersect		
Subtract		
Exclude Overlap		

*Path 1 is represented by a blue ellipse and Path 2 by the original green polygon.

Compound Path

Compound paths are the result of two or more elements being combined, replacing the bottom-most element to result in a single Path element (see Figure 12.12).

Make Clipping Path

Using any shape converted to path or path element that you create, you can apply that shape to other elements as a Clipping Path element.

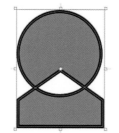

FIGURE 12.12   A compound path result.

A Clipping Path is the result of removing a visible area of one element based on the applied Path area of another.

The following steps show how to use this fun and functional feature:

1. Create or continue to use a Silverlight Application + Website project.

2. Insert an Image into your artboard by adding an existing image item to your Silverlight projects and dragging it onto your artboard.

3. Draw an Ellipse element onto your artboard and position it over your Image where you want to capture inside the clipping region, as shown in Figure 12.13. You can also see in Figure 12.13 that I reduced the opacity of the Ellipse element so I can determine the ultimate clipping location, although a Fill is not needed and is for demonstration purposes only.

4. With both the Image you inserted and the Ellipse element selected, right-click, and under the Path menu item, select Make Clipping Path. You should see a result similar to Figure 12.14.

FIGURE 12.13   The Ellipse element applied in position on the image.

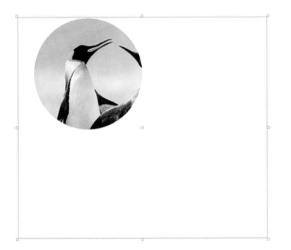

FIGURE 12.14   The resultant clipping path applied to the image.

5. You can readjust your image clip by resizing the image element using the selection tool and the Image element adorners, as shown in Figure 12.15.

You can apply a clipping path to not just images but also other panels, such as the Grid and ListBox, and of course, you can use any shape that you can think up to create the clip.

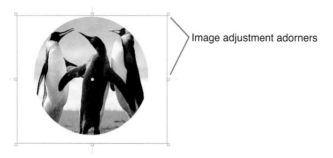

FIGURE 12.15   The Image inside the clipping path adjusted.

The New Silverlight PathListBox

There also exists several more advanced functions that you can perform with paths, such as animating objects around or along a path. In this section, you learn how to use a new Silverlight control called the PathListBox.

The PathListBox represents a lot of functionality that previously would require a developer to write hundreds if not thousands of lines of code to replicate. Using the control can be at times quite a complex set of procedures, but what you learn in the following steps is the basis of working with the control and a collection of objects that you can animate along a Path element.

1. Create a new Silverlight Application + Website project.

2. Draw an Ellipse element on your artboard and set its Width and Height properties to 200. The quickest way to do this is to double-click on the Ellipse element in the Tools panel, which gives you an Ellipse position at the top left of the artboard with a Width and Height of 100. Just adjust the Width and Height and set the HorizontalAlignment and VerticalAlignment properties to Center.

3. Center the Ellipse and ensure that it has some Fill color.

4. Right-click on the Ellipse element, and from the Path menu item on the context menu, select Make Layout Path, as shown in Figure 12.16.

5. On the artboard, it looks like nothing has happened, but if you look at the Objects and Timeline panel as shown in Figure 12.17, you see that a new element has now appeared called PathListBox.

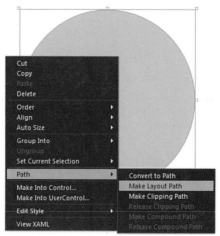

FIGURE 12.16   The context menu options for creating a layout path.

6. For the moment, ignore the Properties of the `PathListBox`; you will investigate them shortly.

Find and draw several `Star` shapes and pepper them around the screen, as shown in Figure 12.18. You could line them all up next to each other; I have simply positioned the stars so I can figure a relative amount that will spread evenly around the `Ellipse`.

FIGURE 12.17   The new PathListBox added to the Objects and Timeline panel.

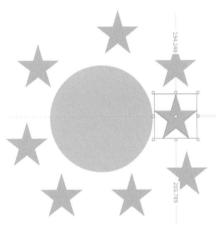

FIGURE 12.18   The random collection of star polygons.

7. In the Objects and Timeline panel, select all the `Polygon` elements representing your star shapes and then drag that collection onto the `PathListBox` element, as shown in Figure 12.19. Ensure the tooltip is indicating that the collection of elements will be moved into the `PathListBox` as child elements.

TIP

The Quickest Way to Duplicate Elements

The fastest workflow to create duplicate elements is to hold down the Alt key and drag an existing element to a new location on the artboard.

8. Your `Star` shapes should now have attached themselves to the `Ellipse` element, as shown in Figure 12.20, and be placed in a random type of spread around the element. Don't worry about this, as you will fix it in a moment with the `PathListBox` properties.

9. With the `PathListBox` element selected, take a look at the Properties panel, and the Layout Paths category specifically, which is detailed in Figure 12.21.

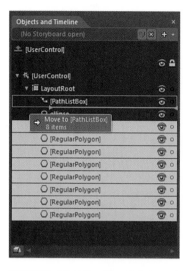

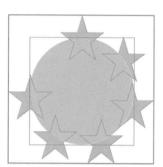

FIGURE 12.20   The polygons attached to the Ellipse path element.

FIGURE 12.19   The Polygons being added as child elements of the PathListBox.

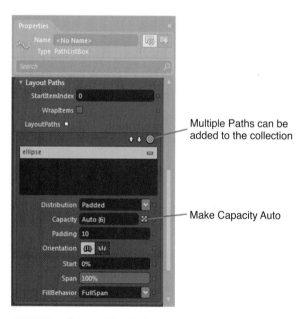

Multiple Paths can be added to the collection

Make Capacity Auto

FIGURE 12.21   The PathListBox-specific properties.

10. Note that the current Distribution property says Padded, so with your mouse, move the value of the Padding property up and down and note the effect that it has on your elements.

11. You could spend a lot of time trying to get all your elements evenly spaced around the Ellipse, and those of you who are perfectionist have probably just tried to do that. Instead, to fix the layout of your stars, select the dropdown of the Distribution property, select Even, and all should be sorted for you. The Padding property has no effect now.

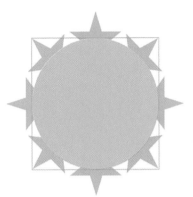

FIGURE 12.22   The orientation change of the polygons to the Path element.

12. Your stars still probably look a little strange, because they are all pointing straight up, so in the Orientation property, select the icon OrientToPath, and you should have a result similar to Figure 12.22.

13. You should now have a play with the Span property; note that this specific value constrain the maximum arc of the Ellipse path that the Polygon elements will cover. It is a percentage of your total path length, so for this example, make sure you return the value to 100% when finished investigating. At the same time, modify the Start property, which in effect changes the location of the first element (in this case, the Star polygon at the top of the Ellipse) to a new % location position on the Path element. Reset that value back to 0% when finished.

14. Select the Ellipse element in the Objects and Timeline panel, removing any color brushes that are applied to both Fill and Stroke properties.

You now have a collection of elements aligned to a Path, inside the PathListBox, which means you are ready to animate that collection around or along the path. In the following section, you create a simple storyboard that will animate the collection indefinitely.

Animating the PathListBox Collection

Animating the child collection of the PathListBox could not be easier. Remember the Start property you played around with? If you move the value all the way up to 100%, you would see that all your elements returned to their start position. That is effectively what you are going to do in your storyboard to create a never-ending animation, which is explained in the following steps.

1. In the Objects and Timeline panel, create a new storyboard using the New function or Storyboard action menu dropdown, as shown in Figure 12.23. Change the name from Storyboard1 to something more meaningful, such as "RotatingStarsInfinity."

FIGURE 12.23 The New Storyboard menu item in the Storyboard action menu dropdown.

2. With the PathListBox element select, add a keyframe at Playhead position 0.000 using the Record Keyframe button, as shown in Figure 12.24.

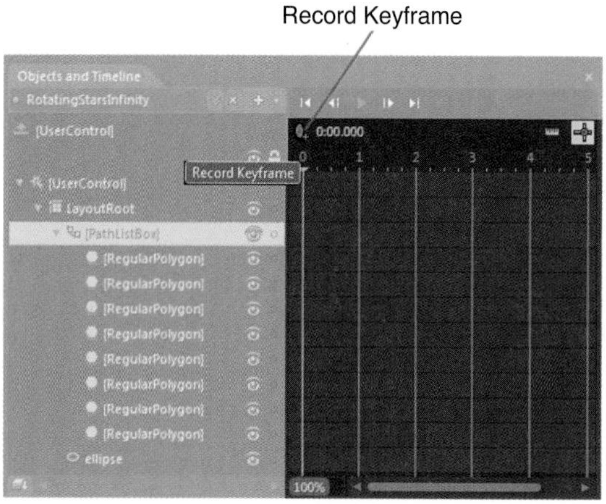

FIGURE 12.24 The Record Keyframe function.

3. Move the Playhead position guide to 3 and then, finding the Start property, change it to 100.

4. You see a new LayoutPath element added to the Objects and Timeline panel with an indication of child elements. Drill down and open all the child elements until you see the Start element, as shown in Figure 12.25.

5. Figure 12.25 also shows that if you right-click on the bar between 0 and 3 for the Start element, you will be presented with a single menu item context menu called

Edit Repeat Count, which you should now select, presenting the Edit Repeat dialog shown in Figure 12.26.

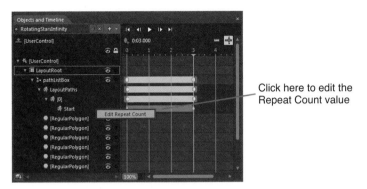

FIGURE 12.25   Where to click to modify the Repeat Count value for the specific animation.

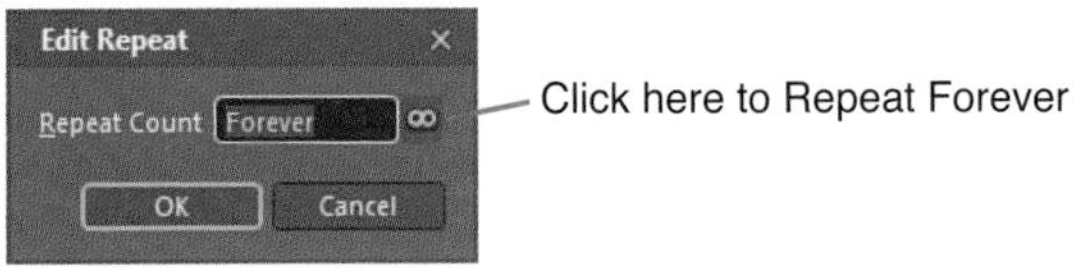

FIGURE 12.26   The Edit Repeat dialog.

6. You can enter an arbitrary number in here, but also note in Figure 12.26 that you can select "Set to forever," which you should do now.

   You are almost done here, but at the present, you don't have anything calling or firing the animation you just created. If you run the application by hitting F5, nothing will happen to your stars. This is easy to fix and requires the use of a Behavior to trigger the storyboard.

7. Close the storyboard using the Close function of the Storyboard action menu.

8. Selecting the PathListBox element again, open the Assets panel and navigate to the Behavior section.

9. Find the Behavior called "ControlStoryboardAction" and drag it onto the '[UserControl]' root element in the Objects and Timeline panel.

10. In the EventName property dropdown, you should select the Loaded event, which is also shown in Figure 12.27.

11. Next, you simply need to select the storyboard you created from the Storyboard dropdown option, also shown in Figure 12.27.

That's all there is to it!

You should be able to now run your
application with F5, and your stars
should rotate forever around the
Ellipse path element you originally
created.

Review of the PathListBox

As the name suggests, the PathListBox
control is a ListBox element, and you
can bind a collection of data, using
elements such as a collection of prices
(in a TextBox) next to a product image,
as shown in Figure 12.28 (see Chapter 9,
"Working with SketchFlow").

The PathListBox is extremely flexible in
what it lets you do to control the
elements shown, and you can also use it
to make text conform to a Path, as
shown in Figure 12.29 (see Chapter 9).

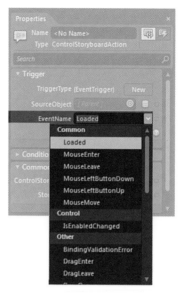

FIGURE 12.27   The Behavior property
options.

Some further resources to help you work
with the PathListBox are shown in
Appendix A, "Resources for Going Further," including a very nice sample solution that
turns the PathListBox into a Carousel-type object as created by Joanna Mason, one of the
Expression Blend team PMs.

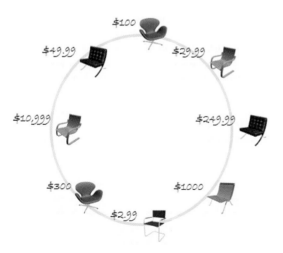

FIGURE 12.28   An example product and price in a PathListBox layout.

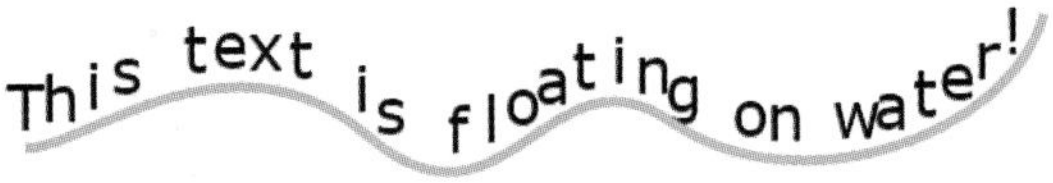

This text is floating on water!

FIGURE 12.29   Text conforming to a path.

The Magic of Effects

Earlier versions of the .Net Framework did include some simple effects that you could use, such as DropShadow and Blur. Unfortunately, those effects were also software rendered, which caused considerable performance loss to an application. Even worse still was the child relation scenario—for example, where an effect was applied to the LayoutRoot, all the child items of the LayoutRoot were also software rendered. It was a killer for the use of effects for sure.

No longer do you have this issue with .Net 4 with full hardware accelerated effects, but you should still use effects wisely in accordance to good design principles.

As previously stated, Expression Blend 4 comes with 15 effects for you to apply in various scenarios, as shown in Figure 12.30.

Effects are for most extremely simple to work with, and in the following example, you apply a simple Ripple Effect to demonstrate so:

1. Create a new Silverlight Application + Website project.

2. Add a Button element to the center of the artboard. Make the button quite large with an increased font size.

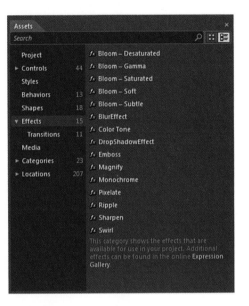

FIGURE 12.30   The Effects category in the Assets panel.

> **NOTE**
>
> **What Are Transitions in the Assets Panel?**
>
> You will also note that a sub-category of effects is "transitions" (as shown in Figure 12.30), which is discussed in detail in Chapter 9.

3. Open the Assets panel and locate the Effects category, and then the Ripple Effect.

4. Drag the Ripple Effect directly from the Assets panel to the button on the artboard or the Button element shown in the Objects and Timeline panel.

5. You see in Figure 12.31 that the Properties panel now shows the four associated properties of the `Ripple` Effect you can modify at will to see the Effect that is applied to the `Button` control.

FIGURE 12.31   The Ripple Effect applied to a Button control.

The `DropShadowEffect` Effect is shown in Figure 12.32 and again demonstrates how simple using effects in Expression Blend is.

FIGURE 12.32   The DropShadowEffect Effect applied to a Button control.

You can now animate the `Ripple` Effect in a storyboard by changing any of those four property values also.

Effects are simple and fun to use. Remember that you can animate most, if not all, the properties that are applied to them as well.

> **WARNING**
>
> **Only One Effect at a Time!**
>
> Unfortunately you can apply only one effect to a control at any given time; so, for instance, you can't have a DropShadowEffect

Summary

In this chapter, you have seen how simple it is to work with the new `PathListBox` element in Silverlight. You can certainly expect to see its use widely in future creations from people, as the functionality it provides allows for a stunning range of impressive visualization scenarios.

You have also used the very simple Effects features of Blend, which can add that certain little piece of flare to your application. Use Effects with caution, though, as too many can and will annoy your end user.

As with all good things in life, moderation is the key!

CHAPTER 13

Skins, Themes, and Resource Dictionaries

Themes and skins are one of those topics that people love talking about, but then sometimes get confused as to what is the difference is between the two, as well as how to correctly package them for reuse.

In this chapter, you will be working with Resource Dictionaries (RDs) to understand how you can apply skins to controls or create a default skin.

You will also download the Silverlight toolkit and see just how simple it is to work with the various themes that are available with it.

Does It Come in Blue?

The Silverlight or WPF platform version you are running is what will determine if your control set supports themes or has, at the very least, an easy mechanism for implementing them.

You must understand that there is a difference between the themes that can be applied in Silverlight and in WPF. Again, these are governed by the control sets that are available in your chosen platform and the mechanism by which the control is defined from the code level up.

Resource Dictionaries

One of the peculiar things about Resource Dictionaries and how people use them is that, almost always, they are used as a storage mechanism for what is perceived to be large Style storage spaces.

Users generally forget that they can store almost any property value in an RD, from a BorderThickness to a CheckBox check (Boolean value, to be technically correct).

Most new users to Blend tend to try to stick everything in a single RD, with no logical breakdown or categorization present, which becomes unwieldy and awkward to maintain.

The key (no pun intended) to working with Resource Dictionaries like all solution resources is to plan how you will share and distribute those resources contained within them—even if at the outset of your solution creation, you have no intention of doing so. It's just good practice.

The following steps demonstrate my preferred method of creating a separate project that contains all RDs. I call this a Resource Vault, as it enables you to share all resources across any project you add to your solution, as well as easily change out the RDs at design time. Your developers can also add the relatively simple code to load new RDs at runtime should it be a requirement.

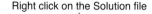

Right click on the Solution file

FIGURE 13.1   How to add a new project to the solution.

1. Create a new Silverlight Application + Website solution.

2. In the Project panel, right-click on the solution and select to add a new Project, as shown in Figure 13.1.

3. Select to add a new Silverlight Control Library project, as shown in Figure 13.2, naming it something meaningful. Note that I have appended my project name with "ResourceVault," as I typically store these projects all together for future reuse.

   You will now be presented with a new project in your Project panel, and it should be automatically populated with a user control called MainControl.xaml, as shown in Figure 13.3.

4. Open the Project menu and select to build the project.

The first step to using this new project is to reference it within your main working project. When you just opted to build your project, a new type of file called a "DLL" was created that contains all the contents of the new project. Referencing this new DLL file is what provides a link to any of the resources you add to it, into your existing solution.

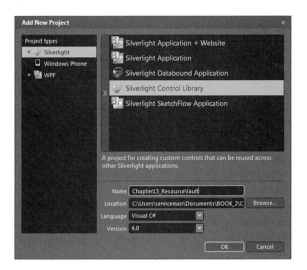

FIGURE 13.2   The project that you should add to your solution.

FIGURE 13.3   The newly added project into the solution.

There are two methods available to reference this new content:

1. A file reference, which is where you would link directly to the DLL file just created.

2. A project reference that lets you work with the source directly.

If you are going to send your resources to someone else to use in the future, you can just send them the DLL file. They don't need to open or change any of the resources you are sharing with them—at least not in your file—but they will be able to copy those resources locally to modify them.

In this scenario, you want to work with a project reference, so you can create new resources and modify them as you go. The following steps show you how to add a Project reference.

1. In the Project panel, locate the working project you first created and find the "References" folder, which is represented by a silver-looking icon.

2. Right-click on that References folder, and you see the two options mentioned previously.

3. Select the Add Project Reference option, which then provides you with your new project available to reference, as shown in Figure 13.4.

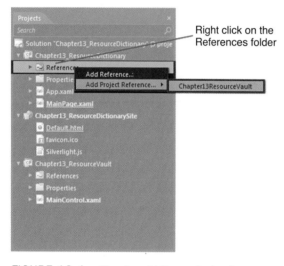

FIGURE 13.4   How to add the project reference.

Once completed, you will now be able to see your project reference inside the References folder, as indicated by the .csproj extension shown in Figure 13.5. If you have created a file reference, you would naturally see a .dll extension in its place.

At any time, you can right-click on the reference inside the References folder and opt to remove the reference. This doesn't delete your file, but merely removes the reference link.

WARNING

References Are One Way!

You have now referenced one project to another, which is a one-way reference. You cannot now reference the main project from the ResourceVault or this will cause what is known as a circular reference. A circular reference means that one object could reference another object in another project, which then references that same object from the previous project—and around it goes into a never-ending cycle of reference that breaks programming logic and therefore is not allowed.

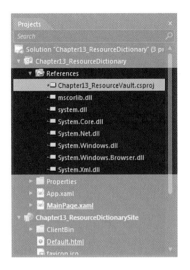

FIGURE 13.5   The new reference added.

What Is the Difference Between a Skin and a Theme?

Generally speaking, a *skin* is referred to as the collection of visual Styles applied to an individual element. A *theme* contains a collection of skins for many controls—not the controls themselves.

Throughout various chapters in this book, you have worked with Styles visually. In most occasions, you have worked locally to the scene or user control, directly placing the resources created without much regard for their reuse.

Setting Up the ResourceVault

Within Expression Blend, you can create Styles and work with them directly in the context of the scene you are working in, or you can store those Styles in a RD. There is a significant difference in the editing experience depending on the option you choose; the vast majority of time, it is much easier to work locally within a scene first and then store your resource in the RD when you are completed the editing experience. It is for this reason that I opt to keep the MainControl.xaml file that is automatically created in the project and use it as a scrapbook in many ways.

In my experience, it is always better to define meaningful collections of RDs that are descriptive and refer to the contents inside them. Thus, in the following sample, you are going to create a series of empty RDs for future use.

You can create Resource Dictionaries at many points while using Blend, as various dialogs pop up, as well as directly from the File menu -> New Item:

1. Right-click on the ResourceVault project and opt to Add New Item.

2. Select Resource Dictionary from the New Item dialog and name it Colors.xaml, as shown in Figure 13.6.

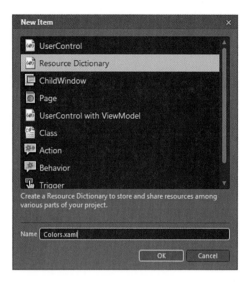

FIGURE 13.6   The Resource Dictionary entry in the New Item dialog.

3. Click OK to close the dialog.

4. Perform this step again, creating a `Controls.xaml` Resource Dictionary.

When you open the Resources panel, you should see that your two Resource Dictionaries are now present, as shown in Figure 13.7.

Working in Context of the Resource Dictionaries

In the following sample, you are going to create a simple resource to work with: a `Button`. You also learn how to reuse the skin within the context of your scene and then the solution. First, you are going to create a series of color resources and then a brush resource for use with the `Button`, working directly in the Resource Dictionaries:

1. If closed, reopen the `MainControl.xaml` file in your ResourceVault.

> **WARNING**
>
> **Be Careful What You Select!**
>
> Make 100% sure that you select a Resource Dictionary in the New Item dialog and not a User Control. It's an easy mistake to make if you are working fast. You can tell the difference between the two inside the Projects panel because an RD has no code-behind file as a User Control does, so there is no arrow next to the item shown in the project.

FIGURE 13.7   The current collection in the Resources panel.

2. Add a `Border` element to the scene, rounding the corners to your choice.

3. Select the `Background` property for the `Border` element in the Properties panel.

4. Select to use a SolidColorBrush.

5. Make a choice of a nice aqua blue color.

6. Select the Convert Color to Resource button, as shown in Figure 13.8.

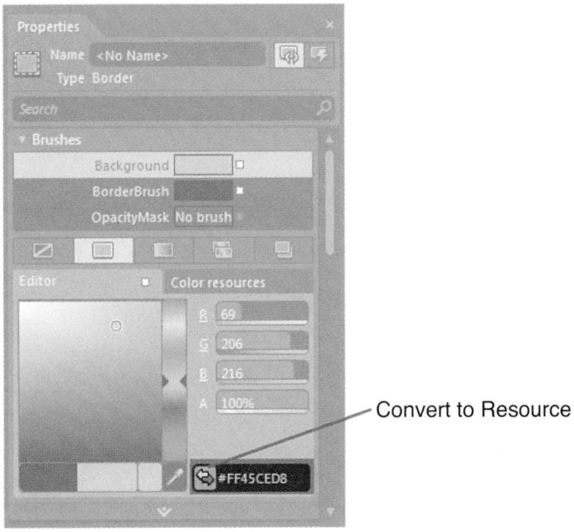

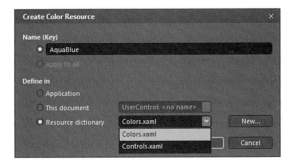

FIGURE 13.8   Where the Convert to Resource button is.

7. You should now be presented with the Create Color Resource dialog, as shown in Figure 13.9.

FIGURE 13.9   The Create Color Resource dialog.

Also shown in Figure 13.9 is the Name (or Key) I have given to the resource. Note that the Resource Dictionary option is selected, and the available Resource Dictionaries are shown in the dropdown box (also note that you can create a new RD here as well).

8. Select OK to add the new resource.

You should now see that in the Properties panel, your Background property for the Border element is referencing the new color resource. Also, the Resource panel now shows the representation inside the Colors RD, as shown in Figure 13.10.

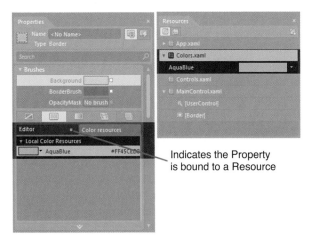

Indicates the Property
is bound to a Resource

FIGURE 13.10   The new resource both referenced in the Properties panel and present in the RD.

Also shown in Figure 13.10 is the green box that is now present on the Editor tab to indicate that the property is bound to a resource.

The following steps show you how to use the referenced resources.

1. In the Properties panel, click on the Editor tab to return to the color palette editor.

2. Create a new color that is a dark blue.

3. Convert this color to a resource, storing it in the Colors RD, and name it DarkBlue.

4. Return to the Editor tab, this time changing the Brush *type* to a GradientBrush.

5. By default, you have two GradientStops available for the Gradient definition. Select the one on the left and then select the Color resources tab.

6. Select the AquaBlue resource and notice that the Editor tab Advanced Options box has turned green to indicate the binding.

7. Select the right side GradientStop and repeat the process of binding to the DarkBlue resource, as shown in Figure 13.11.

From this point on, if you want to change the colors used by the GradientBrush, you can change the colors directly in the RD by selecting the color in the Resource Dictionary. This opens an editor similar to the Brushes category of the Properties panel, as shown in Figure 13.12.

FIGURE 13.12 The in-resource editing experience for the color.

FIGURE 13.11 The GradientStops bound to the Color resources.

What is really quite cool is to now create a Brush resource from the GradientBrush you have just created, which maintains the links through to the individual color resource as well:

1. Select the Advanced Options button of the Background property and select the Convert to New Resource... option, as shown in Figure 13.13.

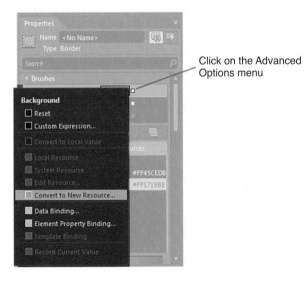

Click on the Advanced Options menu

FIGURE 13.13 How to create a new Brush resource.

2. You are now presented with the Create Brush Resource dialog. Name your Brush a descriptive name and then, next to the Resource Dictionary option, select the New button to create a Brushes RD.

3. Select the new RD as the location to store the resource and click OK to close the dialog.

FIGURE 13.14   The updated Resource panel.

Figure 13.14 shows how your Resources panel should now look, with your collection of color resources and the new Brushes RD containing your GradientBrush resource.

Try editing one of your colors now to view the live changes that are made as you change your selection.

Resource Allocation Viewing

Because you have only a few resources now in your solution, it is very easy to work with them and to remember which elements are using which resources. As your dictionaries grow, however, and other members of your team add to the collection, you might need to narrow in

> **NOTE**
>
> **Resource Bound GradientBrushes Are Not Editable**
>
> One of the only issues with binding the resources all the way through the RD collection like you have just done is that the color resources are not able to be animated. This is a defect in the platform and apparently will never be fixed. Unfortunately, the only workaround you have if that is your use case is to set the GradientStop colors manually.

on the exact resources that are being used. For this task, you can change the view of the Resource panel to show exactly that information:

1. Ensure that you have the Border element selected in the Objects and Timeline panel.

2. In the Resource panel, select the "Show resources used by the selected element" button, as shown in Figure 13.15.

3. Select the "Show all resources" button to return to the previous view.

Working in Context of the Scene

Working with colors is straightforward, as the editing experience directly in the Resource panel is similar to that of the Properties panel. Now you are going to create the Button and view the difference of scene context and resource context:

1. Select the Border element.

2. Right-click and select the Make Into Control... menu option.

3. You should be presented with the Make Into Control dialog. Search for the Button control *type* and give it a meaningful name, such as PrimaryButton1, as shown in Figure 13.16.

4. Leave this resource to be defined in "This document," as also shown in Figure 13.16.

5. Click OK to close the dialog.

Show all resources

Show resources used by the selected element

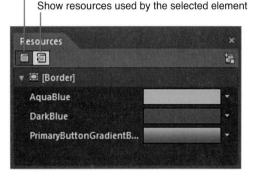

FIGURE 13.15 The selected element resource usage.

You should now see that you have a Button resource available at the bottom of your Resource panel. Above that, you should see the UserControl element, which represents your current scene; nested within it is your new PrimaryButton1 skin, as shown in Figure 13.17.

FIGURE 13.16 The Make Into Control dialog.

FIGURE 13.17 The new resource is shown.

13

You could now drag that resource straight onto the artboard to create a new instance of a Button with your skin automatically applied if you need to.

You will also note that your Objects and Timeline panel is inside the template of the Button control, enabling you to change the controls or Style as desired. If you did modify the control now, you would still see the changes on the artboard, which would look normal; but what happens if your skin is not located in this scene?

The following sample demonstrates the difference:

1. Select the PrimaryButton1 skin in the Resources panel.

2. Right-click and opt to "Cut" the resource. You are presented with the Existing References Found dialog, as shown in Figure 13.18.

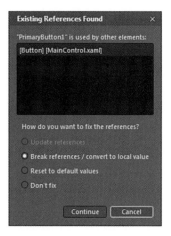

FIGURE 13.18   The Existing References Found dialog.

The dialog shows all the other elements that are referencing that skin or resource and provides you with several options to fix the reference.

Update References

Blend attempts to update all the elements that use the reference to point to the new location of the reference or remove the reference.

Break References / Convert to Local Value

This option takes a copy of the referenced skin and creates a local copy of the resource.

Reset to Default Values

This option removes the reference completely and, in this case, the Button element returns to a default button.

Don't Fix

This option leaves the reference in place:

1. Select Don't fix.

2. Click Continue to close the dialog. The Button reverts to its default, as shown in Figure 13.19. An error now shows in the Results panel, indicating that the reference is broken.

FIGURE 13.19   The broken reference to the skin.

3. Open the Resource panel.

4. Select the Controls Resource Dictionary.

5. Right-click and select Paste; you should see that the reference to the skin is now restored.

6. In the skin resource you have just pasted into the Control RD, you should see an image next to it, which is in fact a Button enabling you to edit the resource. Select that Button to edit the resource in the context of the Resource Dictionary.

Note that several things have now changed in the Blend user interface. You no longer have an artboard, just a representation of your control in the middle of the screen. Your Objects and Timeline panel has you editing the Style directly.

You can work in this context, but you don't really have an understanding of the size of the element you are working with. Most importantly you won't be able to see any additional elements in your scene that you might be trying to style with the same continuity.

You can scope up on the Objects and Timeline panel to exit the editing experience. You might not return to your artboard because you are in fact inside the Controls.xaml file, so you need to double-click on the MainControls.xaml file to return to your artboard.

Multiple Style Resources Within a Single Skin

Sometimes you can't escape the out-of-context editing view. This is particularly hard when working with much more complex control skins, such as the ComboBox or a ScrollBar, where you need to dive down through several control Styles to edit certain Buttons and Borders and their Styles contained within.

To get a better understanding of this complexity, the following sample takes you into the outer layer of the ScrollBar skin:

1. Open the Assets panel and search for a ScrollBar element.

2. Add it to your artboard, drawing it in the default vertical appearance.

3. Right-click on the ScrollBar and select the Edit Template -> Edit a Copy... menu items, as shown in Figure 13.20.

4. Leave the default Style name and location; click OK to close the dialog.

5. In the Objects and Timeline panel, scope up and out of the ScrollBar template.

6. Open the Resource panel.

7. Select to show the resources used by the selected element at the top of the Resources panel, as shown in Figure 13.21.

FIGURE 13.20   Where the current Style can be edited as a copy to the local scene.

As you can see in Figure 13.21, by default you have eight Style resources that come with the ScrollBar element. You can edit each one individually directly in the Resources panel, and that takes you to the out-of-context editing experience, which makes the job all the more difficult.

The other concern that you should have is that the names of all the new Styles from the ScrollBar skin are generic and are shared by other controls. So, if you make one of those templates red—for example, the RepeatButtonTemplate—if you edit another control that shares the generic naming convention of the RepeatButton, it will turn red as well and might look completely out of place.

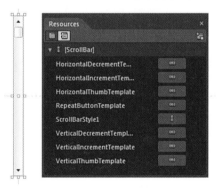

FIGURE 13.21   The multiple Styles used by the default skin of the ScrollBar element.

The golden rule here is to remember to give new or copies of generic Styles a meaningful name that is relevant to the skin that you are editing.

You must also remember to cut and paste all the Styles into the Resource Dictionary if you intend on sharing the skin.

Using the ResourceVault in Your Solution

Now that you have created some simple resources and added them into your ResourceVault project, you can begin to use them in other solutions.

At the start of this chapter, you created a project reference to the resource vault. One of the side effects of performing that step first is that each Resource Dictionary you created was by default added to the App.xaml file, and therefore has already become available globally to your main solution, which is the resource panel (see Figure 13.22).

FIGURE 13.22   The links to the Resource Dictionaries already in the App.xaml file.

In other words, you could indeed create a Button element in your MainPage.xaml file, and the skin you created would be available for use right away as detailed in the following steps.

1. In your original project, open MainPage.xaml.

2. Add a Button element to your artboard.

3. Right-click on the button and select Edit Template ->Apply Resource -> PrimaryButton1, as shown in Figure 13.23.

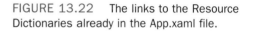

FIGURE 13.23   The resource link available automatically.

What happens if you didn't have that reference applied from the start, or if one of your team just sent you a completed Resource Dictionary, or if you just got a DLL file containing the vault?

The following sample replicates this scenario:

1. Delete the Button element you just added to the artboard.

2. Open the Resources panel.

3. Drill open the App.xaml item.

4. Right-click on each of the three Resource Dictionaries and select Delete to remove the link, which shows a warning dialog onscreen that doing so may cause an issue. It is OK to continue with the action.

5. Draw a new Button element on the artboard.

6. Right-click on the Button and select Edit Template. Notice that you no longer have the option to apply the skin resource.

   You can relink a Resource Dictionary directly back to the App.xaml file if you intend to use the skin resource globally in your solution, but in this scenario, you are going to link directly to the scene that you are working in.

7. Open the Resources panel.

8. Locate the UserControl element at the bottom.

9. Right-click and select Link to Resource Dictionary ->Controls.xaml, as shown in Figure 13.24.

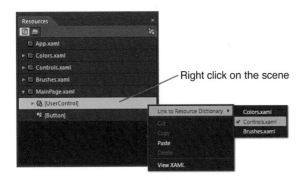

FIGURE 13.24   How to link to the Resource Dictionary.

10. Right-click on the Button element in your artboard and select Edit Template->Apply Resource->PrimaryButton1.

Are you surprised that your Button element doesn't look quite right? This is because the Colors.xaml and Brushes.xaml files are not linked to your scene.

To show that resource resolution works across the scope of your solution, you can relink the App.xaml file to both the colors and brushes Resource Dictionaries:

1. Open the Resources panel.

2. Select the App.xaml element.

3. Right-click and select Link to Resource Dictionary -> Colors.xaml.

4. Do the same for the Brushes RD.

Your button skin should now resolve correctly.

Creating a Default Skin

Creating a default skin is very simple. Remember that when you created your resource, you gave it a name or key value of PrimaryButton1. The result of giving the skin a name is that it must be explicitly referenced by a Button element in order to be used. If you had created a skin and opted not to give it a key value, it would then become the default Style applied to those *types* of elements within the scope of the RD reference.

It is simple to create that now without having to go through the creation of the Style process again:

1. Right-click on the button and select Edit Template->Edit a copy....

2. You see the Create Style Resource dialog, as shown in Figure 13.25.

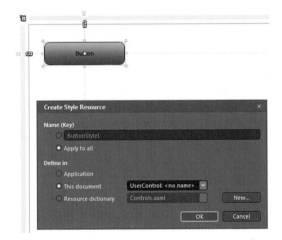

FIGURE 13.25   The Creation of the default Style.

3. Ensure that you click on the Apply to all radio button.

4. Leave the setting to Define in This document, also shown in Figure 13.25.

5. Click OK to close the dialog.

   You are automatically entered into template editing mode, where you can scope up and out of directly in the Objects and Timeline panel. Notice that a new element

[Button default] is added to the Resources panel under your UserControl representing this scene.

6. Add a new Button element to the artboard.

Your skin is applied to the Button element as soon as you add it.

Using Themes in Expression Blend

As discussed at the start of this chapter, a theme represents a collection of skins or Styles.

There are several sites on the Internet that can provide you with themes for any of the platforms that you are working in, and you will find that they are quite simple to implement in your solution:

1. Go to the following URL:

   http://goo.gl/EkWy4

2. You should see a selection of themes that are available in the Silverlight platform.

3. Close any open versions of Expression Blend.

4. Click on the Downloads button, and you can then download the toolkit.

   Download the toolkit and install it, following the instructions that are provided on the CodePlex site and installation screens.

5. Open Expression Blend.

6. Create a new Silverlight Application + Website solution.

7. Open the Assets panel.

8. Type the word "theme" into the search box, and you should see that all the themes from the toolkit are now available to you, as shown in Figure 13.26.

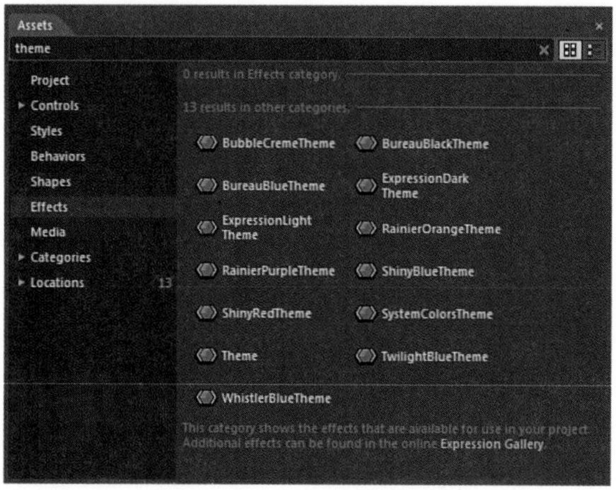

FIGURE 13.26   The theme collection available in the Assets panel.

The usage is very simple, as the theme is applied as a ContentControl into your scene. You simply use the entire theme as the base panel to add the rest of the control element to, and those newly added elements automatically inherit skin provided by the theme (if available):

1. Ensure that you have the LayoutRoot element selected in the Objects and Timeline panel.

2. Double-click on the ShinyRedTheme from the Assets panel.

FIGURE 13.27   The newly added Theme panel.

3. You now see a small panel added to the artboard, as shown in Figure 13.27.

4. Select this element in the Objects and Timeline panel.

5. Open the Properties panel and set the Theme element size to stretch the entire width and height of the artboard.

6. Add a new Grid element to the center of the artboard, which is a child element of the [ShinyRedTheme] element inside the Objects and Timeline panel.

7. Draw a new Button element into the Grid.

8. Draw a new RadioButton element into the Grid.

9. Draw a new ScrollBar element into the Grid.

10. Draw a Slider element into the Grid.

You should now have an artboard that looks similar to Figure 13.28.

13

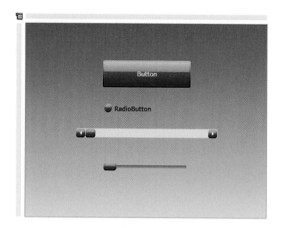

FIGURE 13.28   The theme applied to the new elements added as child elements of the Grid and Theme panel.

Summary

In this chapter, you have learned how to effectively use the Resources panel to manage skins and the collections of Styles that they might contain. You have also learned how to use them wisely in a separate project, as well as how to reference and then reuse those resources accordingly.

You have also implemented themes provided in the Silverlight toolkit, which makes using generic control sets simple inside a Theme panel.

Managing your resources can become a very big challenge if you allow it to get out of control, especially if you are editing a lot of custom control elements that share common Style components. For this reason, naming and placing of resources is key to your success.

CHAPTER 14

Advanced Controls

Introduction

What constitutes an advanced control? This is a subjective topic in some senses, but for this book, it is not necessarily about a control with advanced features, but more about controls that you need to work with at a deeper property level than simple values applied to properties that the control supplies.

This chapter is not about working with the more advanced controls (as some of them could almost have a book written entirely on them), but more of a sample view to the types of controls that are available.

Also provided are some links to help you find out more in-depth information if you are interested in working further with those controls.

The WPF and Silverlight Toolkits

The WPF and Silverlight toolkits are an invaluable addition to the platforms, providing extended and additional controls that the Microsoft development teams have created out of band (out of normal release cycles).

Links

Several of the controls shown in this chapter are from the toolkits, which can be downloaded from the CodePlex home pages at the following links:

http://wpf.codeplex.com/

http://silverlight.codeplex.com/

The DataGrid Control

The DataGrid control was a late edition to the Silverlight collection provided by Microsoft and in truth was added due to the take up and direction of Silverlight toward providing functionality for line of business (LOB) application development.

When you add a DataGrid element to a solution, at first all you see is a big blank box, and you are left trying to determine where you should start.

As a starting point to working with the DataGrid, you can create a sample data set and drag it straight onto a DataGrid element, which will then automatically populate the control with random content, as shown in Figure 14.1.

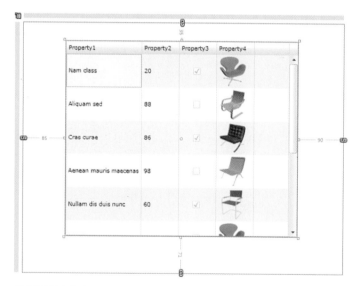

FIGURE 14.1   The DataGrid element populated with sample data.

You are then able to modify various properties and templates of the DataGrid element and visualize what effects those changes are making.

The DataGrid contains one of the largest exposed property sets of all controls. Looking quickly at the Brushes category of the Properties panel for a DataGrid, as shown in Figure 14.2, shows you just how much flexibility you have when determining the style of the control.

Other categories in the Properties panel also contain larger than normal collections of properties, as well as the Advanced Properties areas. You should explore all of those properties and experiment with what those property settings provide.

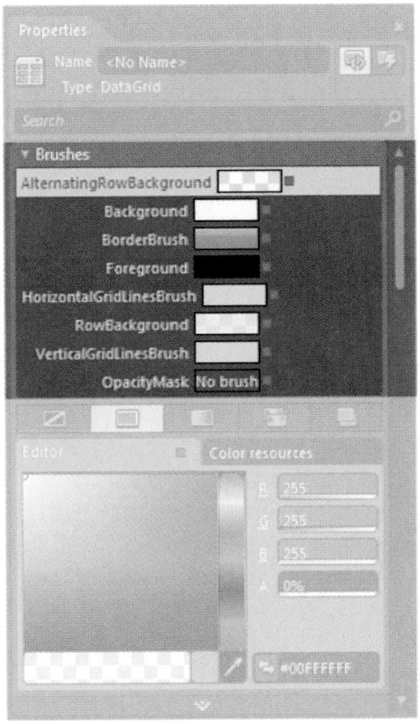

The DataGrid Template Array

The DataGrid element is an inherently complex control as it deals with DataTemplates, selected items, rows, columns, headers, cells, and numerous other points of definition.

Accessing the Style template has, for the most part, been extracted outwardly to save you from having to work with a horrendous level of depth to get to some of the detail of those areas. To find them, you need to look in the generated template collection, as shown in Figure 14.3.

FIGURE 14.2   The large Brushes property collection available for the DataGrid element.

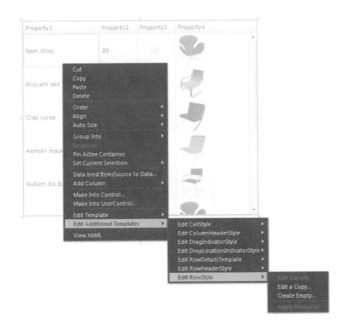

FIGURE 14.3   How to access the many generated templates.

You get an astounding amount of functionality be default in the DataGrid element, as shown in Figure 14.4, which displays the running solution. The figure shows the ability to sort any of the columns and reorder them, as well as edit the cell values. The properties that control this functionality are located in the Advanced Properties of the Common Properties category of the Properties panel.

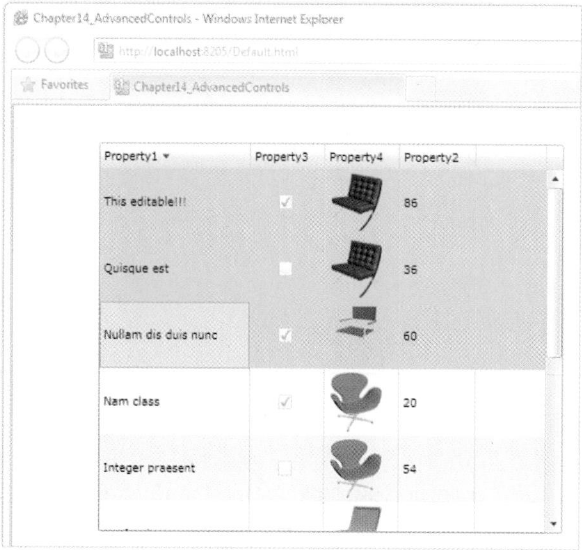

FIGURE 14.4   The level of interaction available to the default DataGrid element.

Link

For explicit information regarding the control, please review the following link:

http://goo.gl/ciXty

The DataForm

Interestingly, quite a number of people who have been using Expression Blend for a while don't realize that there is indeed a DataForm control that works directly in the editor.

The usage can be complex with customized data sources attached to the control, but in terms of generating a simple and easy-to-style form automatically, the DataForm gets you a result very fast.

As with the DataGrid element, simply draw the element on your artboard and then drag a data source collection onto the control, and automatically the fields are created for you, as shown in Figure 14.5. You can now create a style that works with the form type by editing the style templates from the generated content.

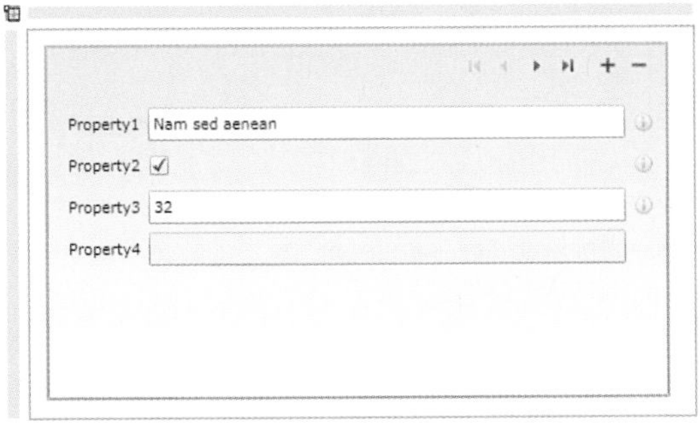

FIGURE 14.5   The simple DataForm control.

Link

A great video on using the DataForm is produced here by Mike Taulty:

http://goo.gl/jALSY

Silverlight Charts

A robust set of charts are available for Silverlight that are quite hidden in the Asset panel after you install the Silverlight toolkit.

You can locate the control in the Asset panel by searching for the Chart and drawing the element directly onto the artboard. This results in a default visualization containing a very basic Column Series chart, as shown in Figure 14.6.

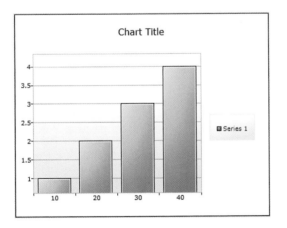

FIGURE 14.6   The default chart element.

What is a little disappointing is that the addition of data to fill the chart visualization is not directly supported in the Properties panel, and you need to then work at the XAML or code level to create a series of points to inject into the series. Listing 14.1 shows an example of the XAML used to display sample data.

LISTING 14.1   The Sample XAML to View Data

```
                    <toolkit:Chart Margin="88,52,88,69" Title="Chart Title"
d:IsHidden="True">
                        <toolkit:ColumnSeries DependentValuePath="X"
IndependentValuePath="Y">
                            <toolkit:ColumnSeries.ItemsSource>
                                <PointCollection>
                                    <Point>1,10</Point>
                                    <Point>2,20</Point>
                                    <Point>3,30</Point>
                                    <Point>4,40</Point>
                                </PointCollection>
                            </toolkit:ColumnSeries.ItemsSource>
                        </toolkit:ColumnSeries>
                    </toolkit:Chart>
```

Even more hidden are the chart visualization series types that are supported by the Chart element. There are approximately 15 available, and you can find them by searching for the term "Series" in the Asset panel.

Figure 14.7 shows the BubbleSeries implemented using the same PointCollection structure as referred to in Listing 14.1.

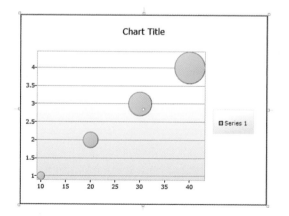

FIGURE 14.7   The BubbleSeries in the Chart element.

Link

Rudi Grobler has put together a great CodeProject article on using the chart control, which can be found here:

http://goo.gl/xsPlb

InkPresenter

The InkPresenter control is a panel that you can use to allow the user to draw directly onto the interface in a simple and effective way.

As you see in Listing 14.2, the crux of working with the InkPresenter is injecting a Stroke collection into the control.

LISTING 14.2   The Code for Collection the Mouse Input and Converting That Into Strokes for the InkPresenter to Present

```
private Stroke inkStroke = null;

        private void inkPresenter_MouseLeftButtonDown(object sender,
MouseButtonEventArgs e)
        {
            inkPresenter.CaptureMouse();
            this.inkStroke = new Stroke();

this.inkStroke.StylusPoints.Add(e.StylusDevice.GetStylusPoints(inkPresenter)); ;
            this.inkStroke.DrawingAttributes.Color = Colors.Red ;
            inkPresenter.Strokes.Add(this.inkStroke);
        }

        private void inkPresenter_MouseMove(object sender, MouseEventArgs e)
        {
            if (this.inkStroke != null) {
this.inkStroke.StylusPoints.Add(e.StylusDevice.GetStylusPoints(inkPresenter)); }
        }

        private void inkPresenter_MouseLeftButtonUp(object sender,
MouseButtonEventArgs e)
        {
            this.inkStroke = null;
        }
```

I am sure you can come up with much more creative uses for the control than I have, as shown in Figure 14.8.

Link

There is a great article in a MSDN article that takes you through creating an entire solution using the InkPresenter:

http://goo.gl/0iYXH

14

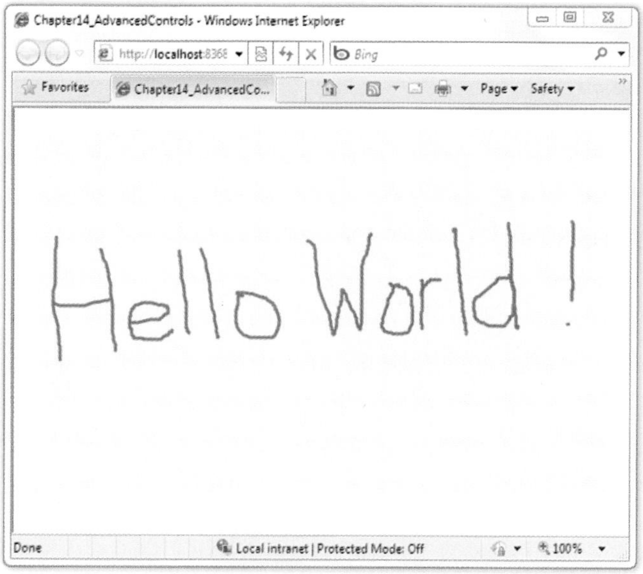

FIGURE 14.8   A simple InkPresenter in action.

AutoComplete Textbox

This handy control enables you to bind a collection of `strings` to the `ItemSource` property either in XAML or in code, as shown in Listing 14.3. As you would expect, the usage is a letter is typed into the control, and a dropdown of matching values is available for selection, as shown in Figure 14.9.

LISTING 14.3   A Simple Code Sample Injecting Some Country Names into the Control

```
public partial class AutoComplete : UserControl
{
        public AutoComplete()
        {
                // Required to initialize variables
                InitializeComponent();
        this.LoadCountryData();
}

        private void LoadCountryData()
        {
        ObjectCollection Countries = new ObjectCollection();
        Countries.Add("Abkhazia");
        Countries.Add("Afghanistan ");
        Countries.Add("Aland Islands ");
        Countries.Add("Albania ");
```

LISTING 14.3   Continued

```
            Countries.Add("Algeria ");
            Countries.Add("American Samoa ");
            Countries.Add("Andorra ");
            Countries.Add("Angola ");
            Countries.Add("Anguilla ");
            Countries.Add("Antigua and Barbuda ");
            Countries.Add("Argentina ");
            Countries.Add("Armenia ");
            Countries.Add("Aruba ");
            Countries.Add("Australia ");
            Countries.Add("Austria ");
            Countries.Add("Azerbaijan ");

            this.AutoBox.ItemsSource = Countries;
        }
    }
```

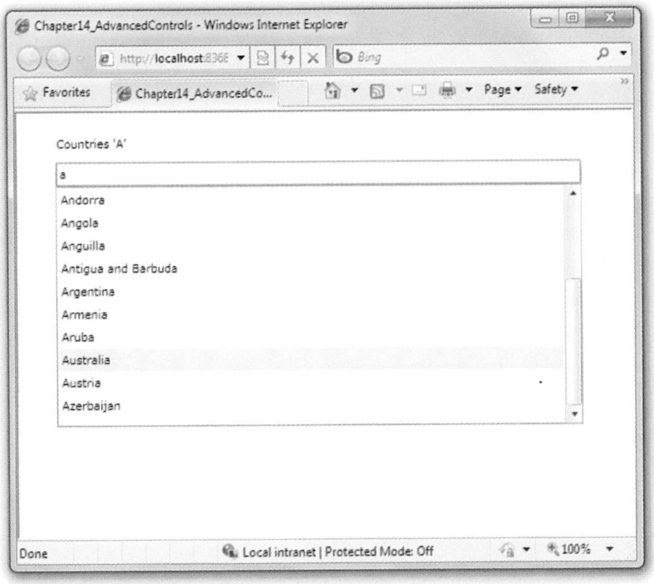

FIGURE 14.9   Tthe AutoComplete Textbox control in action.

Link

More information can be found on the AutoComplete Textbox and its usage at the Silverlight toolkit home page:

http://goo.gl/D850L

WPF Extended Toolkit

Brian Lagunas has created an extended toolkit for WPF that contains some controls ported to WPF from Silverlight and some controls that Brian just wanted to share. The toolkit contains several controls that are very useful in certain use cases, so two of those controls are showcased here to entice you to take a further look.

Magnifier

The `Magnifier` is an effect that is applied against `UIElements` to produce, as the name says, a magnification of a visual.

Simply download and install the extended toolkit and then reference the DLL file in your solution to access the control.

Open the Asset panel and search for the effect by name, dragging it directly onto the element in the artboard or the Objects and Timeline panel. You have several properties of the effect that you can change to suit in the Properties panel, as shown in Figure 14.10.

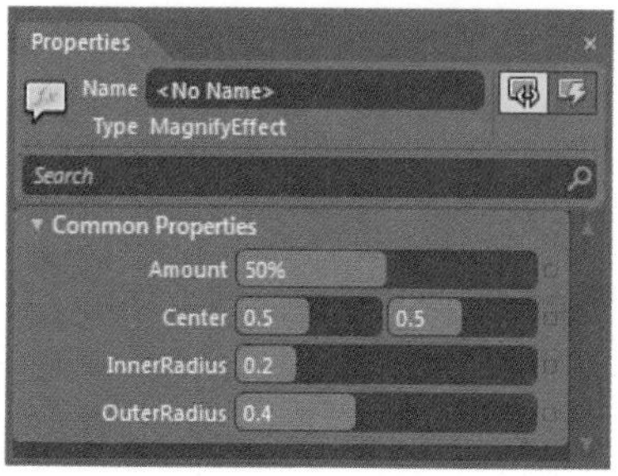

In the sample solution, I have added a simple image file and then applied the `MagnifyEffect` to the image, as shown in Figure 14.11.

FIGURE 14.10   The effect properties available.

FIGURE 14.11   The MagnifyEffect in action.

MaskedTextBox

Of particular use to those creating line of business (LOB) applications, this simple
MaskedTextBox provides a welcome feature in enabling you to lock down the specific
input into the control.

As with any additional TextBox element,
you simply draw the element on the
screen and then locate the Mask property
to which you can specify a large variety
of mask operations, as Brian Lagunas
details in the documentation of the
control.

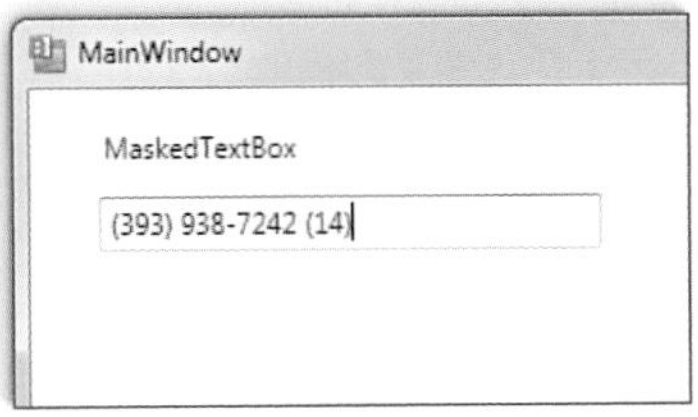

The simple sample shown in Figure
14.12 displays how the MaskedTextBox
has a specific pattern of input that has
been set in the Mask property.

FIGURE 14.12   The MaskedTextBox in
simple usage.

Link

You can find the download to the Extended toolkit and all the supporting documentation
at the following CodePlex home page link:

http://goo.gl/3Kx35

Summary

You by now are able to work with most components provided in the platforms that Blend
supports. It is recommended that you download trial versions of controls where possible
and ensure that they provide an adequate design time solution and not just developer
support.

There are literally hundreds of controls available, both from commercial component
manufacturers and from plenty of open source offerings that are a great augmentation to
your toolkit in general.

Windows Phone 7

This chapter almost never made it into the book. After all, the primary goal of this book is to teach you how to use Expression Blend 4 as a tool for all platforms and not just a specific one, such as Windows Phone 7 (WP7).

I justified it in the end because I think it's important for a number of reasons—the least of all being that you need to see the differences in Blend when using different platform project types. Also, Microsoft kindly gave me a mule (test) device several months before launch, so I felt compelled to spread the goodness.

In this chapter, you create a working application for WP7, reviewing some of the functionality that the platform offers, but most importantly, how Expression Blend helps you to produce such an application using some very sweet design templates and a touch of code magic at the end.

> ### NOTE
>
> **What You Need for This Chapter**
>
> The Windows Phone 7 Emulator is very good at easing you into this type of development without the need to purchase a device. All the tools and software provided by Microsoft is free and readily available.
>
> All you need to provide is the creativity!

And on the 8th Day...

Las Vegas, Nevada.

Mix 2010 had a very different feel about it—more so than some that had passed before.

There was a definite air of expectation, for most knew what was coming, but still there was a tingle of excitement for those of us working with Silverlight. We were anticipating the unveiling of Windows Phone 7 and the Silverlight version that was built to run on it.

People squashed into the main auditorium and were noticeably restless. There was a young kid named Sterling Quinn working his magic with a mad spinning Yo-Yo thing. Amazing as it was, I felt the crowd was about to turn and start throwing things.

Finally, lights down... action time—queue "The Gu."

Windows Phone 7 Series, as it was originally called (they dropped the Series bit after complaints about people running out of breath saying it), was stunning. It was fresh, and it was just what Microsoft needed to unveil to revive a flagging mobile device scenario. The Expression Blend team and many others had worked very quickly over the previous weekend to put together the Add-In for Blend. That is how late in the day it all was, but it all ran like clockwork. Scott Guthrie demonstrated creating a RSS-Reader application in about 8 minutes and people were understandably very excited.

> **NOTE**
>
> **Why Connecting the Dots Matters So Much**
>
> Going back to the "connect the dots" scenario I rambled about in Chapter 1, "Expression Blend 4 Overview," it was hard for Microsoft to sell the vision of three screens and the cloud previously (see Figure 15.1), without a compelling mobile device solution. Now they have one, and the best thing about it for you and I is that it runs Silverlight as the primary OS interface. It also runs XNA, but that's another book.

FIGURE 15.1   The Microsoft 3 screens and cloud sales graphic.

Mix 2010 was decidedly more technical than previous years, and Microsoft has taken some flak for that, but at the end of the day, it's hard to deep dive and really explain a product unless you go into the details of how the platform runs on the phone and what features are available.

Style and Substance with Metro

What was interesting about releasing WP7 at Mix is that Mix is a conference aimed at Rich Internet Application (RIA) developers/designers, the Web, and connected Web technologies, so it stands to reason that Microsoft would talk a little about design practices. In fact, they had quite a few sessions on design for WP7, and at the heart of that was Microsoft's new design style called Metro.

Metro was detailed in explicit depth, which was really refreshing to see; not only was it presented as a new Style, but the complete understanding of thought behind it was detailed. They even produced a very nice style guide, as shown in Figure 15.2, which adds that little touch of class required to really sell it to designer folks.

FIGURE 15.2   The cover of the WP7–Metro design guide.

Metro as a design style is very clean, very clear, and essentially is modeled on the same visuals that you see at airports, as shown in Figure 15.3. This makes use of special customized font libraries that Microsoft commissioned under the Segoe family of fonts called Segoe WP.

> **NOTE**
>
> **Metro Just for Phones?**
>
> Metro as a design style is going to make larger inroads with respect to Microsoft product design guidelines. Several other products (such as Surface2) will have Metro as the design style recommendation.

FIGURE 15.3   A familiar airport sign found almost globally.

Segoe WP is a beautiful font and really well thought out as to how it will work with the phone. Little details like the amount of curve added to certain characters (to add to visual clarity on the limited screen resolutions) are all encompassed with the font family.

Font usage in WP7 is particularly important and based on the font usage inside the Zune player, an example of the UI shown in Figure 15.4. Also combined with this is the use of parallax animations, which give horizontal depth to content as it's swiped from side to side.

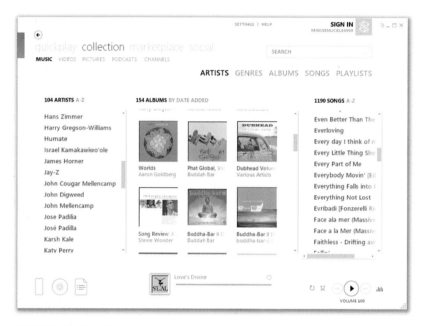

FIGURE 15.4   The proven UI from inside the Zune player desktop client.

The Zune software and entertainment solution is now rolled into the phone OS, and indeed gone is the tired, old, non-working disaster called Active Sync. You will now use a Zune software interface to sync your phone with your computer, and it works very well. Zune takes it all a step further for Microsoft in terms of connected scenarios as well, because you will be able to register to the Zune marketplace to purchase music, films, and various media, distributed across your phone, your x-box, and your desktop.

NOTE

Was Zune All That Bad?

OK, so if you read the press, Zune was a failure. But if, like me, you owned a Zune, you most likely can't understand why anyone would call it a failure. The software is beautifully designed, and the device as a whole just works. The fact that I didn't pay for my Zune doesn't discount the fact that I really like the device and the entire experience that accompanies it.

My advice is to download the PDF design guidelines for Metro and have a read-through. There are some really great bits to pick up on, and it will make designing and developing for WP7 feel all the more intuitive (see http://go.microsoft.com/fwlink/?LinkID=183218).

Tools and Add-Ins

Out of the box with Expression Blend 4, you can't just start creating WP7 applications. You need to download a series of add-ins and tools to make it all work for both Expression Blend and Visual Studio 2010. These add-ins give you not just a project template to work with and the font family collection, but you also get a fully functioning phone client with installs of Visual Studio Express and XNA Studio 4.0.

The phone client that runs on your desktop is not a simulator, but a special version of the actual OS (as shown in Figure 15.5), which makes creating and then deploying solutions to the end device that much easier because you pretty much know just from testing on your desktop what works and what doesn't. The caveat to that is that you can't easily test things like accelerometer, unless you have some crazy setup that lets you shake the hell out of your machine.

FIGURE 15.5   The Windows Phone 7 desktop client trying to "hear" a voice command as occurs with a real phone device.

> **WARNING**
>
> **Latest Release Tools and Add-Ins**
>
> You should always look at http://msdn.microsoft.com/en-us/library/ff402535(VS.92).aspx to find the latest versions and make sure you read the requirements especially around what must be pre-installed in order for the SDK tooling to work.
>
> At the time of writing, Expression Blend 4 for Phone final release was located via this URL: http://go.microsoft.com/fwlink/?LinkId=185584

Installing the tools package from Microsoft shouldn't take too long, but as shown in Figure 15.6, quite a few parts are adding during the download and install.

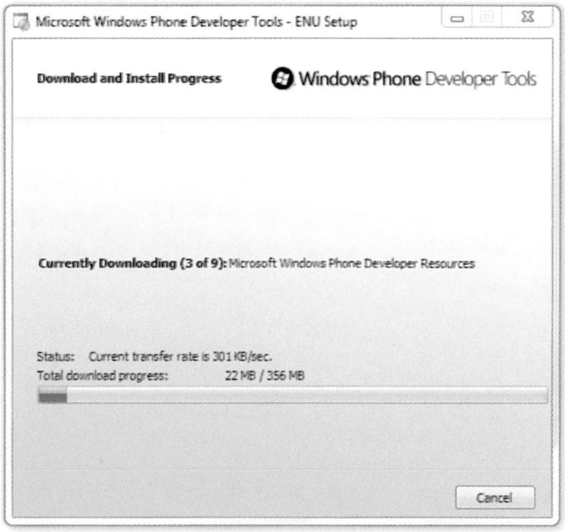

FIGURE 15.6   The Windows Phone 7 Developer Tools install.

When this is complete, running Expression Blend 4 and Visual Studio 2010 will give you several new project types specifically for the phone, as shown in Figure 15.7 and Figure 15.8, respectively.

Before running and creating any applications if you have a WP7 device, you will need to register the device and yourself with the WP7 Marketplace developer portal found at http://developer.windowsphone.com.

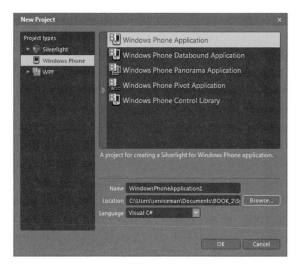

FIGURE 15.7   The newly installed Windows Phone 7 projects inside Expression Blend.

FIGURE 15.8   The newly installed Windows Phone 7 projects inside Visual Studio.

After you have completed that, you can then search for and run the "Windows Phone Developer Registration" application, which requires you to log in with your Windows LiveID, as shown in Figure 15.9.

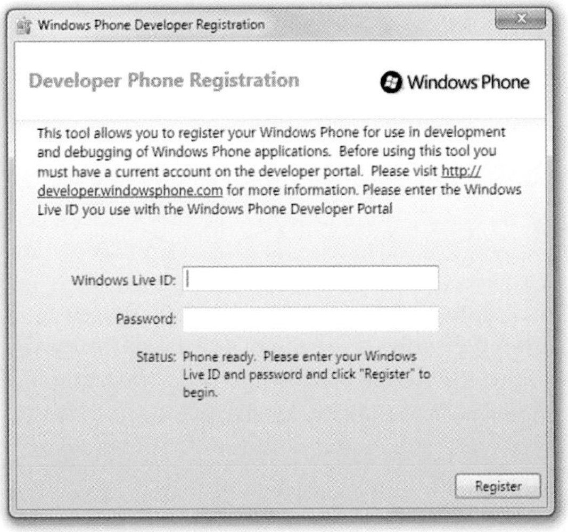

FIGURE 15.9   The device registration application.

After you have completed your market-place registration, you can then create and sideload your solutions onto your phone.

Additional Tools

Just when you thought you were complete, there are now three specific downloads you need to make in order to follow along with this chapter and get the most out of designing and developing for WP7.

WARNING

Make Sure You Read the Terms and Conditions!

You should always do this as a matter of course, but in the case of WP7 marketplace, I encourage you to really be aware of what you are signing up to. In typical Microsoft fashion, it would appear the bean counters and business analysts have had a field day making a mess of the billing scenarios and what exactly it is you get with your sign-up fee.

Layered Photoshop Templates

The first download is located at http://go.microsoft.com/fwlink/?LinkId=196225.

This download contains layered Photoshop template files that will help you to design against the guidelines for WP7. It's a great start when designing your solution, and you will see some samples from the collection in the following section.

Silverlight Toolkit for Windows Phone

The second download is located at http://silverlight.codeplex.com/releases/view/55034.

This download contains the Silverlight for Windows Phone Toolkit. This has a collection of controls and behaviors provided "out-of-band" by Microsoft teams. This download is required for the next download to work correctly.

NOTE

Samples and Source Code

You will also see an additional download that contains samples and source code for each, which you should also review. This contains an awesome array of sample controls and gesture support scenarios. The sample solution home page is shown in Figure 15.10.

WP7 Design Templates for Expression Blend

The third download is located at http://wp7designtemplates.codeplex.com/.

This download contains an Expression Blend solution that provides the WP7 Design Guidelines in active XAML templates. This provides you with a super-fast track for creating panels and experiences matched precisely to the design guidelines along with some of the WP7 controls, such as ToggleSwitch, that are not available elsewhere.

FIGURE 15.10   The sample solution and the features it contains.

NOTE

Why Is Working with the Design Guidelines Important?

Microsoft has taken the approach that you, as the designer and developer of your Windows Phone 7 application, are responsible for the end results being an exciting, efficient and ultimately rewarding experience for your end users. Realistically, you could ignore the guidelines completely and go to town on your very own train smash of a solution.

Working with the guidelines is the recommended path because after all, the experience of the phone has been precisely designed to work in a smooth and compelling way, and the design guidelines help you to expose the power of the framework in an intuitive and transferable way. You want your end user to almost not have to "learn" your application, and the way to achieve that is through consistency against the other experiences they may already have had with the operating system and the device itself.

The other reason is that with the downloads you just completed and installed, most of the heavy lifting has been done for you, which means more time working on the delivery and finesse of your solution.

To check that you have everything installed correctly and that you are ready to work through the rest of this chapter, you can open the WP7DesignTemplates solution directly in Expression Blend by navigating to the .sln file in Explorer and then right clicking for the context menu and opening in Blend, as shown in Figure 15.11.

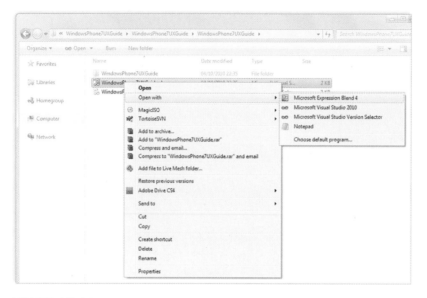

FIGURE 15.11   The handy "Open with" option in Windows Explorer.

After you have the solution opened within Blend, you should first build it using the Project menu -> Build Project option. Everything should build right away without issue.

The very first place to look in the opened solution is inside the Pages folder where you will find a file called "WP7 Design Templates.xaml," which is partially shown in Figure 15.12. Open the file and have a thorough look around it, taking in the notes and descriptions of all the panels and collections.

You will notice in the rest of the "Pages" folder that there are several individual examples of elements such as Buttons, Sliders, and Dialog boxes.

FIGURE 15.12   The detailed collections of the WP7 Design Templates file.

Building a Simple WP7 Application

The following sample walks you through creating a simple solution for Windows Phone 7 using the design templates that you have downloaded, as well as the toolkit features:

1. Open the `WindowsPhone7UXGuid. sln` file in Expression Blend if you don't already have it open.

2. Open the WP7 Design `Templates.xaml` file.

3. Locate the List View sample showing the small grid, as shown in Figure 15.13.

4. Select an element in the template on the artboard, which should help you locate the parent grid of the items (listview_small_grid), as shown in Figure 15.14. The collection in the Objects and Timeline tree is pretty substantial, so double-check that you have the right control selected.

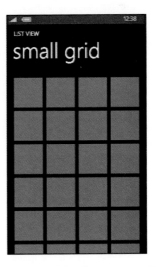

FIGURE 15.13   The small grid view element.

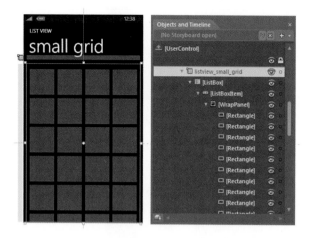

FIGURE 15.14   The parent grid selected with the Objects and Timeline tree.

5. Open a new instance of Expression Blend.

6. Create a new Windows Phone Pivot application, as shown in Figure 15.15.

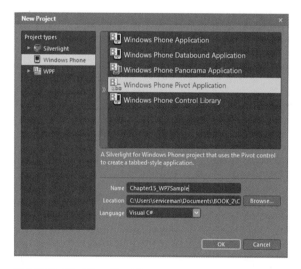

FIGURE 15.15   The Windows Phone Pivot application location.

You will be given a default view of a Pivot application when the solution is created, which contains two pivot screens named first and second, respectively, along with some sample data. Figure 15.16 shows the opening page of the solution.

This project structure is ready to run as a solution in the Windows Phone 7 emulator, and you should try this now to ensure that the emulator and the solution is correctly running. Run your project by clicking F5.

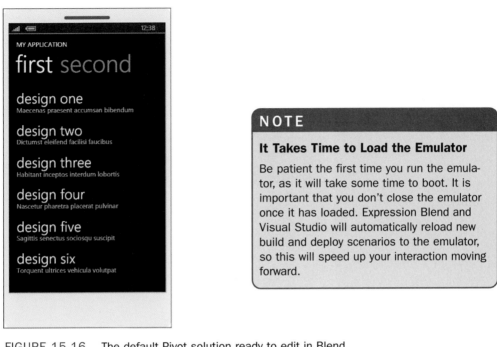

NOTE

It Takes Time to Load the Emulator

Be patient the first time you run the emulator, as it will take some time to boot. It is important that you don't close the emulator once it has loaded. Expression Blend and Visual Studio will automatically reload new build and deploy scenarios to the emulator, so this will speed up your interaction moving forward.

FIGURE 15.16   The default Pivot solution ready to edit in Blend.

Expression Blend will build the solution and then launch the Windows Phone 7 emulator, as shown in Figure 15.17. You will also notice that Blend displays a dialog telling you the status of that loading, which is also shown in Figure 15.17.

Have a play with the simple Pivot solution and the emulator swiping the screen as if you were using your fingers.

After you have finished exploring the emulator and solution, return to your solution in Blend—remember that you shouldn't close the emulator; just minimize it for the time.

In the following steps, you will review the Properties for the PhoneAppicationPage.

1. Open the Objects and Timeline panel.

2. Select the [PhoneApplicationPage] element at the top, which is the root element of this page.

3. Open the Properties panel, Brushes category.

When you click on the Foreground brush, notice that it is bound to a resource called PhoneForegroundBrush, as shown in Figure 15.18. This is important to note, as these bindings are active to the phone settings, and by using these resources correctly, your solution will automatically present the user's settings, such as theme and accent colors.

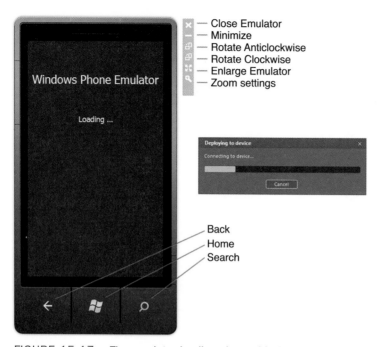

Close Emulator
Minimize
Rotate Anticlockwise
Rotate Clockwise
Enlarge Emulator
Zoom settings

Windows Phone Emulator

Loading ...

Deploying to device
Connecting to device...
Cancel

Back
Home
Search

FIGURE 15.17   The emulator loading along with the communication status from Expression Blend.

You will notice that the Background brush has no such binding. The black background you are seeing is the background property of the LayoutRoot grid element that you will look at shortly.

The following steps demonstrate the Orientation Property of Windows Phone 7.

1. Open the Common Properties category and find the SupportedOrientation property.

   Notice that by default, this value is set to Portrait, which means that when your solution runs in the emulator or on a Phone device, the solution will not change its rotation to suit the position of the phone. You have a choice between just running you solution in

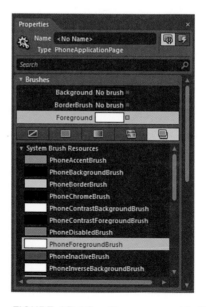

FIGURE 15.18   The resource binding of the Foreground brush property.

Portrait, Landscape, or
PortraitOrLandscape, which
enables both scenarios, as shown in
Figure 15.19.

2. Change the SupportedOrientation
property to PortraitOrLandscape,
which enables a change to be
shown in the solution on rotation
of the device or emulator.

3. Select the LayoutRoot element in
the Objects and Timeline panel.

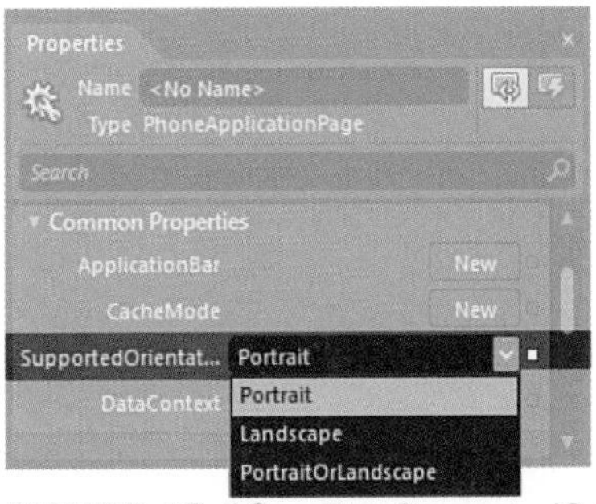

FIGURE 15.19 The SupportedOrientation options.

4. Open the Brushes panel and select the Background property.

The color applied to the Background property is white, but with all the opacity removed from it. It is important to note that the Background property must be set to a brush of some description in order to generate the correct events in the OS that the user is selecting or possibly dragging on the control.

The following steps show you how to change the Background brush applied to the solution.

1. Set the Background property to have a GradientBrush applied.

2. Select the left-hand GradientStop and bind it to PhoneBackgroundColor in the resources tab.

3. Select the right-hand GradientStop to be bound to the PhoneAccentColor resource, as shown in Figure 15.20.

4. Drill down into the LayoutRoot element and select the Pivot element.

5. Select the Foreground property and bind it to the PhoneAccentColor resource.

6. Open the Common Properties category.

The two most important properties to note here are the Items (Collection) property, which contains the PivotItem collection and the Title property. These enable you to set the Application title, as shown in Figure 15.21.

FIGURE 15.20 The application of the PhoneAccentColor resource to the LayoutRoot element.

In the following steps, you will reference the Windows Phone 7 toolkit.

1. Drill down into the first PivotItem in the child elements of the Pivot element.

2. Find the element called FirstListBox, select, and delete it.

   At this point in the solution, you need to ensure that you are referencing the Toolkit DLL; this supplies the WrapPanel control that you want to use to implement the small grid view that you selected in the design template instance of Expression Blend.

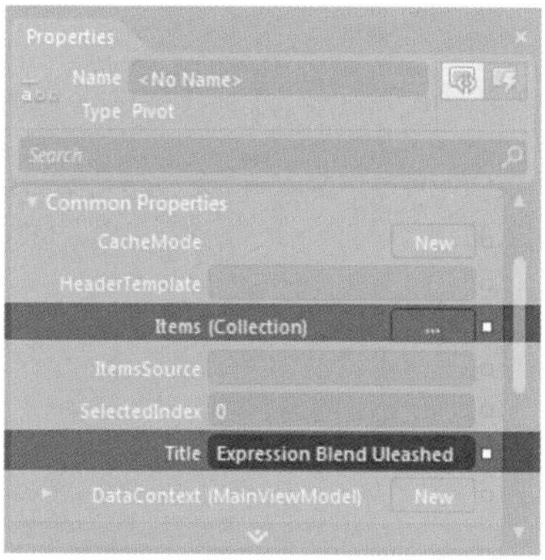

FIGURE 15.21 The Common Properties of the Pivot element.

3. Inside your project, locate the References folder and right click, selecting Add Reference.

   The DLL file should be located at:

   C:\Program Files\Microsoft SDKs\Windows Phone\v7.0\Toolkit\Nov10\Bin

4. Select the Microsoft.Phone.Controls.Toolkit.dll file to include it as a reference.

5. Save and run your solution with F5.

6. Open the original instance of Expression Blend containing the WP7 Design Templates file where you had selected the listview_small_grid element.

7. Right-click on the Grid element in the Objects and Timeline panel and select Copy.

8. Return to your new instance of Expression Blend, located the first PivotItem element and right-click to paste the listview_small_grid element into it, as shown in Figure 15.22.

You can now close down the WP7 Design Template solution to free up some resources on your machine.

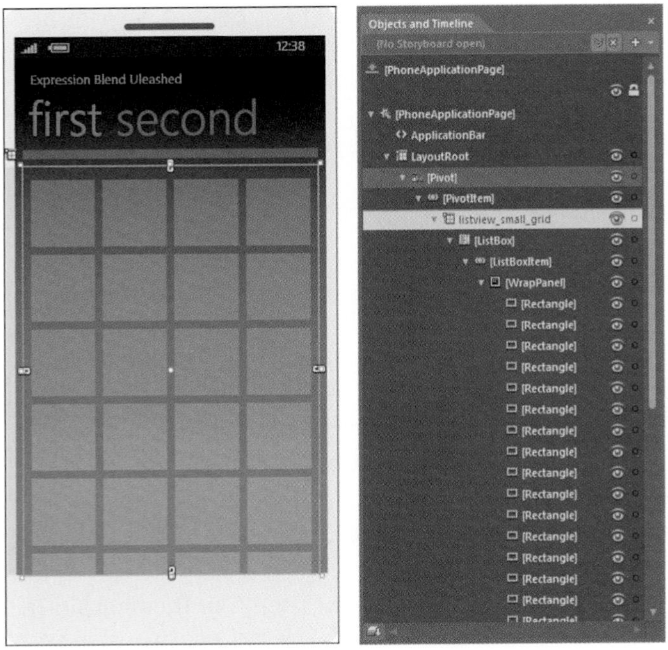

FIGURE 15.22   The copied elements pasted into the solution.

The ListBox items contain a template for displaying the Rectangles that are making up the template at present. You are going to use this as a basic layout template for the background of the solution:

1. Open the Data panel.

   You see that a sample data source is already present that provides data to the default templates that Blend created.

2. Add a new set of sample data.

3. Keep only one property of the sample data source.

4. Change the Property1 property type to an image.

5. Edit the sample values of the data source and set the property to contain 50 records, as shown in Figure 15.23. You want enough sample data to fill the grid to determine that the usage will be correct with large data sets.

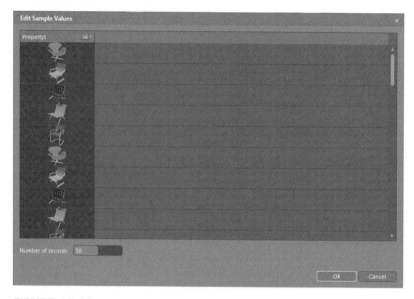

FIGURE 15.23   The sample data source being set to contain 50 images.

6. Drag the sample data source collection directly onto the listview_small_grid element, which should result in a new ListBox element being created.

7. Set the new ListBox element size to fill the entire space of the listview_small_grid element with the Margin properties all set to 0, as shown in Figure 15.24.

The obvious problem now is that your ListBox element is not laying out the elements in a WrapPanel format, as was contained in the small Grid list view that you are using as a template.

The following steps show you how to overcome this.

1. Right-click on your new ListBox element and select Edit Additional Template -> Edit Layout of Items (ItemsPanel)->Create Empty…, as shown in Figure 15.25.

2. Leave everything as default in the Create ItemsPanelTemplate Resource dialog and click on OK.

3. Notice that in the template, a single StackPanel element is under the ItemsPanel. Open the Assets panel and search for a WrapPanel element.

FIGURE 15.24   The new ListBox element applied to the scene.

FIGURE 15.25   How to edit the ItemsPanel of the ListBox.

4. Delete the `StackPanel` and replace it with the `WrapPanel`; notice that instantly the image elements in the `ListBox` are now in the correct wrap scenario, as shown in Figure 15.26.

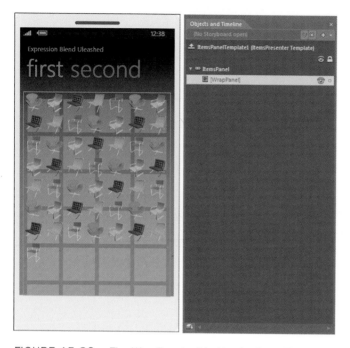

FIGURE 15.26   The WrapPanel added to the ItemsPanel template and the resulting layout change in the ListBox.

5. Scope up and out of the `ItemsPanelTemplate`.

Your solution is getting closer, with all that remaining is for you to set the items to present correctly as per the design template.

6. Right-click on the `ListBox` element and select to Edit Additional Templates ->Edit Generated Items (ItemTemplate) ->Edit Current.

You now are inside the `ItemTemplate`; note that the `Image` element is inside of a `StackPanel` element. In order to fulfill the design template requirement, you need to add a `Rectangle` behind the image element and work with the sizing of the elements to get them correct.

7. Right-click on the `StackPanel` element in the `ItemTemplate` selecting Change Layout Type -> Grid.

8. Set the `Grid` element to `Width` and `Height` 99.

9. Set the `Margin` value to 12 from Left and 12 from Top, as specified in the WP7 design guidelines for spacing.

10. Add a new `Rectangle` element as a child of the grid.

11. Select the `Fill` property of the `Rectangle` and bind it to `PhoneSubtleColor`, which is a semi-transparent fill.

12. Select the `Stroke` property and remove the brush applied.

13. Send the `Rectangle` element to the back behind the `Image` element.

14. Select the `Image` element.

15. Set the `Image` size to be `Auto` for both `Width` and `Height`, set it to `Stretch` both Horizontally and Vertically, and remove any `Margin` property values.

16. Scope up and out of the `ItemTemplate`.

17. Select the `ListBox` element and set its Top `Margin` property to `8`, which should line up the collection perfectly with the template behind.

18. Select the original `ListBox` element containing the design template and delete it, which will complete your design, as shown in Figure 15.27.

FIGURE 15.27   The ListBox element lined up correctly as per the design template.

Change the Theme in the Emulator

The nice thing about the Metro design is that you should have a very nice solution working with all accent colors.

Run the solution now and look at how it works in the emulator as you would expect:

1. Click on the Windows logo in the emulator to return to the home screen.

2. Click on the arrow at the top right of the emulator screen to view the optional menu.

3. Click on Settings.

4. Click on theme.

5. Change the Background to Light.

6. Change the Accent color to that of your choice.

You can now navigate around the
emulator and restart your solution,
which you should see has presented
with the correct theme and accent, as
shown in Figure 15.28; I have selected
the light background with a lime accent.

Adding Rotation Animation Support

Now that your solution is presenting the
data in the way you intended, one of
the annoying little issues is that when
you rotate the phone emulator using the
emulator buttons, the perspective
changes as you intended, but it just
snaps to the new view with no animation or transition to smooth the experience.

Fortunately, the Windows Phone Toolkit
you downloaded and installed previously contains a handy helper built in
to enable such transitions, and the code
that is required to implement it isn't too
difficult to understand.

FIGURE 15.28   The inherited theme and
accent in the application.

Add the code that is provided in Listing 15.1 to your MainPage.xaml.cs file and then run
your solution again to test that the transitions work.

LISTING 15.1   Code to Provide the Functionality to Transition Smoothly Between Orientations

```
public partial class MainPage : PhoneApplicationPage
{
    // Constructor
    public MainPage()
    {
        InitializeComponent();

        // Set the data context of the listbox control to the sample data
        DataContext = App.ViewModel;
        this.Loaded += new RoutedEventHandler(MainPage_Loaded);

        this.OrientationChanged += new
➡EventHandler<OrientationChangedEventArgs>(MainPage_OrientationChanged);
        this.CurrentOrientationSetting = this.Orientation;
    }
```

LISTING 15.1   Continued

```
        private PageOrientation CurrentOrientationSetting;

        void MainPage_OrientationChanged(object sender,
➥OrientationChangedEventArgs e)
        {
            RotateTransition newRotationTransition = new RotateTransition();

            switch (e.Orientation)
            {
                case PageOrientation.Landscape:
                case PageOrientation.LandscapeRight:
                    newRotationTransition.Mode =
                        (this.CurrentOrientationSetting ==
➥PageOrientation.PortraitUp) ?
                            RotateTransitionMode.In90Counterclockwise :
                            RotateTransitionMode.In180Clockwise;
                    break;
                case PageOrientation.LandscapeLeft:
                    newRotationTransition.Mode =
                        (this.CurrentOrientationSetting ==
➥PageOrientation.LandscapeRight) ?
                            RotateTransitionMode.In180Counterclockwise :
                            RotateTransitionMode.In90Clockwise;
                    break;
                case PageOrientation.Portrait:
                case PageOrientation.PortraitUp:
                    newRotationTransition.Mode =
                        (this.CurrentOrientationSetting ==
➥PageOrientation.LandscapeLeft) ?
                            RotateTransitionMode.In90Counterclockwise :
                            RotateTransitionMode.In90Clockwise;
                    break;
                default:
                    break;
            }

            PhoneApplicationPage currentPhoneApplicationPage =
➥(PhoneApplicationPage)(Application.Current.RootVisual as
➥PhoneApplicationFrame).Content;

            ITransition transition =
➥newRotationTransition.GetTransition(currentPhoneApplicationPage);
```

15

LISTING 15.1   Continued

```
            transition.Completed += delegate { transition.Stop(); };
            transition.Begin();

            this.CurrentOrientationSetting = e.Orientation;
        }

        // Load data for the ViewModel Items
        private void MainPage_Loaded(object sender, RoutedEventArgs e)
        {
            if (!App.ViewModel.IsDataLoaded)
            {
                App.ViewModel.LoadData();
            }
        }
    }
}
```

Your solution should now handle any orientation on both the device and the emulator, as shown in Figure 15.29.

FIGURE 15.29   The reverse orientation of the emulator and the solution correctly presented after a transition.

You can continue to work through the design templates provided in the sample solution, implementing controls as you go by simply copying and pasting between two solutions.

Using the Panorama-type solution is just as simple as this Pivot solution has been, with the only primary difference being that the Item panels are side by side. The default Panorama template is a little more colorful (I don't know why); as you work through the properties of the PanoramaItem elements, you will see the repetition in features.

Summary

In this chapter, you looked at the resources available to Windows Phone 7 designers and developers, including the sample solutions and design templates that make building phone applications a relatively simple task.

You then created a simple solution, looking at how Expression Blend can make it very quick to get a design style-compliant composition together, as well as some code to help implement transitions for the phone orientation, using the Windows Phone 7 Toolkit downloadable from the CodePlex site.

Windows Phone 7 is a fun and exciting platform to build for and changes the way in which you would attack a web- or desktop-based solution. There are hundreds of great blog posts and content available for Windows Phone 7 already, which is set to rise as the phone OS and subsequent updates are implemented throughout 2011 and beyond.

15

Resources for Going Further

I have a few hopes for this book—none higher than having you in a comfortable zone when opening and using Expression Blend.

This book had to be about the tool itself and not about a specific platform, the XAML scripting language, or the .NET coding language of choice. If you feel comfortable using the tool and the available functionality that it surfaces for the various platforms, you can right now start working on your choice of supported platform from WP7, Surface, or any of the rich platforms available, such as Silverlight and WPF.

In this chapter, you find links to resources for everything from XAML to the recommended development design pattern called M-V-VM (Model-View-ViewModel).

Finding Out More...

No doubt you can spend an endless amount of time searching websites for answers to your questions, so hopefully this compilation helps get you there faster.

Short URLs

Some of the resource links are long and a pain to retype. I have shortened all URLs using the Google URL-shortening tool.

Links

Regardless of what resources you are looking for when using Blend, your first port of call when wanting answers should be the Microsoft Expression Blend + SketchFlow forums hosted here:

http://goo.gl/GH5vt

You might just bump into me there!

Expression Blend Resources

You should take the time to explore the home of Expression Blend from Microsoft. The Learn Expression Blend section of the Products section contains some excellent videos and papers to get you even deeper into using the tool.

Links

You can find the Learn Expression Blend collection here:

http://goo.gl/TstRu

As a general rule, you should also check out CodePlex, the home of open source solutions from Microsoft, located here:

http://www.codeplex.com

I also advise you to look at code project for more details around developing for all the supported platforms, as well as some very detailed tutorials on how to achieve more advanced solutions. Code project has a massive repository of content and is located here:

http://www.codeproject.com/

How to create a carousel using the `PathListBox` in Silverlight is a fantastic tutorial that will help you learn more about this new controls usage and features is located here:

http://goo.gl/SG8Ml

SketchFlow Resources

SketchFlow is an interesting proposition mostly for designers, but I am convinced that as more and more developers begin to use the solution, the more they will see the benefits of designing an application before just heading into coding.

Spending as much time as possible in SketchFlow during the design phase is really an investment in a great end result, and I would advise you to research the subject further.

Links

A great book, *Dynamic Prototyping with SketchFlow in Expression Blend*, written by Microsoft's Chris Bernard and Sara Summers, is located here:

http://goo.gl/Ux7MA

XAML Resources

You haven't spent a lot of time reading XAML or understanding how the script is part of the magic that makes rich interface solutions work throughout the platforms mentioned in this book. There are several reasons for that decision; once again, it comes down to forcing you to use the tool rather than hand coding a script that is both inefficient to do by hand, compared to using Blend, and proven to be error prone in the first instance.

There will be times, however, where you need to get your hands dirty and hand-crank the XAML.

Links

My recommendation for going further with XAML is to read the amazing book *Programming WPF*, by Chris Sells and Ian Griffiths:

http://goo.gl/oKGqo

I read the original resource cover to cover, and it not only was brilliantly written, but it also explained very clearly the concepts behind how XAML works and provides a much deeper understanding of data binding and deep templating.

You will also find a rather in-depth description of XAML here:

http://msdn.microsoft.com/en-us/library/ms752059.aspx

Silverlight Resources

Silverlight as a platform has evolved rapidly from version 1 through to its current version of 4; already at the start of 2011, you begin to see information focused on Silverlight 5.

Pay attention to the platform that blog posts and examples are targeting. Silverlight 3 is not too bad when porting to 4, but any previous versions will be a tough job.

Links

For assistance and good resource information, you should always try searching the Silverlight forums located here:

http://www.silverlight.NET/

There are also several video tutorials under the Learn section of the Silverlight site here:

http://goo.gl/wCZVv

You should also check out *Silverlight 4 Unleashed* by my friend, Laurent Bugnion, found here at Amazon:

http://goo.gl/xWfZH

WPF Resources

The grandfather of all the XAML-based platforms, you are bound to find an extremely large amount of content to help you work with WPF. The platform has spawned several books diving into separate areas of study, from control development through to coding patterns specifically designed to work with WPF.

Links

The first stop I would point you to is *WPF Unleashed* by Adam Nathan. This was a very successful book, clearly written and expertly crafted to teach you everything you need to know to work with the WPF platform. You can find it here:

http://goo.gl/o1gxX

Christian Mosers has also created a very thorough website full of insightful details and tutorials around the Windows Presentation Foundation. The site can be found here:

http://www.wpftutorial.NET/

If you are interested in creating highly customized WPF control, the book *WPF Control Development Unleashed* from another friend of mine, Pavan Podila, is an excellent resource. You can find that book here:

http://goo.gl/RWchA

Windows Phone 7 Resources

Windows Phone 7 has a lot of resources added by a thriving initial community, and you are sure to find details around most scenarios that you might want to research.

The Expression Blend forum also contains plenty of information on how to use Blend against the WP7 platform; as mentioned previously in this book, this is currently a cut of Silverlight 3 with extensions specifically built for the phone.

Links

You can head to the official site for Windows Phone 7 development, found here:

http://create.msdn.com/en-US/

You should also take a good look through the Windows Phone 7 development blog at:

http://goo.gl/E9Ip4

Surface Resources

Microsoft Surface is an interesting and exciting platform to design and develop for, but unfortunately, as a platform, it suffers from an almost-closed solution. This is just a result of poor messaging from Microsoft because the platform is open and available to people to develop for, even without a device.

Developing for Surface is very similar to a standard WPF solution, with the added extensions and controls that are available for the platform exposing all the features of touch and interactive physical objects with the device.

I was fortunate enough to be a part of the first and second Surface TAP programs, which enables me to actively work with Surface on an almost-daily basis through my employer, Splendid.

Links

A good source of development resource is located at the official Surface development forums here:

http://goo.gl/wYyiW

You should also check in at the Surface sites developer portal for more resources, located here:

http://goo.gl/7N2BD

C# .NET Development Resources

.NET as a development platform has been around for the better part of a decade now and is extremely mature. Reportedly, there are some 26 million developers around the world working on one or more form of the .NET platform using one of the many languages that are compatible.

C# was the focus of this book from a coding perspective. Although there is nothing wrong with writing in Visual Basic, C# is the most widely used of the .NET-compliant languages commercially—thus the decision to focus on C#.

Links

If you are new to C# or programming in general, I would suggest you take a look at the book *Sams Teach Yourself C# in 24 Hours* by James Foxall and Wendy Haro-Chun. You can find that resource on Amazon, located here:

http://goo.gl/7N2BD

You should also head to the collection of forums provided by Microsoft at the following location:

http://goo.gl/bY9In

M-V-VM Resources

Model-View-ViewModel is a design pattern recommended as the basis for most XAML-based solution development, which is a highly contentious issue for a lot of folks. One thing for sure is that the design pattern as a guide to good software development does introduce some very succinct, if not complicated, scenarios and concepts to gather.

Links

You can find a good overview of M-V-VM here from Microsoft:

http://goo.gl/6X8nS

There are lots of different implementations of the pattern, and you are advised to review which ones provide you with the best solution for your task at hand. One location I would check out is the mvvmlight home page on CodePlex, which was created by Laurent Bugnion. You can find that here:

http://mvvmlight.codeplex.com/

Summary

Moving forward, you will see Microsoft produce similar tooling as Expression Blend for languages and scripts such as HTML5 and a new high-performance UI platform from Microsoft (codenamed Jupiter), which will also be XAML based. It's very difficult to take all those scripts and languages on board and to be efficiently working within their boundaries right away.

Now that you have learned Expression Blend, you can start creating user interfaces and experiences faster.

Good luck, and remember to have fun!

Index

Q–R

T

How can we make this index more useful? Email us at indexes@samspublishing.com

X-Y

Z

UNLEASHED

Unleashed takes you beyond the basics, providing an exhaustive, technically sophisticated reference for professionals who need to exploit a technology to its fullest potential. It's the best resource for practical advice from the experts, and the most in-depth coverage of the latest technologies.

informit.com/unleashed

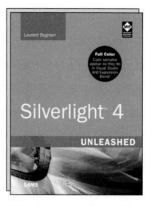

Silverlight 4 Unleashed
ISBN-13: 9780672333361

OTHER UNLEASHED TITLES

Visual Basic 2010 Unleashed
ISBN-13: 9780672331008

ASP.NET 3.5 AJAX Unleashed
ISBN-13: 9780672329739

Microsoft Visual Studio 2010 Unleashed
ISBN-13: 9780672330810

Microsoft Exchange Server 2010 Unleashed
ISBN-13: 9780672330469

Windows Server 2008 Hyper-V Unleashed
ISBN-13: 9780672330285

System Center Operations Manager (OpsMgr) 2007 R2 Unleashed
ISBN-13: 9780672333415

System Center Configuration Manager (SCCM) 2007 Unleashed
ISBN-13: 9780672330230

Microsoft SharePoint 2010 PerformancePoint Services Unleashed
ISBN-13: 9780672330940

C# 4.0 Unleashed
ISBN-13: 9780672330797

Microsoft Dynamics CRM 4.0 Unleashed
ISBN-13: 9780672329708

Microsoft Dynamics CRM 4 Integration Unleashed
ISBN-13: 9780672330544

LINQ Unleashed
ISBN-13: 9780672329838

Windows Communication Foundation 3.5 Unleashed
ISBN-13: 9780672330247

Windows Server 2008 R2 Unleashed
ISBN-13: 9780672330926

Microsoft System Center Enterprise Suite Unleashed
ISBN-13: 9780672333194

Microsoft Expression Blend Unleashed
ISBN-13: 9780672329319

Microsoft SQL Server 2008 Reporting Services Unleashed
ISBN-13: 9780672330261

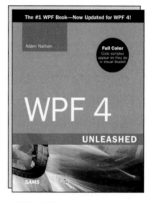

WPF 4 Unleashed
ISBN-13: 9780672331190

Microsoft SQL Server 2008 R2 Unleashed
ISBN-13: 9780672330568

informit.com/unleashed

FREE Online Edition

Your purchase of **Microsoft® Expression Blend® 4 Unleashed** includes access to a free online edition for 45 days through the Safari Books Online subscription service. Nearly every Sams book is available online through Safari Books Online, along with more than 5,000 other technical books and videos from publishers such as Addison-Wesley Professional, Cisco Press, Exam Cram, IBM Press, O'Reilly, Prentice Hall, and Que.

SAFARI BOOKS ONLINE allows you to search for a specific answer, cut and paste code, download chapters, and stay current with emerging technologies.

Activate your FREE Online Edition at
www.informit.com/safarifree

> **STEP 1:** Enter the coupon code: MHOJZAA.

> **STEP 2:** New Safari users, complete the brief registration form.
> Safari subscribers, just log in.

If you have difficulty registering on Safari or accessing the online edition, please e-mail customer-service@safaribooksonline.com